RECONCEIVING INFERTILITY

RECONCEIVING INFERTILITY

*Biblical Perspectives on
Procreation and Childlessness*

Candida R. Moss and Joel S. Baden

PRINCETON UNIVERSITY PRESS
PRINCETON AND OXFORD

Published by Princeton University Press,
41 William Street, Princeton, New Jersey 08540
In the United Kingdom: Princeton University Press,
6 Oxford Street, Woodstock, Oxfordshire OX20 1TW

press.princeton.edu

Jacket art: Sandro Botticelli (Alessandro di Mariano di Vanni Filipepi, 1444/5–1510), *Annunciation*, tempera on panel, Galleria degli Uffizi, Florence, Italy. Bridgeman Images

ISBN 978-0-691-16483-0

Library of Congress Control Number: 2015935300

British Library Cataloging-in-Publication Data is available

This book has been composed in Linux Libertine O

Printed on acid-free paper ∞

Printed in the United States of America

1 3 5 7 9 10 8 6 4 2

For John and Adela

CONTENTS

PREFACE   IX
ACKNOWLEDGMENTS   XI
INTRODUCTION   1

Chapter 1: The Matriarchs as Models   21

Chapter 2: The Blessing and the Curse   70

Chapter 3: Mother Zion and the Eschaton   103

Chapter 4: The Son of God and the
           Conception of the New Age   140

Chapter 5: Chastity, Marriage, and Gender
           in the Christian Family   171

Chapter 6: Barrenness and the Eschaton   200

Conclusion   229

NOTES   239
BIBLIOGRAPHY   291
PRIMARY SOURCE INDEX   313
SUBJECT INDEX   325

PREFACE

This book is intended for a wide range of potential audiences. As academics, we hope that it will make a contribution to the critical study of the Bible and its cultural contexts, and so be of use to our colleagues in the academy. We have, however, written it in such a way that, without sacrificing any detail or argumentation, it may be accessible to quite different groups of readers. Because we are dealing with a topic that has present and practical real-world ramifications, we hope also to reach audiences in arenas that deal in practical ways with infertility: medical professionals, social workers, counselors, therapists, and clergy. And, of course, we have written this book in the hope that it might be of use to those who suffer from infertility themselves, and seek ways to understand their experience within the context of a biblical and religious framework.

In the following pages we open to discussion anew the question of how the Bible, in both the Old and New Testaments, might speak to the condition of infertility. No singular argument is imprinted on the text; rather, we work through case studies of texts and themes, each of which contributes a different perspective on the issue. As scholars and historians, we are committed to reading in a historically responsible way, with attention to the ancient cultures from which the biblical texts emerged and the potential range of meanings that we might plausibly attribute to the biblical authors. At the same time, we recognize that the meaning of the text remains flexible, even given these constraints, and so our readings are self-consciously creative, in the sense that we actively try to dive deeply into the well of interpretive possibility.

This book is not an exhaustive treatment of every reference to infertility, children, or the family in the Bible. The dominant picture of infertility that emerges from reading the Bible is that infertility is a problem that is fixed by, and usually caused by, God. If earlier studies of the family and children in the Bible mention infertility at all, then they invariably summarize the problem in these ways and in a few sparse sentences. Implicit in these studies is a Victorian view of the family and a position that infertile couples offer, at best, anomalous evidence for the study of the family. Just as such approaches are selective in their definition of the family and fertility, this book is selective in its treatment of infertility in the Bible. It is not our intention to rehearse a master narrative in which infertility is a divine curse, nor do we claim that such a belief is not present in the biblical text—it is. Rather, we show that even in the ancient world and the Bible there were diverse ways of interpreting the experience and significance of infertility. And our hope is that the results will be of use even today.

ACKNOWLEDGMENTS

We are indebted to our editor, Fred Appel, who enthusiastically embraced the project and our vision for the book with sincere interest and great care. We are, as always, appreciative of our fleet of graduate research assistants—Justin Buol, Laura Carlson, Ashley Edewaard, Liane Marquis, Joshua Noble, Mary Young—who gathered primary materials and read drafts with good humor.

Our colleagues at Notre Dame and Yale have created positive work environments that allow us to pursue our work and interests happily and productively, for which we are ever appreciative. All the more so our families, who are sources of lasting support.

We are grateful to Meghan Henning and Anna Rebecca Solevag for providing us with prepublication drafts of their work. Thanks to Blake Leyerle for supportive and generative conversation, and to David Frankfurter and Michelle Morris for sharing unpublished work. The anonymous readers of the manuscript made suggestions, large and small, that improved the work immeasurably.

The research for this book was supported by grants from the Institute for Scholarship in the Liberal Arts at the University of Notre Dame.

This book is dedicated to John and Adela Collins, who, over years of advising, mentoring, and friendship, have acted as our professional and spiritual parents. We would not be where we are today without them—nor would we want to.

RECONCEIVING INFERTILITY

Introduction

> Bring the child forth and do it with all your might! If you
> die in the process, then pass on over, good for you! For you
> actually die in a noble work and in obedience to God.
>
> —MARTIN LUTHER, 1522

During her campaign to become chancellor of Germany, Angela
Merkel was accused of being an unfit representation of womanhood. Although married, Merkel was (and remains) childless, and
in the context of running for public office, her apparent choice
was interpreted as a calculated career move. One indiscreet insin-
uation in the media was that her lack of children demonstrated
a deficiency of the kinds of natural instincts commonly found in
women.[1] She was viewed with suspicion, and some questioned
whether she adequately represented women or even human beings in general.[2]

The vilification of childless women is nothing new. While the
texture and contours of the childless woman have been reshaped
and the childless hag recast as the "career-driven professional,"
social attitudes to childless couples are at best ambivalent. As the
discourse of "having it all" continues to beat the tension between
career and family into our cultural consciousness, it drowns

out the fact that, for many, this choice is illusory and luxurious. What these characterizations obscure are the wide variety of experiences that lead a person or a couple to remain childless. Underneath the shrill rhetoric of culture wars fought over politicized families and concerns about overpopulation, underpopulation, consumption of global resources, and environmental ethics, there is little visibility for those who are biologically unable to reproduce.

CHILDLESSNESS AS DISEASE, DISABILITY, AND SOCIAL STIGMA

It might seem clear from the title that this book is about the physical inability to have children. Certainly this is true and represents the starting point from which this book was conceived. But this inability, and the lived experience that stems from it, is less easily defined than it might initially appear. In the modern world, "childlessness" denotes merely the absence of children. The term has intimations of loss and bereavement, but technically applies to anyone without children; whether this is by choice, by circumstance, or by biology is undetermined. Although the self-designation "child-free" implies resolute choice, the ambiguity surrounding childlessness arouses suspicion and sometimes judgment. Alternatively, the terms "barren" and "infertile" can be used to describe a biological state or condition. These terms are gendered and usually applied to women, are rooted in agricultural imagery, and presuppose a definite state. If we say that a person is "barren," we assume that she is, as a fact of her very existence, unable to conceive children. The term "sterile" is more masculine but can also be used as a verb to denote the process by which a person—male or female—is rendered infertile. Sterilization might be forced on a person or it might be elective, but in either case it presumes a distinction between those who are made infertile and those who simply "are" infertile.

At the margins of all of these commonly used, sharply drawn medical categories are blurred boundaries. The distinction between sterility and contraception is obscured in contexts in which modern couples choose sterilization—tubal ligation or vasectomy—as a form of contraception. The difference between "abnormal" biological infertility and "natural" biological infertility is a matter of menopause. Even with menopause, the distinction between normal and abnormal is grounded in age. A woman who experiences menopause under the age of forty is medically different from a woman who goes through the same experience a few years later.

All of these categories are complicated by the social contexts that produce the diagnosis and label of infertility. In contemporary society, the identification of infertility belongs first and foremost to the medical world. But identifying a childless person as infertile involves cultural ideas that are not limited to the medical world. The process of formalizing medicalization relies upon both accurate diagnostic tools and procedures and the existence of medical treatments. In the majority of cases, a person is categorized as "infertile" only in the event that he or she is actively attempting to have children, has thus far proven unable, and, crucially, has consulted a doctor about his or her procreative abilities. This last step is further complicated by the fact that medical testing is religiously unacceptable to many. Thus a person or couple might be actively trying to conceive, be encountering difficulties, and yet be ineligible for formal diagnosis. They would instead inhabit a liminal space in which they hoped for children but had not yet had them.

This liminal position of trying unsuccessfully to have children without a medical diagnosis of infertility may sound marginal, but historically it is the experience of most couples. With the exception of those who never go through puberty, are rendered impotent or sterile through castration or other surgical intervention, or have other diagnosable impairments, all people are uncertain of their procreative status up until the point at which they conceive and then give birth.[3] They may assume that they are fertile, but they cannot be sure until they are pregnant. Similarly they may suspect that they are infertile, but—divine intervention notwithstanding—the resolution of this suspicion comes only with menopause and advanced age. Men and women who have biological conditions that make it impossible for them to procreate but who never attempt to have children would never be diagnosed as infertile.[4]

All of this draws our attention to the recognition that infertility, even as a medical condition, is socially constructed from a wide variety of cultural ideas regarding religion, age, patriotism, biology, gender, and so on. Whatever biological impairments a person may or may not have, procreative abilities become relevant only in the event that he or she is trying to have children. Infertility is not the concern of the pediatrician. In those who are sexually active but trying to avoid conceiving, undiagnosed infertility might actually be an advantage. Only in the context of wanting to have children does childlessness evolve into infertility. The identification of childlessness as infertility involves much more than medicine.

In this regard infertility as a description of childlessness embodies perfectly the modern definition of a disability. One of the fundamental premises of critical disability theory is that what qualifies as a disability depends on the cultural ideas that we use to narrate and interpret physical, cognitive, and emotional differences. When we identify some of these differences as "disabilities," we are usually describing more than just a medical diagnosis. We are also accounting for political, religious, sexual, and legal factors, among others, related to the social and environment context in which these differences present themselves. Moreover, as we will discover through this book, discussions of disability can help us to express a variety of cultural ideas, including ideas about gender, divine activity, marriage, family, and the eschaton. Disability is a cultural product that involves ideas about a wide variety of social structures, institutions, and experiences.[5]

With respect to infertility, social context is especially important. Accessing the lived experiences of infertile couples, and thus quantifying the stigmatizing effects of being identified as or self-identifying as infertile, is fraught with difficulty. For a variety of reasons, including socioeconomic and religious considerations, only approximately half of infertile individuals worldwide seek treatment at all. Social-scientific studies of the experience of infertility are based exclusively on those couples actively seeking treatment. Many such studies have focused on psychological distress and thus narrowed the scope of their investigation to infertile couples or individuals actively in psychiatric care, a sample group that automatically limits itself to those experiencing distress.[6]

What this means for this project is that sociological studies of the experience of infertility underrepresent both those who are infertile by the medical definition but do not intend to have children,[7] and those who do not seek treatment because they are unable to do so.[8] Of this second group, individuals and couples who are opposed to reproductive technologies on religious grounds are especially underrepresented.[9] We can empathize with the dilemma facing researchers: they can work only with the data available to them. All the same, the voices of those who are without children and hold religious views that prohibit them from seeking certain forms of medical treatment are muffled in the very studies designed to assist them.

To the broader and shifting bases for the stigmatization of infertile couples and individuals in the workplace and society in general we can add the pressure that infertile couples face from family members, whether their partner, in-laws, grandparents, or siblings. The dilemma is an ancient one: fifth-century bishop John Chrysostom wrote that a daughter is the source of many sleepless nights to her father, who lies awake worrying that she might be childless, past her prime and unmarried, or repulsive to her husband.[10] This same sentiment is found at a remarkable distance of space and time: a Chinese proverb holds that "there are three ways one can dishonor one's parents, with childlessness being the foremost."[11] Modern studies of infertility reveal that, in societies that foster tight-knit extended families or permit polygamy, the social pressures applied to infertile wives are increased. Infertile women experience higher rates of alienation in social situations that place a higher premium on reproduction.

We should add that the distinction made by critical disability theorists between those stigmas based on various physical deformities, those associated with perceived blemishes of character, and those described as "tribal stigmas" (race, religion, nationhood) are broken down in religious contexts.[12] The assumption that "infertile women are stigmatized because of abnormal bodily function" is sometimes challenged in religious communities.[13] This might be an adequate description of the stigmatization of the openly infertile, but it fails to address the social situation faced by the ambiguously childless.

By neglecting the complex forces that contribute to childlessness and by rehearsing a simple picture of (in)fertility, some religious groups only exacerbate the problem. In a sermon delivered in June 2014, for example, Pope Francis castigated those married couples "who don't want children, who want to be without fruitfulness."[14] These couples, he went on to say, have been blinded by a "culture of well-being" into thinking that "it's better not to have children. . . . That way you can see the world, be on vacation, you can have a fancy home in the country, you'll be carefree." While he attempts to make a clear-cut distinction between childlessness by choice and infertility, he is oblivious to the complicated issues we have just described. Given that infertility is an "invisible disability," all childless couples, including the infertile, are socially disabled by his stigmatization of childlessness as selfish. Francis's default assumption seems to be that childless couples have simply made a lifestyle choice. The complexities of lived childlessness are obscured by the binary he reproduces. In religious communities opposed to the use of contraception but situated in larger communities in which contraception is widely available, this kind of deviant familial model is likely to be perceived as the result of an immoral lifestyle choice. A physical deformity is, in this context, read and understood as a blemish of character. The fact that diagnosis can elude members of certain religious denominations means that they are perpetually in limbo—or worse.

CHILDLESSNESS AND GENDER

The assessment of childlessness and responsibility is acutely gendered. While Merkel's candidacy was not affected by the speculation, childless women in modern society continue to be the subject of intense personal scrutiny. In 2014 Ayaka Shiomura, a Japanese politician, was heckled in parliament as she called for an increase in support for pregnant women. Leaders of the opposing majority party called out, "Get married!" and "Can't you have children?"[15] The content of the comments was curious; paradoxically, her advocacy for pregnant women led her opponents to conclude that she is infertile. Womanhood continues to be associated with motherhood, and with the assumption that motherhood is the highest state of womanhood. Those women who fail to meet these social expectations are subject to additional scrutiny. They are, even in the twenty-first century, characterized as "unmaternal," as inadequate representations of women, as selfish, and as bitter.[16] This characterization is, in some cultures, even embedded in the language: in Japan and Korea, the term for an infertile woman translates as "a woman made of stone."[17]

For women in the workplace there is no socially acceptable family situation. While women of a childbearing age are treated as potential liabilities, childless women encounter their own problems. Sociologist Caroline Gatrell has remarked that employers see female employees who do not have children as "cold, odd and somehow emotionally deficient in an almost dangerous way that leads to them being excluded from promotions that would place them in charge of others."[18]

To an extent, the presumption of guilt is typical of Christian—and more broadly cultural—norms that evaluate the kind of person a woman really is on the basis of external features. Like dress, hairstyle, and makeup choices, family life is taken as an indication of innate femininity and morality. Although similar prejudices exist in the evaluation of male family life and appearance, the crude hyperspeculation about morality related to childbearing, and the unstated assumption that childlessness is a matter of choice, continually and repeatedly lands squarely in the lap of the nonmother. Thus while successful childless women are assumed to be embittered, selfish, career-hungry feminists, similar accusations are not laid against childless men. More often than not, when men are childless it is assumed either that the man's wife is just the kind of "cold" feminist described above or that the couple (again, probably the wife) is infertile.

Paradoxically, the stigmatization that women seek to avoid by openly self-identifying as infertile is only reinforced when women "out" themselves. An individual woman can choose to disclose her fertility status, but in doing so she unwittingly reinforces a system that judged her inadequate and potentially immoral.

POLITICS, PATRIOTISM, AND PRODUCTION

In a 1903 article titled "Barrenness: Its Cause, Curse, and Cure," a certain Reverend James G. Evans remarked that barrenness "leads to immorality and domestic infertility . . . breeds brazenness; makes heartless; makes criminals and murderers . . . depopulates the state; retards the growth of the church; injures society." The solution? According to Evans, it was to "give children a value, and recompense the woman who bears; encourage production."[19]

Infertility is not a matter only of familial pressures, personal disappointments, and cultural stigmatization; it is subject to and shaped by legal and political pressures. Procreation and population growth are issues of state and national importance. The family is the unit by which society is built and nations prosper. Rev. Evans, in calling for infertility to be recognized not merely as a challenge for the individual but as a challenge to society at large, is not alone. The intermingling of the family and state has its own storied history.

Strategies of governmental population management vary. From China to Ceaușescu, intrusive policies that have destructive effects on citizens' lives run the gamut from encouraging growth to limiting expansion. Selective programs of sterilization for the sake of the nation—targeting immigrants, epileptics, alcoholics, and those with low IQs, among others—are equally horrifying.

Even in the absence of overt public policy, state structures implicitly determine and respond to cultural conceptions of the "right kind" of family. Economic social structures place a premium on procreative abilities. The US tax code not only favors married couples, but also makes provisos for dependent children under the age of twenty-four and offers child credits, child care tax credits, adoption credits, and earned income tax credit.[20] This is to say nothing of tax breaks for educational savings accounts, tuition programs, and higher education tuition deductions. While these programs are often adjusted by income, they are adjusted also by the number of children present in the household. These allowances encode the idea, normative to our society, that children are a social good.

Conversely, those who have trouble conceiving "naturally" face an onslaught of financial penalties. Reproductive technologies and testing often stand outside the realm of ordinary health care provisions. The situation can be more extreme when couples are seeking to adopt. While no one can doubt the good intentions behind those formal procedures by which adoptive families are evaluated and regularly checked on, adoptive parents are subjected to additional scrutiny by society as a whole. They are examined in ways that those who reproduce biologically are not. The process itself can be lengthy, and is one in which personal finances play a key role. Couples can increase their chances of adopting either by paying advertising costs and/or the cost of living expenses and medical fees for birth mothers, or by adopting privately abroad. While the system can be galling for any couple, it privileges conventional families and wealthy couples.

PROCREATION AND NATURE

The high value that modern societies place on fertility and reproduction has biological roots. But the language and ideas used to express the value of the family, and particular models of the family, are often religious. For individuals struggling with infertility, religious communities are often a natural place to turn for solace, validation, consolation, and meaning. This process is complicated by two factors: the politicization of the family and human sexuality over the past fifty years, and the deeply religious and biblically based commandments to reproduce.

Since the 1960s there has been a revolution in societal attitudes to sex, women's roles, and familial life. These social trends
have been equated with developments in contraceptive technologies, feminism, relativism, and secularization and, as such, have
been rejected as immoral by some religious groups. In pushing
back against these wider social trends, some have seen the traditional model of the family as the last bastion of social values
and morality.

When large families become a marker of morality and fidelity, childless families become associated with secularization and
feminism. The subtle social stigma attached to women, in particular, for failing to procreate melds patriotism and procreation
into one. It extends the biological shortcomings and perceived
character flaws of infertile couples into moral and political subversion. Conversely, larger families are highly valued as traditional, principled, and religious.[21]

In the countercultural apologetics of large families and divine
fecundity, pregnancy and childbirth are conceived of as preferable. Certain kinds of births, those that take place in the home
rather than the hospital, for example, or that forgo pain-killers,
are explicitly described as "natural." In a social context that in-
terprets childbirth as natural, it is easy to take for granted the
idea that childbearing is a simple human process rather than—as
was the case until well into the twentieth century—a potentially
deadly event in the life of a woman.

This depiction of pregnancy and childbirth as natural further
exacerbates the characterization of infertile women as violators
of the laws of nature. Procreation is, of course, a part of the natural order. It is a vital part of the survival of the species. This does
not, however, necessarily mean that pregnancy is easy, safe, or
good. The idea that natural is equivalent to good and healthy is
misleading. Many things are natural and dangerous. Snakes are a
natural part of creation, but they do not make good playmates or
theological conversation partners.

Although this perspective is not always religious, it is fostered and fed by biblical understandings of childbirth and mothering. Tradition holds that the pain that women experience in childbirth is the result of the sinfulness of Eve in the Garden of Eden. In Christianity, the sin of Eve can be juxtaposed with visual images of Mary, the mother of Jesus. Since the Renaissance, the postpartum Mary has been depicted as placid, calm, and content. Medieval descriptions of her experience of conception, pregnancy, and childbirth describe it as pleasurable and at times even erotic. The subtle and deeply entrenched association of "natural childbirth" with moral superiority lingers in modern discourse of pregnancy. Against these idealized portraits of natural motherhood, the infertile woman or woman who experiences difficulties carrying to term appears unnatural, complaining, and self-absorbed.

READING INFERTILITY IN THE BIBLE

The Bible is read as an academic text, a work of literature, and a spiritual and theological handbook. When it comes to infertility, however, these disparate readings have coalesced around a single idea: that God instructed humanity to "be fruitful and multiply." The simple association of fertility with divine blessing, both in the Bible and in its subsequent interpretation, led and leads to a master narrative of infertility as equally originating from the deity, often, if not always, as a form of curse or punishment.

The presence, and perhaps even dominance, of this sharp perspective in the Hebrew Bible is not in question. The traditionally most revered women from the Hebrew Bible are those whose fertility is specially marked by having overcome barrenness with divine assistance, the matriarchs of Genesis and Hannah, the mother of Samuel. Fertility is a near constant in the various divine and familial blessings in the text, beginning in Genesis 1 and appearing again in the divine promise to the patriarchs. The

Psalms equate a fertile wife and a large family with the very definition of happiness for those who follow the path of God (Ps 128:3).
On the negative side, in the story of Hannah in 1 Samuel 1, both
her rival wife Peninnah and the narrator declare that Yahweh
had "closed her womb" (1 Sam 1:5–6). Although there is no explicit language of curse or punishment here, Peninnah levels the
accusation against Hannah as a taunt: she implicitly creates a
hierarchy of social acceptance in which the fertile woman out-
ranks the infertile, a hierarchy in which Yahweh, by being named
as agent, is implicated. The prophet Hosea calls for God to pun-
ish Ephraim with "a womb that miscarries" (Hos 9:14). The un-
productive womb thus becomes a symbol and signal of divine
wrath. On the male side, men who are reproductively disabled
are prohibited in Deuteronomy 23:2 from participating in the
cult, which in biblical terms at least means separation from the
heart of Israelite society.

While miraculous births are rarer in the New Testament, the
master narrative remains the same in the writings of the Jesus
movement. Agricultural barrenness continues to be a metaphor
for spiritual failure (Jas 2:20). In a clear allusion to the matriarchs of the Hebrew Bible, Elizabeth—the elderly and formerly
"barren" mother of John the Baptist—conceives and gives birth
late in life (Luke 1:36). The story might be read as suggesting
that such miracles are available to followers of Jesus. Certainly
the author of Hebrews read the birth of Isaac to the formerly
infertile Rebekah as a prototype for faithfulness (Heb 11:11).
But perhaps the most difficult teaching on fertility is found in 1
Timothy, in which the author writes that women "will be saved
through childbearing, provided they continue in faith and love
and holiness, with modesty" (1 Tim 2:15). While any number of
scholarly and pastoral interpretations have tried to reinterpret 1
Timothy, the starkness of the language and imagery cannot be
easily dismissed.[22] The pseudo-Pauline association of women's

salvation with childbearing or—as some have read the passage—child rearing, binds the fate of female followers of Jesus to their procreative and maternal abilities.

The association of divine blessing and fertility reverberates throughout the entire corpus. As part of the covenant, God promises Abraham offspring as numerous as the heavens. And, by the time we reach the theologically weighty question of salvation in the pastoral epistles, the vindication of women is explicitly tied to their ability to bear children. Taken together, these texts contribute to a master narrative running throughout the Bible in which fertility is a sign of divine blessing, procreation an obligation, and infertility a sign of divine judgment and moral failure.

Numerous spiritual and religious self-help books and manuals have been written to address the experience of alienation and failure experienced by those who are unable to reproduce biologically. Whereas in the past infertility was frequently linked to sin, the majority of these books direct their readers away from personal culpability toward a more general and cosmic sense of brokenness. Simultaneously, however, these books reinforce the biblical idea that personal transgression is the potential root of distress. To offer just one example, a book from 2005, *Infertility in the Bible*, offers the following statement: "We see that infertility can be a divine decree, a punishment for a specific philosophical error that caused you to make a mistake (i.e., a "sin"). That's a possibility for any of us, and it pays to take it seriously. Happily, the constructive response to infertility is the same whether the infertility stems from divine punishment or whether it's the result of the laws of nature: look for a character flaw in yourself related to having children, understand what mistake you're making, and hope that your new insight will lead to divine intervention now that you are no longer blinded by goals that contradict God's plan."[23] While it may not be the author's goal, the statement "infertility is not always punishment for sin" is immediately followed by instructions to the implied infertile reader to "look for a character flaw" in himself or herself. This sort of advice is found in many other similar publications, but religious manuals cannot shoulder the blame alone. Studies have demonstrated that, in the absence of diagnosis or cure, some infertile couples have interpreted their infertility as divine punishment for having had premarital sex.[24]

When it comes to the evaluation of infertility in biblical texts, scholarly readings have not diverged sharply from conventional religious understandings. The basic premise that disability or disease is divine judgment from God for sin is as entrenched in the academy as it is in the pulpit.[25] This is what, in critical disability theory, has come to be known as the "religious model" of disability: the notion that disability is divine punishment. Yet this label, it should be noted, is misleading in certain ways. Certainly today it would be inaccurate to say that religious understandings of disability necessarily entail concepts of sin and punishment. More important for our purposes, the "religious model" suggests that as we look back in history we should *expect* to find that the more "religious" cultures of the past, particularly in the ancient world, held to this notion of disability as divine judgment. Yet this is prejudicial, and paints the diverse intellectual and religious sensibilities of the past with a single wide brush. A pointillist technique is more appropriate to the historical situation.

When it comes to infertility, the standard "religious model" is grounded in the assumption—derived from Genesis—that pregnancy, childbearing, and procreation are unequivocal goods, that childlessness that is chosen is intrinsically different from childlessness that results from biological impairment, and that women are responsible for infertility and childlessness. While these assumptions might appear reasonable, and might even be generally true, they are in need of reassessment.

THE PURPOSE OF THE BOOK

This book is neither a synthesis of biblical views of fertility and family nor an overview of fertility in the ancient world. It is self-consciously selective. It does not treat every single mention of infertility in the Bible, nor every possible text or ancient analogue that might impinge on the topic. Nor does it deny the presence or even dominance in the biblical text of the master narrative of infertility described above. We are seeking not to supplant, but to add; not to contradict, but to contribute. This book rereads in a historically responsible way a multifaceted text, the Bible, that has been unilaterally interpreted as negatively assessing the experience of infertility.

We have chosen to focus our story on the canonical Bible because these are the texts that formed the bedrock for later Jewish and Christian thinking about infertility, and because these are the texts that have cultural, religious, and imaginative power for readers today. At the same time, the Bible was not created ex nihilo and is never read outside of time and space. In their canonical form the books of the Bible are literary snapshots of broader, sweeping, and sophisticated processes of reasoning. Cultural conversations about infertility preceded, followed, and surrounded the elegant frames in the modern biblical canon.

Part of the process of reading biblical stories about infertility is placing them into the ancient context in which they were written. This process involves engaging, where applicable, ancient religious, medical, political, and legal texts pertaining to pregnancy, childbirth, marriage, and inheritance. It also means broadening the scope of the project to include discussions of adoption, constructions of the family and "fictive kinship" in the ancient world, and understandings of ideal bodies in relationship to the divine. Ancient Near Eastern, Egyptian, Greek, and Roman authors had a great deal to say about these issues and operated from assumptions very different from our own. In the history of scholarship, our understanding of this comparative material has been colored by traditional readings of the biblical material. Informed by recent critical biblical scholarship on disability, we seek to do the opposite. Our task is to read this contextual material afresh in order to disrupt the homogeneity present in modern assessments of the "biblical" or "ancient" view of fertility.

In some instances, especially in our treatment of the New Testament authors, this means turning to unexpected places: to stories and concepts that may not initially seem to be relevant to the question of infertility. The prevalence of adoption in the ancient world, negative understandings of pregnancy, and the development of Christian notions of nonbiological families allow us to see how infertility became a nonissue for some early Christians and why barrenness was on occasion even idealized. By situating conventional understandings of infertility in the context of these broader discourses relating to the family and childlessness we will catch glimpses of an imagined world predicated on family, but not on procreation.

What we hope to reveal is that, even in the Bible, childlessness need not be the hallmark of impiety, immorality, divine abandonment, or divine punishment. While it is largely presented as negative, it is on other occasions assumed or neutral. In some cases childlessness is a part of the divine plan, is embedded in creation, or serves as eschatological foreshadowing. There are junctures in the text where real thought is given to an alternative form of divinely authorized family. And by the time we reach Paul the celibate life seems actually to be preferred.

The organization of this book reflects our conviction—a conviction shared by the majority of biblical scholars—that the Bible is a collection of voices. It is an assortment of views assembled by fortune as well as tradition. Despite the fact that all of our authors are, so far as we know, educated men, they reflect the opinions of diverse groups and individuals whose lives were separated from one another by centuries, empires, social context, and fundamental spiritual convictions. Even within the "Old" and "New" Testaments there is disagreement and difference.

Depending on a scholar's or reader's own worldview, it is possible either to harmonize or to cacophanize these voices, to weave them together into an ornate tapestry or to expose the broken threads and unsightly hermeneutical knots that mar the canvas. Our intention is to do neither of our things but, rather, to highlight the diversity of voices about infertility in the biblical record. The impressive variety of these perspectives militates against any attempt to find any sustained argument running from Genesis through Revelation. We do not attempt to replace one dominant reading with another. To that end, the reader will notice that the arguments and claims made in one chapter of this book may be quite different from those made in another. These are case studies, and as each text or theme under discussion is distinct, so too are the potential ramifications to be drawn from it.

The resistance to harmonization and cacophanization is not only an attempt to do justice to the evidence and the historical circumstances in which the Bible was produced. It is also an effort to preserve, for those whose lives do not mirror the conventional religious narrative of fertility as God's blessing, the conflicting, competing, and diverse emotions and reflections that they might have about and on these experiences.

In pushing back against the dominant narrative of fertility, this book runs the risk of inadvertently rehearsing some of the more problematic arguments of second-wave feminism. In disrupting the idealization of women as mothers, feminism allowed for a woman's worth to be unshackled from her procreative capabilities. It created a structure in which biologically infertile women and women who choose to be infertile could be valued. It is worth pausing to acknowledge the enormity of this contribution. At the same time, the movement that sought to deconstruct a woman's desire to bear children, and treated that desire as the byproduct of patriarchal discourse, did not allow room for maternal desire or reproductive technologies.[26] The dominant narrative of women as defined by their procreative abilities (or, as 1 Timothy would state it, "saved through childbearing") was replaced with a new narrative in which maternal desire itself was rejected.

As third-wave feminists pointed out in their critiques of their predecessors, this new narrative did not allow space for women, or men for that matter, to feel conflicted or divided about their situation. The move to replace one strong monolithic view with another is replicated in other arenas in which marginalized or liminal identities are formed. In conversations surrounding deafness, for example, the deaf lobby is often criticized both for opposing the selective termination of deaf fetuses and for funding research into curing the conditions that lead to deafness. The accusation that is made is that the deaf lobby is "inconsistent" or, worse, "hypocritical." It is important to note that similar accusations are pointedly not made against those who fit into the culturally defined group of "normal" and (thus) dominant bodies. Our culture continues to identify emotions with women, but it is culturally acceptable for men to perform the roles of either the "sensitive modern man" and the "stoic male" without being subjected to high-brow accusations of hypocrisy. Consistency is evidently the hobgoblin only of marginalized minds.

The same breadth of expression, experience, and inner conflict permitted to the "normal" should be extended to the atypical. By illuminating the diversity of ancient opinions about childlessness—recognizing the neutral and the positive alongside the conventionally negative—and by resisting the desire to set these opinions into a single monolithic narrative, we aim to supply resources for the wide varieties of life experiences that lead to childlessness and the wide variety of responses that even a single person might have to these circumstances. It is an effort to puncture the wall of the proscriptive and to allow for a multiplicity of interpretations that mirror the multiplicity of emotions and lives.

Even as this book is methodologically historical, it has in its sights the embodied experience of childlessness. The subject matter of this book is not a set of abstractions, and the book itself is not an academic thought experiment intent on dislodging truisms merely for the sake of doing so. Smoothing over biblical tensions either by elevating infertility over fertility or by presenting a singular counternarrative to the dominant narrative of fertility would do injustice both to the diverse experiences of childlessness today and to the biblical record. In this quest for polyphony, therefore, historical responsibility and embodied reality meet.

If a single word or thought can summarize the thrust of our argument, it is this: childlessness in the Bible is divinely sanctioned—insofar as the word "sanction" means both to endorse and prohibit. Social-scientific studies of infertility have suggested that women who are diagnosed as infertile are able to restructure their definition of family to include child-free lifestyles and adoption, and report that their lives are greatly improved on account of these changes.[27] The intent of this book is to broaden the conventional understanding of the biblical perspective in order to reveal the diversity of biblically endorsed notions of family, parenthood, and fertility.

CHAPTER 1

The Matriarchs as Models

In the Israelite hill country, toward the beginning of the eleventh century BCE, there lived a woman named Hannah. Though her name meant "grace" or "favor," she hardly considered herself either graced or favored. Her husband Elkanah loved her, to be sure, but she was childless. To make matters worse, Elkanah had another wife, common enough in those days: a woman named Peninnah, who had given birth to many children, sons and daughters. Living under one roof with her husband, her husband's other wife, and her husband's other wife's children, Hannah would have been reminded of her unhappy situation almost every moment of every day. But it was particularly evident during the family's annual pilgrimage to the great sanctuary of Shiloh, the home of the revered Ark of the Covenant, the place where Israel could communicate most directly with its God.

Every year, Elkanah would take his household to Shiloh to offer thanks for their mutual well-being, by sacrificing an animal from his herd or his flock, burning its innards on the altar, donating some of its meat to the local priests, and consuming the remainder of the animal with his family in a rare bountiful feast. Hannah may well have wondered what well-being she had to be thankful for, given her daily misery. Her feelings would only have been compounded by the traditional practice at the feast itself: as Elkanah divided up the meat among his household, Hannah's childless solitude was made tangibly manifest, as Peninnah received multiple portions for herself and her children while Hannah was given one lonely portion, to be shared with no one.[1]

The mere objective facts of her life were no doubt hard enough. But, adding insult to injury, Peninnah could not refrain from taunting Hannah over the fact that Hannah's barren state was God's doing. Said in God's holiest sanctuary, this accusation had real force behind it. Elkanah attempted to soothe Hannah: "Why are you so sad? Am I not dearer to you than ten sons?" (1 Sam 1:8).[2] Yet for Hannah, even this question must have cut deeply—after all, her rival Peninnah had both Elkanah and children; she wasn't forced to choose. And with Peninnah's taunt ringing in her ears, Hannah had every right to wonder if there wasn't some truth to it: what good would Elkanah's love be—what good is anything—if God himself had turned against her?

Of the five narratives of barren women in the Hebrew Bible—the others being the matriarchs Sarah, Rebekah, and Rachel and the unnamed mother of Samson—the story of Hannah is by far the most fully rendered. And yet it is told in a mere eight verses at the beginning of 1 Samuel. We know of Hannah's internal torments only from later in the chapter, from the story of her heartfelt prayer, where we are told that she is "wretched," that she lives in "suffering," that she is "a very unhappy woman," that she experiences "anguish and distress" (1 Sam 1:10–16). We know, then, how Hannah feels about her infertility, all of which is eminently understandable. But the description at the beginning of the chapter leaves much unsaid, and many questions unanswered.

The narrator gives us virtually no information about Hannah: where she comes from, what she looks like, who she is as a person—the only description we are given is that she has no children. When we turn to the other barren women in the Hebrew Bible, we find the same descriptive brevity at work, with only minor variations. In Genesis 11, we learn that Abraham has taken a wife named Sarah, of whom we are told immediately and without any further introduction that she "was barren; she had no child" (Gen 11:30). Rebekah enters the scene in Genesis 24, where she proves herself to be generous and worthy; but in the next chapter, with little warning and less detail, we hear that Isaac has to plead with God on her behalf "because she was barren" (Gen 25:21), her infertile state being relegated to a mere subordinate clause. As with Hannah, we know that Rachel is loved by her husband Jacob, who spent fourteen years working to marry her; yet she speaks not a single word in the narrative of those years. Instead, immediately after she has finally married Jacob, we learn from the narrator that "Rachel was barren" (Gen 29:31). And the poor mother of Samson—she is not even given a name, but is known to us only as the wife of Manoah, introduced in the text thusly: "His wife was barren and had borne no children" (Judg 13:2).

The exclusive quality of infertility—the sense that it is the only aspect of these women that is worth mentioning—is not limited only to the narratorial voice. Not only is infertility Hannah's defining descriptive feature, it also seems to be all anyone can speak to her about. Before she bears Samuel, every word Hannah speaks, in her prayer and her dialogue with the priest Eli, is related to her distress. Her rival, Peninnah, taunts her about her infertility. The only words Elkanah speaks to her are an attempt to relieve her sorrow over having no offspring. So too with Sarah: though almost entirely silent in the biblical text before giving birth to Isaac, when she does speak it is either to Abraham, to complain about her infertile status when compared to her handmaid Hagar, or to herself, doubting God's ability to make her pregnant (and then to God, trying to deny her doubts). Rachel's first words, addressed to Jacob, are "Give me children, or I shall die" (Gen 30:1). When she next speaks it is to her sister Leah, requesting some of the mandrakes that Leah's son Reuben had found (30:14). The mandrake is no ordinary plant. It was considered to have potent aphrodisiacal properties—the Hebrew word for mandrake comes from the same root as the word for "beloved," and the plant appears only twice in the Hebrew Bible, here in Genesis and in the highly sexually charged Song of Songs.[3] When Rachel requests the mandrakes, she is requesting them a means of increasing her fertility; having perhaps exhausted other options, she is turning in desperation to the world of dietary medicine. The laser-like focus on each woman's infertility, to the exclusion of nearly every other aspect of her identity, means that infertility is effectively her identity. If women in the ancient world were reduced to vessels for childbearing, barren women were just fragile shells, empty of consequence.

All of these stories, all of these lives, zero in on one salient characteristic, then leave us grasping for explanations. No explicit interpretation of this infertility is provided. By leaving unspoken the full meaning of this bald description—"she was barren"—the text allows, even invites, its readers to project onto and into the story their own understandings. In many ways, this remains the experience of infertility even to the present: so often no more than simply a diagnosis, without any greater explanatory power. The meaning of infertility, the why to its what, is something medicine is unequipped to provide. It is, rather, culturally dependent. The fundamental questions—How do we define infertility? Why does it occur? What does it signify?—are answered differently in different times and places. Because so many of our modern notions come from the Bible, what concerns us here is how they would have been answered in biblical times. That is to say, how would Hannah have understood and experienced her

barrenness? And how can a greater appreciation of ancient ideas
about infertility lead us to reassess some of our own ideas?

THE SOCIAL EXPERIENCE OF INFERTILITY

To fully grasp the narratives of these infertile biblical women, we
need to ask some very basic questions, questions that no ancient
readers would need to ask, for they would already know the answers intuitively, and questions that few modern readers tend to
ask, because they seem perhaps beside the point or because the
answers seem, erroneously, obvious. But, in order to avoid casu-
ally transposing our assumptions onto the ancient and different
world of the Bible, the ostensibly simplest questions are often the
most important.

The question that is least often asked, and one that will recur
throughout this book, is this: why do we—or, better, why do
the biblical authors of these stories—assume that these women
would want to bear children in the first place? There is no need
to rehearse the litany of biblical and other ancient texts that glo-
rify procreation; at the same time, there is no requirement to use
those texts as a filter through which to read everything else. No
one asks, for instance, why Moses's sister Miriam has no children. Should we automatically assume that she *wanted* children?

In the case of Hannah, there is no real doubt, given what we
know of her unhappiness and her desperate prayer. So too Rachel, who exclaims, "Give me children, or I shall die!" (Gen 30:1).
But Sarah, Rebekah, and Samson's mother never express such a
desire in any explicit fashion. As readers familiar with the biblical narrative, we know that they will become pregnant eventually, and so it is easy to understand these characters with that
end in mind—to see them as one-dimensional, singly purposed
figures whose journey is almost exclusively from infertile to fertile—in which case the only way to make sense of their story

arc is to make fertility their goal and infertility the obstacle they must overcome.[4]

And this seems to be what the biblical authors had in mind. When Sarah is introduced solely as barren, we learn something about her past. As we noted in the introduction, infertility only recently became understood as a medical condition. Today we can, in many cases (though certainly not in all), determine whether or not a woman is capable of bearing children with simple tests—test that can be (though rarely are) done even on those women who have no desire or intention to ever have children. Not so in the biblical period. A woman who was not trying to have children could not be called "barren"; there would be no way to know (here one may again consider Miriam). The label "barren" necessarily implies the attempt—and failure—to conceive. It is perhaps no coincidence that of these five biblical women, the only one who does not receive such explicit designation is Hannah, of whom we learn only that she "was childless" (1 Sam 1:2). This description, in theory, could apply equally well to someone who had no desire for children. Yet Hannah is the character who is provided with the most extensive narrative of maternal despair; in other words, her desire to have children is conveyed through the story, whereas for the other women we learn it through a descriptive label.

Let us then grant the biblical authors the assumption that these women all wanted to have children.[5] We can then ask perhaps the more important question: why? It is easy to talk about the fulfillment of God's promise of offspring to the patriarchs—perhaps too easy. Even within the world of the text, Sarah is introduced as barren even before Abraham has received any promise; Isaac, similarly, does not receive the promise until after Rebekah has borne Jacob and Esau; at no point do we learn that Rachel is told of the promise; and Samson's mother and Hannah live many centuries later. In every case, the children are desired without any notion of fulfilling some divine plan. Again, it may seem obvious: of course they wanted offspring. But despite the claims of Proverbs, which attributes to the womb of the barren woman a metaphorical insatiable hunger (Prov 30:15–16), the desire for children, common though it may be, is not a universal biological imperative. It is not enough to simply say that these Israelite women wanted children. It is not enough to say that the Bible valorizes procreation. The attitudes of ancient Israelite women and the literature produced by ancient Israelite men emerged from a common cultural matrix, and it is that which must be interrogated. What was it about Israelite society that supported and emphasized the virtue of childbirth? Why is the Bible so invested in progeny, such that it projects these desires onto its female characters? And do we remain beholden to the same system of values?

THE PRESSURE TO PROCREATE

As we have already observed, there are numerous social forces at work today that enforce an implicit positive valuation of fertility, be they in the realms of religion, employment, or tax policy. Similarly, but even more so, cultural pressure in ancient Israel to produce offspring came from multiple directions and arrived on multiple levels. We may start with the widest circle, the community of Israel writ large. The very historical circumstances of Israel's emergence in the early Iron Age contributed to a cultural emphasis on offspring. Israel came into existence just following a period of general urban collapse and population migration across the ancient Near East.[6] Though the cause of this phenomenon remains unclear, the sudden decline may have driven a compensatory baby boom to replenish existing communities or to more firmly establish nascent ones.[7] For Israel, a newcomer in the Canaanite context, demographic expansion was important in its own right: families and clans required a certain population to gain an economic foothold, to ensure the proper transmission of inherited property, and to provide for a measure of self-defense if necessary—both Samson and Hannah's son Samuel, after all, became famous fighting off the threat of the neighboring Philistines.[8] In relatively broad sociological terms, therefore, the matriarchal stories emerge from a context in which, given the historical and cultural situation, childbirth was particularly valued.

Then there are the considerations at the level of the household. Hannah and her family were almost certainly agriculturalists or pastoralists, as was the overwhelming majority of the populace.[9] The economy was primarily household-based, and as has always been the case in such circumstances, the more hands to work the better. (We may take as exemplary the shepherding work done by Jacob's sons [Gen 37:2].) It has been estimated that children could begin contributing to the work of the household as early as age five or six.[10] In ancient Israel there was a particular need for supplemental agricultural help: the hill country, where Hannah and most Israelites lived, was particularly difficult to farm. Stone terracing, to prevent the soil from slipping down the hillside during the rainy season, and cisterns, to collect the rainwater before it rushed into the valleys, were necessary for agriculture to be carried out in this region. Unlike the fertile plains of the coast, where crops could simply be planted and grow, it was a constant struggle in the highlands to create and perpetuate the conditions amenable to farming. This additional labor came primarily from an increase in family size.[11]

From the perspective of a parent, children were a safety net, as they often are today.[12] The elderly would be supported by their offspring: housed in their children's homes, fed from their children's food.[13] A Ugaritic text describes in detail the responsibilities of a son to his father: protecting the father from slander and ill intentions; helping him stand while drunk; offering sacrifices on his behalf; plastering his roof; washing his clothes; and of course performing his burial.[14] On a less tangible—but equally important—plane, children were also required to support their ancestors in the afterlife. The practice of caring for one's deceased ancestors, known as the cult of the dead, is well and widely attested in the ancient world.[15] Those deceased ancestors, in turn, were understood to ensure the fertility of their attentive descendants, thereby reinforcing the ritual practices around the gravesite.[16]

From the viewpoint of the family patriarch, children were viewed as necessary because without them one would effectively disappear from history. The ancient Near East was predominantly illiterate; for one's name to live on after one's death, there had to be someone to keep it alive. Memories and stories, which could be curated only in the minds of one's offspring, took the place of letters, photographs, and home videos. It was up to the son to maintain the memory of the family.[17] Numerous biblical texts attest to the common ancient anxiety of being forgotten.[18] Absalom sets up a monument to himself precisely because, as he says, "I have no son to keep my name alive" (2 Sam 18:18). The wise woman from Tekoa who confronts David over his treatment of Absalom tells the same story, envisioning what will happen when her only son is killed: "They would quench the last ember remaining to me, and leave my husband without name or remnant upon the earth" (2 Sam 14:7). Most important for our purposes is God's promise to Abraham: "I will make your name great" (Gen 12:2). This does not mean fame, at least not exclusively; it is the standard divine promise to the patriarchs of offspring.[19] Abraham's name will be great because a nation will come forth from him, a nation that will retell his story and keep his name alive—and so, indeed, it came to pass.

In short, ancient Israelite economy and custom effectively demanded offspring. A family could survive neither literally nor figuratively without children to sustain it. Couple these deeply felt needs with the relatively high infant mortality rate—estimated to be a staggering 50 percent[20]—and it is easy to see how ancient Israel came to value childbirth so highly. It is no coincidence that the biblical authors made "be fruitful and multiply" (Gen 1:28) the first words God speaks to humanity.[21]

Recognizing the social forces that went into the biblical valuation of fertility, however, we might also observe that virtually none of these are applicable today. We suffer, in broad terms, from overpopulation, not from underpopulation; agriculture is, to say the least, no longer the dominant livelihood; having taken the Bible's advice, we no longer practice any cult of the dead; in a world in which our Facebook pages remain online even after we've died, memorialization through offspring hardly seems so pressing; and the infant mortality rate is no longer 50 percent, but, in America at least, stands currently at 0.6 percent.[22] In short, the social context from which the biblical emphasis on fertility emerged has not been perpetuated down to the present; and yet the valuation of childbirth, and the related views of those who cannot bear, has remained with us.

THE RISKS OF INFERTILITY

Hannah lived in a culture that heavily emphasized fertility. What, then, would she have felt upon realizing that she might be unable to conceive? Surely disappointment and sorrow; but also, in a manner peculiar more to the ancient world than to our own, a very real fear. It is meaningful that infertility is frequently aligned in the Bible with other positions of social vulnerability, such as poverty: "He raises the poor from the dust/lifts up the needy from the refuse heap. . . . He sets the childless woman among her household/as a happy mother of children" (Ps 113:7, 9), or widowhood: "May he consort with a barren woman who bears no child/leave his widow deprived of good" (Job 24:21). A woman who was unable to conceive was immensely vulnerable, her life susceptible to being overturned in any number of ways.

For the wealthy, at least, this dangerous social position could be alleviated somewhat by elevating a maidservant to the rank of concubine and having the slave girl bear children in the wife's name, the path taken by Sarah and Rachel. Elsewhere in the ancient Near East, such practices were inscribed into ancient law, in the form of marriage contracts, such as we find from Nuzi: "Puzur-Ištar married Ištar-lamassi. . . . If Ištar-lamassi does not behold an infant within three years, he will buy a maid-servant and take her (as a concubine)."[23] Such a practice would preserve the infertile wife's official status, but could also cause rifts in the fabric of the home, as the example of Sarah and Hagar amply demonstrates. The infertile wife would be willing, however, to endure the social discomfort within the household in exchange for the long-term benefits of having children in their own names. Sarah and Rachel offer their servants to their husbands for the sake of the family line, to be sure, but also, and quite explicitly, so that they themselves might be "built up" through this form of surrogacy (Gen 16:2; 30:3).

Alternatively, there was, in the customarily polygamous ancient world, the risk of the husband taking a second, fertile, wife—as Hannah knew all too well.[24] Again, from Nuzi: "Kelim-ninu has been given in marriage to Shennima. If Kelim-ninu bears children, Shennima shall not take another wife; but if Kelim-ninu does not bear, Kelim-ninu shall acquire a woman of the land of Lullu as wife for Shennima."[25] Note that in this case, it is actually the infertile wife's responsibility to find a fertile replacement for herself. In another text, a man looking to acquire a second wife states his reason plainly: "I have no child; I desire a child. Please give me your daughter in marriage."[26] In rabbinic law, it is actually required for a man to take another wife if, after ten years, his first wife does not bear at least one son.[27] While a second wife might solve the genealogical problems of the husband, it threatens to turn the infertile wife into little more than a burden for the rest of the household, as Hannah may well have felt each time she received her lonely portion.

Most often, we may guess—though no biblical narrative exemplifies it, for obvious reasons—infertile marriages ended in divorce, as in ancient Egypt, where infertility was aligned with infidelity as a rationale for the husband dismissing his wife.[28] There is an Egyptian text that admonishes the reader to "not abandon a woman of your household who does not conceive and give birth"[29]—a statement that is indeed thoughtful, but that at the same time betrays the existence of a customary practice. Divorce in the ancient world, including ancient Israel, was devastating for the woman. She would be returned to her father's house, where she would be a drain on her family's resources long beyond the time when she would have been expected to have left. She would be tarnished with the social stigma of divorce, making it harder for her to marry again—and if it was known that she was infertile, remarriage would likely be impossible; at least it was according to rabbinic law, which states that a man is prohibited from marrying a barren woman.[30] The biblical laws of divorce make clear that the husband can dismiss his wife for virtually any reason: "She fails to please him because he finds something obnoxious about her, and he writes her a bill of divorcement, hands it to her, and sends her away from his house" (Deut 24:1).[31] It was that simple, and that harsh.

Hannah—and any woman in ancient Israel—would have known that these were the possibilities awaiting her should she prove to be infertile.[32] Only the rare situation of the surrogate concubine was tolerable, if not palatable, as it resulted in a child in the infertile wife's name. When a surrogate was not possible, however, as was the case with Hannah, then there was more to be feared than either a fertile rival or the shame of divorce. When Hannah and Elkanah and Peninnah passed away, who would remember them? Who would tend to the family tomb? It would be the children of Peninnah, in whom Hannah had no share. Hannah, like every woman, required children to preserve the family name—hers included—and to maintain the ancestral cult, so that she would be firmly established as part of her husband's household in the world to come. If no offspring carried her name, if no children offered sacrifices and libations on her behalf, she would be as forgotten in the afterlife as she felt in her unhappy home.[33]

Having a child who bore one's name was essential. So much so, in fact, that even the rare woman who chose not to bear a child herself still felt the need to have one borne for her. In the ancient Near East, almost the only women for whom pregnancy was undesirable were priestesses, who were generally expected not to bear children while holding their offices. For some, this might mean taking up the priesthood later in life, after their children were already raised; for others, however, it could mean taking up celibacy from an early age and never bearing children at all.[34] There were no such priestesses in ancient Israel, but they were prominent in Mesopotamia. Priestesses who chose the route of celibacy would take virtually the same course of action as did the barren matriarchs Sarah and Rachel: they would give slave girls to their husbands, that offspring might be born in their names.[35] Those women who did not give birth—whether by choice or not—all saw the value of having children.

Thus when Hannah expresses her desire to bear a child, it is not just the economic, historical, or familial pressures upon which she is acting. She is acting for herself. Why does Hannah long for a child, when Elkanah already has many by Peninnah? Similarly, why is it important for Sarah to bear a child? Abraham already has a son, Ishmael. Why should Rachel care if she is barren or not, when Leah has provided Jacob with son after son? These children are desired not for the sake of the continuity of the father's name, nor for the economic well-being of the household—those issues have already been resolved. They are, rather, for the safety of the mother's social position and for the continuity of her name; for her status, now and in the afterlife. Even Leah, who already has four sons, offers her handmaid Zilpah to Jacob so that even more children can be born in her name. This is, again, not for the sake of Jacob, who by that point has eight sons already, but for Leah: she is looking to improve her status, not his.[36] As one scholar has put it, "Within the world of these women, it is possible to achieve personal security only through an abundance of sons."[37] Or as the rabbis said, more succinctly, "Who secures the woman's position in her home? Her children."[38]

Another subtle but forceful indication in this direction is found when we look closely at the prayers and pleas for fertility in our stories. All prayers, of course, are offered to Yahweh; but who does the offering? In the cases where a couple has no children to begin with, it is the man: Abraham (Gen 15:2) and Isaac (Gen 25:21). Their prayers are for their names and their lineage, for the family and the upholding of God's promise to become a great nation.[39] But when there are already children in the household by another wife, it is the woman who pleads: Rachel (Gen 30:1) and Hannah (1 Sam 1:11). They cry for themselves.

This view of the matriarchs cuts against the conventional gender division regarding the desire for offspring. Generally, it has been thought that men want children, sons in particular, for reasons of inheritance, lineage, and legacy—concepts that have, historically, been predominantly the male domain—while women mostly express a biological maternal urge, that warm feeling that comes from holding an infant in one's arms. Although there may be truth in these stereotypes, they are in no way exhaustive. From the perspective of the ancient Israelite woman, those warm biological feelings are a luxury; far more was at stake, including aspects of identity and legacy that have often been associated more with men than with women. But for these women (and for so many women since), in the absence of even the possibility of a professional career or a life apart from their households, having children was the means to and signal of cultural success.

The emphasis on offspring was felt from the individual through the familial all the way to the communal and even national level, on fronts economic, social, and religious, extending from the present into the indefinite eschatological future. It is no wonder that Rachel exclaims, "Give me children, or I shall die!"—though there is no small irony in the fact that when Rachel does die, it is in childbirth.[40] (It is hard not to read Rachel's cry in light of her death: the truth of the matter is, in fact, "Give me children, *and* I shall die.") The same language is used to describe the experience of infertility to this day,[41] and was echoed across the ancient Near East: in Mesopotamia, a man wrote of his infertile wife that she was "neither dead nor alive."[42] Some Mesopotamian texts suggest that humans who are incapable of reproduction might actually become a demon.[43] A midrash states, "Four are regarded as dead: the leper, the blind, the childless, and the impoverished."[44] The rabbis imagined Hannah saying, "Before he gave me a son, I was one of the dead; now that he has given me a son, I have been reckoned with the living."[45] Infertility left one socially and existentially separate—among the community but not part of it—in this world and in the world to come.[46]

GENDERING INFERTILITY

Hannah's isolation was acute. And though Elkanah's attempts to reassure her of his affection were certainly lovely in their way, they may well have only highlighted for Hannah just how alone she was.[47] For, despite his love, Elkanah could never share in Hannah's feelings: in the ancient Near East, before there were any tests to establish whether it was the husband or the wife who was infertile, the responsibility for fertility fell almost entirely on the woman.[48] Using a metaphor common to both Egypt and Mesopotamia, one scholar poetically stated the situation thusly: "The reproductive process involved the planting of the male seed in the female field. If this was accomplished and yet there was no conception, the fault lay not in the seed but in the field."[49]

The "if" of the last sentence quoted above represents the only circumstance in which responsibility for childlessness fell on the husband rather than on the wife: not male infertility, which seems to have been virtually unknown, but rather male impotence, the inability to achieve or maintain an erection.[50] For the latter, there were numerous suggested treatments. "If a man's 'heart' does not rise for his own woman or for another woman"—note that it is ensured that the man is not simply bored with his wife—he is to sacrifice to Ištar, or mix iron ore with oil and rub his body with it, or tie a rope around his waist, or recite an incantation over a bag filled with animal parts and gold and silver beads.[51]

The fact that there are numerous texts explicitly relating to male impotency, but none for male infertility, suggests the possibility that male impotency was in fact the functional counterpart to female infertility in the ancient Near East.[52] Each represented the quintessential visually defining sexual act of the gender: erection for the man, and pregnancy/childbirth for the woman.[53] Yet we know that there is an element invisible to the naked eye, and that men are just as likely to be infertile as women. And here the gender equality shifts precipitously against the woman: for so long as the man delivered the seed, the absence of offspring would be blamed on her, and she would be the one to suffer the consequences.

She may not have been happy about such a determination, of course—Hannah's silent response to Elkanah's kindness speaks loudly. In the Hittite "Story of Appu," the protagonist is childless, and his wife, after yet another attempt to conceive, blames him for their condition: " 'You have never taken me correctly! Have you taken me correctly now?' " Though Appu's wife is given the freedom to assign responsibility in an unconventional direction, the text returns us to the normative stance with Appu's response: "You are only a woman of the usual female sort and consequently don't know anything!"[54] To a certain extent, this is not so far from the interchange between Rachel and Jacob: "Give me children, or I shall die!," she cries, to which Jacob angrily responds, "Can I take the place of God?" (Gen 30:1–2). In both stories blame is explicitly or implicitly leveled at the husband, who redirects it to the unknowing or the unknowable. These texts, from very different times and places in the ancient Near East, together attest both to the potential for an alternative explanation and to the standard cultural rejection of such an alternative. The woman remains the focus.[55]

The closest the Hebrew Bible comes to recognizing the possibility of male infertility is in the law of levirate marriage. According to Deuteronomy 25:5–10, if a husband dies without an heir, his widow is to be married to her husband's brother, and the first son that she bears will be accounted to her deceased first husband. The law centers on the question of inheritance rights and land possession, but it also depicts a situation in which a couple has been married for an indeterminate period and has no sons—a situation in which we would assume fault to lie with the woman. Yet when her husband dies, she is not only permitted but required to remarry for the sole purpose of having children, therefore raising the possibility that the lack of offspring was the deceased husband's fault: if she is to remarry for the purpose of bearing a son, then the childlessness of her previous marriage could hardly be due to her infertility. It is this legal circumstance that lies behind the famous story of Ruth, who, according to Ruth 1:4–5, had been married, without children, for around ten years—and who, of course, proves to be perfectly fertile when she eventually marries Boaz.[56] Of course, it is possible that what is imagined here is impotence rather than male infertility; and given that the law relates specifically to a couple without a son, it may be imagined that we are dealing here not with childlessness but rather with an abundance of daughters.[57] Similarly, when in Deuteronomy 7:14 God promises that Israel's obedience will be rewarded with an absence of any barren man or women (*'aqar we'aqarah*), there is no way to know whether the masculine adjective *'aqar*, which appears only here in the entire Bible, indicates infertility or impotence—especially if male impotence was imagined to be the functional partner to female infertility. Though there may be whispers of male infertility in the Hebrew Bible, they are decidedly shouted down by the standard ancient Near Eastern paradigm in which the woman was to blame.[58]

In this we can see the difference between infertility as a medical condition and infertility as a social experience. In the ancient Near East, there was no such thing as "biological" infertility. There was only the culturally determined conclusion that childlessness is to be laid at the woman's feet. While there are no explicit statements of this sort in the Hebrew Bible, it is safe to say that, given the near ubiquity of closely related texts from across the rest of the ancient Near East, ancient Israel would have partaken of the same set of basic notions. Indeed, the fact that every one of these biblical stories is about a barren woman rather than an infertile man—even while it is the man to whom God makes the promise of offspring—testifies to the casual assumption that infertility was a fundamentally female condition. Hannah suffered alone.

Again we may note that although the situation has changed, the experience of the infertile woman has essentially remained. We are often capable now of determining whether infertility lies with the man or with the woman. We do have such a concept as "biological" infertility. And thus we know that, perhaps unsurprisingly, men and women are equally responsible for difficulties in conception and pregnancy.[59] And yet, in the absence or failure of medical tests—or, more commonly, when the results of those tests are not announced to the world—it remains the default assumption, as it was in the ancient world, that infertility is a female problem.

THE SHAME OF INFERTILITY

When we read of Hannah's misery and anguish, we understand that it is sorrow born not merely of being unable to fulfill a biological desire. As Jeremy Schipper has observed, her infertility is in many ways "more . . . a social experience than a biological anomaly."[60] Far more than in most modern societies, Hannah lived in a world that was practically designed to make infertile women feel outcast and alone.[61] As has ever been the case, the constant confrontation of the infertile mother with the fertility of her neighbors was a source of pain. In the Bible, this pain is highlighted by the cultural and literary custom of polygyny, such that Sarah and Rachel and Hannah all live in the same home, literally face to face, with the living embodiment of their anguish.[62] Rachel, in naming Joseph, makes clear what infertility feels like: "God has taken away my disgrace" (Gen 30:23), she says, using a Hebrew word, *ḥerpa*, that is used elsewhere in the Bible to denote uncircumcised men (Gen 34:14), men with their eyes gouged out (1 Sam 11:2), cowardice (1 Sam 17:26), a rape victim (2 Sam 13:13), and the collapsed walls of Jerusalem (Neh 2:17).[63] The experience of infertility in ancient Israel was utterly crushing.

What is important about Rachel's word choice is that "disgrace," both in Hebrew and in English, is a social term. There can be no disgrace, no *ḥerpa*, without other people before whom one feels shame—without other people to do the shaming. And such shaming is present in the biblical story, of course. Hagar looks down on Sarah: "her mistress was lowered in her esteem" (Gen 16:4). We are given no details, but for Sarah to have known Hagar's feelings, the maidservant must have acted in an openly disrespectful manner.[64] The clearest example of the sort of social stigmatizing that Rachel calls *ḥerpa* is that which befalls Hannah: "Her rival, to make her miserable, would taunt her because the Lord had closed her womb" (1 Sam 1:6).[65] There is nothing ambiguous about Peninnah's intentions: "to make her miserable." Nor is there any doubt as to the superior social position in which Peninnah stood. Though Hannah was the favored wife of Elkanah, Peninnah, as mother of Elkanah's children, was untouchable. The very fact of her fertility gave her an unbeatable edge in status. Similarly, Hagar, though merely a maidservant, felt herself empowered by her fertility to look down on her mistress. And though it seems morally wrong, she was technically right: by carrying Abraham's child, she became the indispensible female member of the family. The status of fertility outweighed the status of maidservant. Sarah might have wanted to expel Hagar from the house—as we know, she would eventually do just that. But Sarah was able to remove Hagar only once she herself had given birth to Isaac. Then, and only then, did Hagar become dispensable. As long as Hagar was the sole fertile woman in Abraham's home, the best Sarah could do was make her life miserable.[66]

It is worth asking the ethical question: granting, for the moment, that Peninnah may be right that Hannah is a victim of God's will—after all the narrator has confirmed the facts in the immediately preceding verse—is she justified in mocking Hannah? Perhaps surprisingly, in biblical terms the answer is probably yes. In the common biblical model shaming is a perfectly reasonable, perhaps even desirable, behavior.[67] When God brings misfortune on those with whom he is angry, there is often an explicit determination that the victim should be made an example of, publicly humiliated. Incest is called "a shame, a reproach"; those who commit incest are to be excommunicated "in the sight of their kinsfolk" (Lev 20:17). A girl who, on her marriage night, is found not to be a virgin is to be stoned publicly, at the entrance to her father's house (Deut 22:21). Idolaters will be "driven back and utterly shamed" (Isa 42:17). The Psalmist calls for the shame of his enemies to be exposed like clothing: "My accusers shall be clothed in shame, wrapped in their disgrace as in a robe" (Ps 109:29). Prophetic condemnations against foreign nations often invoke the shame they will experience among the peoples of the world: of Tyre, "The Lord of Hosts planned it to defile all glorious beauty, to shame all the honored of the world" (Isa 23:9); of Babylon, "Your nakedness shall be uncovered, and your shame shall be exposed" (Isa 47:3); of Moab, "Moab is shamed and dismayed; howl and cry aloud! Tell at the Arnon that Moab is ravaged" (Jer 48:20). Note particularly Isaiah's reproach to the Phoenician city of Sidon: "Be ashamed, O Sidon! For the sea—this stronghold of the sea—declares, 'I am as one who has never labored, never given birth!'" (Isa 23:4). Childlessness is linked with shame; shame is in fact commanded for the city imagined as childless. Infertility is employed as the very epitome of abasement.

And of course Israel itself will be openly shamed by God's own hand: "I in turn will lift your skirts over your face, and your shame shall be seen" (Jer 13:26); "I will make them a horror—an evil—to all the kingdoms of the earth, a disgrace and a proverb, a byword and a curse in all the places to which I banish them" (Jer 24:9); "I will uncover her shame in the very sight of her lovers" (Hos 2:12). If God not only condones shaming, but even practices it against his own beloved people, then those who do the same may merely be emulating the deity.[68]

But shame and guilt, though often intertwined, are not the same thing.[69] So the question remains: even if Yahweh is responsible for Hannah's infertility, how should we understand this divine behavior? Is it somehow ultimately Hannah's fault? And what of Rachel, to whom Jacob replies in anger, "Can I take the place of God, who has denied you the fruit of the womb?" (Gen 30:2)? Did God intervene to stop Rachel from conceiving? If so, why? When? How? These questions have more lasting and pressing interest for those today who take the Bible seriously, because they involve God, rather than ancient social context. To answer them, we need to understand the relationship not between the infertile woman and the society around her, but between her and her deity.

INFERTILITY AND THE DEITY

Peninnah's taunt represents a well-established strand of biblical and ancient Near Eastern thought. In Mesopotamia, an omen text declares that "if a woman's womb has accepted the sperm, but she does not conceive: wrath of the gods."[70] The biblical narrator himself announces of Hannah that "the Lord had closed her womb" (1 Sam 1:5), affirming at least divine agency, if not explicitly divine anger.

Most ancient interpreters fundamentally agreed with this basic statement of the master narrative of infertility, and held that God is directly responsible for rendering women barren. A Jewish work from the second century BCE, *1 Enoch*, could hardly be more blunt: "A woman was not created barren, but because of her wrongdoing she was punished with barrenness, childless shall she die. Why is a woman not given a child? On account of the deeds of her own hands would she die without children."[71] The rabbinic period produced a wide variety of explanations under this general heading. They imagined that God rendered the matriarchs infertile so that they would pray to him: "He said to them, 'My dove, I will tell you why I have kept you childless; because I was longing to hear your prayer.' "[72] Sarah was punished, ironically, for accusing God of preventing her from bearing: "By your life," God said to her, "I am visiting you through the very language that you have spoken."[73] Rebekah was barren because her non-Israelite relatives had prayed for her (Gen 24:60), and God wanted to make sure that the pagans would not think their prayers had any power.[74] Rachel was infertile because God had judged and condemned her.[75] Hannah was made infertile in order that she might be all the happier when she actually did bear a child.[76] They were kept infertile in order to preserve their good looks.[77] They were barren in order to refine them, to test them, to try their strength.[78]

Divine agency is explicit in the Koran: "Allah's is the kingdom of the heavens and the earths; he creates what he pleases . . . he makes whom he pleases barren; surely he is the knowing, the powerful" (42:49–50). Muslim women in modern Turkey tend to blame infertility on some past sin, often, perhaps unsurprisingly, abortion.[79]

This reading, often amplified by the idea not only of divine power but of divine punishment, continues to be restated in modern scholarly work. "However the motif of the barrenness of the matriarchs is to be dated, the theological intention of these texts is clear . . . infertility as punishment, just like children as blessing, is the work of Israel's God."[80] "Childlessness is not merely a distress for the woman; it is also a punishment. . . . It is the outpouring of the wrath of God."[81] "Barrenness and childlessness were at times viewed as either a test or a punishment by God."[82] The Hebrew Bible holds to "the conviction that offspring is granted or withheld by God, and that He must have His reasons for both."[83] "Birth and infertility are part of God's hidden plans."[84] The Bible "makes a connection between barrenness and sin."[85]

Given the centuries upon centuries of readers who have understood infertility within this overarching religious framework, and given the centrality of the Bible as the source of our understanding of God, it is natural to assume that for all of the ancient biblical authors, as well, infertility was thought to be the result of divine punishment. But is this a necessary conclusion—or have we been so overwhelmed by the master narrative that we are unable to see other strands of thought present in the narrative? Has the dominant view of infertility become so ingrained in our cultural understanding of the Bible that we now read the text exclusively through that lens?

SIN AND PUNISHMENT?

The biblical authors were certainly capable of explicitly describing an affliction as divine punishment. King Uzziah is struck with skin disease for illegitimately offering incense in the sanctuary (2 Chr 26:19–20); Elisha's servant Gehazi contracts the ailment for requesting money in exchange for his master's free services (2 Kgs 5:–27); even Miriam suffers for having dared to speak ill of her brother Moses (Num 12:10). The entire nation of Israel endures a three-year famine as punishment for Saul having killed some Gibeonites, who were protected by a divinely sworn oath (2 Sam 21:1–2). Sickness, often fatal, befalls those who have sinned or who are associated with sin: the son of the evil king Jeroboam (1 Kgs 14:1), for example. The principle is expressed in the negative by Isaiah: "None who lives there shall say 'I am sick'; it shall be inhabited by folk whose sin has been forgiven" (Isa 33:24). Innumerable people die as a result of divine wrath, from the rebels Korah, Dathan, and Abiram (Num 16) to Aaron's sons Nadab and Abihu (Lev 10:1–3) to David's unnamed child with Bathsheba (2 Sam 12:15–18) to King Saul (1 Sam 28:17–19) to the entire generation of the Exodus (Num 14:29–35).

Yet there are also many texts in which these same afflictions are provided with no justification whatsoever. The detailed laws regarding skin disease (Lev 13–14) align it not with any negative behavior, but rather with quite positive (if equally impurifying) events, such as sex and childbirth.[86] Famine repeatedly befalls Israel even in the patriarchal era, a period characterized by perfect obedience to God (Gen 12:10; 26:1; 41:54). Biblical figures who are entirely righteous still fall ill: the prophet Elisha (2 Kgs 13:14), King Hezekiah (2 Kgs 20:1), Daniel (Dan 8:27), the unnamed son of the widow of Zarephath (1 Kgs 17:17). Even premature death befalls the ostensibly innocent: the young child of the Shunammite woman (2 Kgs 4:20), for example, or Naomi's husband (Ruth 1:3), or even the great king Josiah (2 Kgs 23:29). Given the clear associations described above of disease, famine, and premature death with divine punishment, it is easy enough to see how biblical interpreters came to believe that such events were always such: they were simply extrapolating from the known to the unknown. Yet these examples challenge the general categorization of all such misfortunes as divine punishment.[87]

This same duality—explicit punishment in some texts and ringing silence in others—is present also in those passages that deal with infertility. On the one hand there is the story in Genesis 20 of Abraham and Sarah's sojourn to a foreign land, in which God causes all of the women in the court of Abimelech, king of Gerar, to become infertile. Here infertility is decidedly a punishment, though it is of the rare anticipatory sort: Abimelech has not in fact done anything wrong yet, as God himself acknowledges. Yet the king requires prophetic intercession on the part of Abraham to spare himself and his household from disaster: "Abraham then prayed to God, and God healed Abimelech and his wife and his slave girls, so that they bore children, for the Lord had closed fast every womb of the household of Abimelech because of Sarah, the wife of Abraham" (Gen 20:17–18).[88] To read this text in isolation, or as paradigmatic, one would think that infertility was, indeed, conceptualized as direct divine punishment for an identifiable wrong.[89]

On the other hand, however, there are the five infertile women we have already met. Not only are there no explicit mentions of any wrong any one of them may have committed that would justify such punishment, there are in fact numerous indicators that point in quite the opposite direction. Sarah is described as barren in the very first verse in which she is the subject. This does not preclude her having done something wrong earlier in her life, in theory. As one scholar suggests, "there was always the possibility that the woman had a 'hidden sin' on her record."[90] (It is revealing that scholarly interpreters prefer to alter and supplement the biblical narrative in order to fit it into their preexisting notion of the nature of infertility.)

In practice, however, what could Sarah have done? Sarah marries Abraham before he is called by God to leave his father's house and start a new life of obedience to Yahweh. When she is first introduced as infertile, she is still as yet unbound by Yahweh's will. Mere idolatry, which we can almost assume she practiced, could not be the cause of her infertility; if it were, then we would expect every woman on earth in the generations before Abraham to have been infertile (which would have been difficult for the continuation of humanity, not to mention the story line). It is, furthermore, difficult to imagine that a woman who was sinful to the point of being punished by God would simultaneously be chosen to bear the line of Abraham's divinely promised descendants—at least not without some form of repentance, or atonement, or even vague recognition of previous wrongdoing. And yet there is not a trace of that anywhere in the text. Sarah is not quite perfect: she famously doubts God's very power to make her fertile (Gen 18:12). Yet, notably, this moment of weakness—the sort of doubting of God's power that, in other circumstances (such as the episode of the spies in Num 13–14), does indeed lead to divine punishment of the most severe sort—occurs, necessarily, only after Sarah has been promised offspring. And Sarah's doubt does not jeopardize her fertility, but instead reinforces Yahweh's determination to bring about what he has promised.[91]

Whereas Sarah enters the first family of Israel even before God takes notice of Abraham, her daughter-in-law Rebekah seems handpicked by the deity. Abraham's servant is promised and provided with divine guidance on his mission to find a wife for Isaac. She is divinely chosen and appointed to marry into the lineage of Abraham, the chosen people. The sign itself is indicative of her character: not only does she give water to Abraham's servant when he asks for it, but she then offers some to his camels as well. Rebekah is described as beautiful in form, and proves herself by her conduct beautiful in character as well, typifying the virtue of hospitality, a virtue valued almost above all others in the ancient world. Finally, Rebekah is given the choice to go with Abraham's servant or to stay in her home; she chooses to go, thereby replicating by her decision the same willful obedience demonstrated by Abraham. All this is to say that the biblical description of Rebekah, in all of its aspects, is entirely positive. And all of this occurs before we are told that she is infertile. To find fault in Rebekah, as a way of justifying her infertility as divine punishment, would be to read aggressively against the text, and indeed against Rebekah herself.

Rachel—Rebekah's niece—is, like her sister and rival Leah, strikingly quiet in the biblical narrative. This is perhaps due to a sudden decrease in available narrative space: after all, in each of the previous two generations there were only two parents and two sons, while this generation sees five parents (Jacob, Leah, Rachel, Bilhah, and Zilpah) and thirteen children (the twelve sons and one daughter, Dinah). With more characters to fill the story, there is necessarily less room for any one of them to play an active role. As a result, we can say significantly less about Rachel's character than we could about Rebekah's. What we can say, however, is that when she confronts her infertility she neither prays, nor repents of any sin, nor confesses any iniquity, nor asks forgiveness of any kind—she doesn't turn to God at all. Displays of virtue, piety, penance, or self-examination do not lead to a divinely wrought cure. And yet God does make her fertile.

Samson's unnamed mother, like Hannah, has no family history, no easily described character, no physical description; she is only barren. Unlike Hannah, or Rachel, however, she does nothing to change her infertile state, at least nothing of which we are told; we enter the story at the moment that a messenger of Yahweh announces that she who was once barren will bear Israel's future savior. What, if anything, had she done to be infertile? What, for that matter, caused her to become suddenly fertile? The story does not tell us, which indicates that, at least within the world of the story, the origins or causes of her infertility are of no import. Again, though it is possible that Samson's mother had sinned in the past and been punished for it with infertility, it is certainly not evident in the story we are told. In fact, what little we do know about her testifies to her keen mind and moral worthiness: even while her husband cowers in fear before the presence of the divine messenger, she correctly perceives that "had the Lord meant to take our lives, he would not have accepted a burnt offering and meal offering from us, nor let us see all these things; and he would not have made such an announcement to us" (Judg 13:23).[92] This is a woman who is confident in her good standing before God.

Finally, there is Hannah. As we already saw, what we know about Hannah is the fact of her infertility and the emotions this state causes in her. But we also know what she says when she prays for a son: "O Lord of Hosts, if you will look upon the suffering of your maidservant and will remember me and not forget your maidservant, and if you will grant your maidservant a male child, I will dedicate him to the Lord for all the days of his life, and no razor shall ever touch his head" (1 Sam 1:11). As with Rachel, what is unsaid here is as revealing as what is said. This is not a prayer of repentance. It is not a confession of wrongdoing. We can recall her emotions, which indicate the same: she is wracked with anguish, with distress, with sadness—not with guilt.[93] She has not been punished for doing anything wrong; rather, she feels as if she has been punished for nothing at all.[94] We may note in contrast a Mesopotamian woman's prayer: "May my God who is angry with me turn back to me; may my transgression be forgiven and my guilt be remitted . . . may my womb be fruitful."[95] Here there is guilt, here there is divine anger, here there is a plea for not only fertility but, as a means to fertility, forgiveness. All of this is absent, consistently, in the matriarchal parallels.

Though there is, in the Abimelech story, a biblical text to support the idea that infertility is divine punishment for sin, there are five biblical texts, five women, all central to the overarching narrative, whose descriptions and stories and words testify to the opposite: that infertility can befall even those who are divinely designated as righteous and worthy. The Wisdom of Solomon refers to the desirability of "childlessness with virtue" (Wis 4:1), a category that would seem to be impossible were infertility and divine punishment inextricably linked. These five women are blameless. They also happen to be infertile.

DIVINE CONTROL

Infertility thus falls in a class of biblical misfortunes, including disease, famine, sickness, and death, that share certain common features. There are two ways that each of these is presented in the Bible: explicitly as divine punishment, or without any explanation whatsoever. If we merely extrapolate from the explicit to the unstated, then it is possible to say that all such misfortunes are directly attributable to God's judgment. But, as we have seen, in many cases this would not only be unwarranted, but would actually be reading against the narrative context. It is also possible to conclude that, since sometimes these misfortunes are indeed divine punishment, in those cases when there is no explicit statement we simply cannot know whether the sufferer did something to deserve her fate. But even this ambivalent conclusion does not take into account the strict dichotomy established in the biblical text: in the cases where an affliction is divine punishment we are never in any doubt as to what the person did to deserve it, while in the cases where we are not told that an affliction is divine punishment we can almost always say with assurance that the person did nothing at all to deserve it.

In other words, we are dealing not with a common phenomenon presented in two distinct forms, but with two distinct phenomena presented in a common form. We are dealing not with infertility (or sickness, or famine, or death) as divine punishment presented in either explicit or implicit fashion, but with two phenomena—divine intervention and mere happenstance—presented in the form of infertility (or sickness, or famine, or death). Death presents perhaps the best analogy: everyone dies, some by accident, or in battle, or from sickness, and some as the result of divine wrath. Divine punishment can, at times, take the form of premature death, just as at times it can take the form of infertility. But we would be mistaken to read all premature deaths as divine punishment, just as we would be mistaken to read all cases of infertility as divine punishment.[96]

One might then assume that the Bible therefore preserves two distinct views of infertility (and the other misfortunes mentioned above): one corresponding to what we would deem a "religious" perspective, in which infertility is divine punishment, and one corresponding to what we might call a "natural" perspective, in which God plays no part at all. But we cannot align our spectrum of possible interpretations with that of the ancient biblical authors. For the ancient Israelites, no part of life was totally divorced from the realm of what we would call "religious." Today we see two standard options for dealing with misfortune: if one thinks that misfortune is supernatural in origin, one addresses it by appeals to the supernatural (prayer, for example); if one thinks that misfortune is natural in origin, one addresses it by appeals to the natural world (such as medicine). But when we look at the Bible, we see that even those misfortunes we might today call "natural" are addressed not with medicine—there are no doctors in the Hebrew Bible—but rather by appealing to God: "For I the Lord am your healer" (Exod 15:26).

"Isaac pleaded with the Lord on behalf of his wife, because she was barren; and the Lord responded to his plea, and his wife Rebekah conceived" (Gen 25:21). Rebekah would have no reason to think that God had caused her infertility, yet it is to God that Isaac turns to cure her of it. We have already seen Hannah's plea that God should grant her a child. Even for those who do not directly address God, it is God who relieves them of their infertility. "Is anything too wondrous for the Lord? I will return to you at the same season next year, and Sarah shall have a son," God tells Abraham (Gen 18:14). Of Rachel it is said that "God heeded her and opened her womb" (Gen 30:22). Samson's mother receives a divine annunciation. Though the initial state of infertility may not be divine punishment, the change to fertility, it is abundantly clear, is the work of the deity. The rabbinic midrash that describes God and the heavenly court debating Sarah's merits does not have them deciding whether or not she should change from fertility to barrenness, but rather from barrenness to fertility.[97]

This is a question, therefore, of control. Even when the origins of a misfortune are unknown, there remains no doubt that God has the power to alleviate it. When Hezekiah falls ill, when his imminent death is even announced by the prophet Isaiah, the king turns immediately to prayer. His prayer—as we might expect from a monarch of whom the Bible said that "there was none like him among all the kings of Judah after him, or among those before him" (2 Kgs 18:5)—contains no expression of guilt; quite the contrary. "Please, O Lord, remember how I have walked before you sincerely and wholeheartedly, and have done what is pleasing to you" (2 Kgs 20:3). Hezekiah does not ask what he had done to deserve the sickness; he does not blame God for bringing it upon him. The origin of the illness is unknown and, fundamentally, unimportant; what is important is that God has the power to end it.[98] And indeed, immediately upon the conclusion of Hezekiah's prayer, God promises him not only a return to health, but even an additional fifteen years of life. God, the text maintains (and all biblical texts affirm), has power over life and death, sickness and health.

But divine power and control does not mean constant and unvaried divine activity. God's ability to harm and to heal does not mean that all harm (or, for that matter, all healing) is directly caused by God. Our modern spectrum ranges from supernatural on one end to purely natural on the other. The biblical spectrum, by contrast, always falls under the umbrella of the supernatural, of what we, from a modern vantage point, would label the "religious."[99] It ranges from supernatural to supernatural, with active divine causation on one end and total divine passivity on the other, and a wide range of possibilities between the two poles. Sometimes God directly causes misfortune; sometimes God is actively passive, allowing misfortune to happen without directly intervening in human history; sometimes God is uninvolved in the initial misfortune but comes to the rescue when called upon; sometimes God is passive from start to finish. But there is no circumstance in which God is not part of the story.[100]

When we view the ancient biblical perspective as a "religious" extreme unto itself, to be contrasted with a modern, secular, medical view of the origin of infertility, the variety of biblical conceptualizations becomes telescoped, their features indistinct. The result is inattention to the details of the biblical evidence and ignorance of the presence of more than one "religious" approach to the question of infertility. But there are distinct and different views held in the Bible, distinct and different explanatory possibilities. Infertility as punishment may have emerged as a dominant interpretation, but closer examination of the biblical material reveals that it did not start that way.

GOD IN THE WOMB

At the heart of the biblical conceptions of infertility—either as divine punishment or, more often, as a state that God has the power to change—is a basic sense of the unknown. In an age long before fertility treatments, before pregnancy tests, indeed even before the fundamental manner in which sperm fertilizes an egg was known, the entire process of conception was a mystery.[101] Of course it should be remembered that much of that mystery remains to this day: we are not always able to identify the reason why a couple is unable to conceive; it is never clear why, even in a fertile couple, one act of intercourse leads to conception while another does not. We tell couples who are just starting to try to get pregnant to "give it another try"; even without fertility treatments it can take some women years to successfully conceive. In the biblical world, these mysteries were both broader and deeper. Why was Peninnah able to bear children when Hannah was not? Why Leah and not Rachel? Why Hagar and not Sarah?

In the absence of almost any—not to mention accurate—biological information about conception, those in the ancient world put the responsibility for fertility on the ultimate unknowable entity: God. (This is a mystery in its original sense: knowledge that belongs to the divine realm and cannot be comprehended by the human mind.) It was not the case, then, that ancient people perceived any gap in their understanding of how the world worked. The workings of the deity were as real to them as the basics of biology are to us. Indeed, we are far more aware of the blank spaces in our understanding of the universe than they were. This is the message of Job: though we may not understand why things happen as they do, this does not mean that there is no reason for them. There is always God, who cannot be interrogated. The wisdom of Ecclesiastes says it clearly: "Just as you do not know how the lifebreath passes into the limbs within the womb of the pregnant woman, so you cannot foresee the actions of God, who causes all things to happen" (Eccl 11:5).

This is not an exclusively biblical view. It is, rather, part of the broader ancient Near Eastern understanding of the deity's role in childbirth, beginning with conception. "Without you," a prayer to the Babylonian moon god reads, "the childless one can receive neither seed nor impregnation."[102] Every Near Eastern culture had at least one, and usually many, deities who oversaw fertility. In one Ugaritic myth, a group of goddesses known as the Katharatu are present and, presumably, active assistants as the protagonist Dan'ilu attempts to impregnate his wife.[103] Amulets could be worn to bring about pregnancy: "Silver, gold, iron, copper, in total twenty-one (amulet) stones, in order that a woman who is not pregnant becomes pregnant: you string it on a linen yarn, you put it on her neck."[104] Incantations could be recited, with titles such as "Incantation for making pregnant a woman who does not bear (children)."[105] Fertility figurines, small household idols, have been found across the ancient Near East and across the centuries. These were, perhaps surprisingly, particularly popular in ancient Israel in the preexilic period (though not exclusively then): small female figures with large breasts, the nearly universal symbol of fertility.[106] A Mesopotamian prayer invokes the deity thusly: "My god, my lord, who created my name, who guards my life, who brings my seed into existence. . . ."[107]

From the Greco-Roman context as well there is also a plethora of magical texts that reveal the anxieties surrounding pregnancy in the ancient world. Appeals for conception,[108] calls for protection from demons during pregnancy,[109] diagnostic inquiries,[110] and appeals for renewed sexual interest that leads to conception have survived from the ancient world.[111] Inscriptions from healing sites, amulets, papyri, and figurines asking for protection during pregnancy were abundant in the Roman Empire. Many of these exemplars bear witness to the desperation of poor urban women to grapple with the origins and dangers of pregnancy and childbirth.[112] Life, and nascent life in particular, was fragile.

God—or, for the ancient Near East at large, the gods—is responsible for the conception, the creation, of new life.[113] In the Hebrew Bible, this comes to expression in a repeated refrain: Isaiah refers to God as the one "who formed you in the womb" (Isa 44:24; 49:5); God tells Jeremiah that he "created you in the womb" (Jer 1:5); the Psalms praise God as the one who "fashioned me in my mother's womb" (Ps 139:13); Job knows that he and his servant were made by the same hands: "Did not he who made me in my mother's belly make him? Did not one form us both in the womb?" (Job 31:15). The Hebrew word most commonly used in these expressions of "forming" in the womb—*yatsar*—comes originally from the context of a craftsman forming an object of wood or clay.[114] But most important for our purposes, it is also the same word used for the creation of the first man: "The Lord God formed man from the dust of the earth" (Gen 2:7). In other words, God's initial act of creating man from dust is replicated in the womb. Just as God created then, so God creates now.

This creation in utero is represented also in the names that many children are given in the Bible, names that testify to the deity's role in bringing them into being. The first human child born, Cain, is named this by his mother Eve because, she says, "I have created [*qaniti*] a man with the Lord" (Gen 4:1). Of her third son Seth she says, "God has established [*shat*] for me another offspring" (Gen 4:25). Eve, of course, does not suffer from infertility; yet she still attributes her children to God's power. There is nothing "natural" about conception. It is emphatically God's doing. "Sons are the provision of the Lord/the fruit of the womb, his reward" (Ps 127:3). Thus when Rachel confronts Jacob, saying, "Give me children, or I shall die," Jacob responds, "Can I take the place of God?" (Gen 30:1–2).

This assignment of divine activity in the process of conception comes through not only in abstracted terms, but in a very specifically realized physical manner. When Rachel becomes pregnant with Joseph, it is said that God "opened her womb" (Gen 30:22). It would be reasonable to assume that this implies that God had previously closed her womb—this is, after all, precisely the language used when God punishes Abimelech's household, "The Lord had closed fast every womb of the household of Abimelech" (Gen 20:18) as well as in the story of Hannah, "The Lord had closed her womb" (1 Sam 1:5–6). Recognition of the active role of God in human conception, however, sheds new light on the language used to describe the transition from a barren state to a fertile one. If God's role in conception is depicted as opening the womb, then it would seem that prior to this moment, the womb was—by default—closed.

Such a conclusion is borne out by the ostensibly common term "open," a term that typically has no particular nuance but which, when God is the subject, is both rare and meaningful. In Psalm 105:41, Yahweh "opened a rock so that water gushed forth," an unusual moment for a rock if there ever was one. Yahweh opens Isaiah's ears (Isa 50:4–5), not thereby changing him from deaf to hearing, but transforming his ordinary human ability to hear into the extraordinary prophetic ability to hear Yahweh's words. Similarly, Yahweh opens Ezekiel's mouth (Ezek 3:27), not thereby changing him from mute to speaking, but transforming his ordinary human ability to speak into the extraordinary prophetic ability to speak Yahweh's words.[115] Most prominent in this regard is Balaam's donkey, in Numbers 22:28: "The Lord opened the donkey's mouth, and she said to Balaam. . . ." The snake of Genesis 3 notwithstanding, it seems a reasonable assumption that in ancient Israel animals were not given to talking; Yahweh opens the donkey's mouth and changes it from its usual speechless state into one of eloquently voiced sarcasm.[116] In other words, when God opens something, he changes it from its usual state to an unusual state.

In the case of the womb, then, the biblical analogies suggest that in fact it is the closed womb that is usual, and the opened womb that is unusual. Again, God's active role in conception is highlighted, even marked as miraculous—regardless of how often it may occur. Such notions are found elsewhere in the ancient world. From Egypt a sizable collection of amulets have been found that depict a god or gods, a uterus, and a key. Though the precise meaning of these amulets remains debated, the imagery and the mechanism are clear. Opening and closing of the womb are beneficial in varying degrees and at different times: the womb must be closed to prevent miscarriage, but it must be opened to allow for delivery. Most important for our purposes, the womb must be opened at the moment of intercourse to allow for conception—which requires that it have been closed before that point.[117] The rabbis state this clearly: "Three keys are in the hands of the Holy One, blessed be he: the keys of resurrection, rain, and the womb."[118] The womb is imagined as a closed chamber, one to which only God holds the key. For a child to be born—and perhaps even for the man's seed to enter—God must turn the key and unlock the door.[119]

This understanding of conception may change how we read some of the biblical language that ostensibly describes God as involved in the preventing of pregnancy: Sarah says that "the Lord has kept me from bearing" (Gen 16:2); Jacob says to Rachel that God has "denied you the fruit of the womb" (Gen 30:2). We might say that these figures are, as in 1 Samuel 1:5, merely representing the dominant concept that God is directly responsible for infertility. But we may also note that their words are fairly passive: it is possible to keep one from bearing, or to deny one the fruit of the womb, by doing nothing at all—merely by neglecting to open the womb in the first place. It is worth noting that in both narratives—as with the story of Hannah—there is a rival to the barren wife: Hagar, Leah, and Peninnah. That is to say: the only times that the Bible uses language that implies a divine hand in causing these women's infertility is when it is establishing a rhetorical contrast between two women, one fertile and one infertile.

The best proof of this concept of fertility is not the opening of Rachel's womb, since, after all, we know that she was previously infertile. It is, rather, that the same is said about Leah, Rachel's fertile counterpart: Yahweh "opened her womb" (Gen 29:31), too.[120] If neither Rachel nor Leah can become pregnant without divine intervention, then it seems possible to argue that, from the biblical perspective, all women are "by nature"—that is, using perhaps more authentic ancient categories, created—infertile. Thus it is not that Rachel is barren while Leah is not, but rather that both are barren to begin with, and Leah's womb is simply opened before Rachel's. There is also Ruth, about whom it is said that "the Lord allowed her to conceive" (Ruth 4:13).

In the imagery—more literal to its original authors and audience than it is to us—of God opening the womb, we should recognize more clearly than is usually the case that responsibility for infertility does not, indeed cannot, lie with the barren woman. Here is a biblical voice, one with ample ancient Near Eastern contextual background, that has been lost in the roar of postbiblical interpretation.

We may ask: if every woman is "naturally" infertile, and needs God to open her womb, why then are we not told in every case of conception that this occurred? It may well be that this notion of how conception works was simply assumed in Israelite society, as it was, in various forms, elsewhere in the ancient Near East, and that it did not need to be explicitly stated. It is notable that when it is alluded to in the Bible, in the creation-echoing language of "forming in the womb" and in the naming of children, it appears in prophetic writings, in wisdom literature, and in narrative, in different sources from different authors—that is, in multiple genres and across many centuries. This suggests that it was not a rare concept, but rather one that existed in the background of the broader culture.

Perhaps the question should not be "why is infertility not mentioned in every case?" but rather "why are these five women specifically mentioned as infertile?" What should be noted is that not only are these five women the only ones who are marked out as barren, but they are also the only ones for whom God's role in bringing about their fertility is explicitly stated. And these are no ordinary women, and they have no ordinary children. Isaac and Jacob and Joseph: these are the patriarchs through whom the divine promise to Abraham to make him into "a great nation" (Gen 12:2) is realized. They are the people Israel. Samson is the savior of that people, promised from birth to be "the first to deliver Israel from the Philistines" (Judg 13:5). And Samuel, the great judge and prophet, is also the midwife of the Israelite monarchy, the anointer of both Saul and David.

It is thus true, as many others have noted, that the infertility of these five women is a means of demonstrating God's power over ostensibly insurmountable obstacles: How could the nation exist if the matriarchs were barren? How would Israel overcome the Philistines? How would it become a great nation? But this is only half of the picture. It is not that these women are somehow different from all others in any (biblically) biological sense. It is that by bringing their "natural" infertility to the forefront of their stories, by making it the central feature of their persons, the biblical authors can thereby emphasize God's direct role in the births of their children. These stories stress God's participation not only in the process of individual conception, but in the process of national conception, in the birth and sustenance of Israel as a people. Let no one think—the Bible is telling us—that Israel came into being and survived by chance alone; it exists by the active intervention of God.

Again, the key to recognizing this message lies not in the explicitly barren matriarchs, but in the only other woman of whom we are told that God opened her womb: Leah, the fertile matriarch. God is equally active in bringing into the world her sons too, the other tribes of Israel. God's role in all human conception is the underlying reality; these stories, including Leah's, highlight that reality, rather than contradict it.

If we say that active participation on the part of God is required for a woman—for all women—to become fertile, then infertility is not divine punishment; it is rather the state in which all women enter the world. Of course, infertility can also be divine punishment, as in the case of the women of Abimelech's court. But note a distinctive feature of that story: when Abraham prays and God restores the fertility of the women of Abimelech's court, there, and only there, is the word "healed," *rāpā'*, used of God's action. Those women were stricken by God, and thus they were healed by God; the barren Israelite women we are discussing in this chapter are never said to be "healed."[121] Another difference, one to which we will return in the next chapter: it is not just one woman who is made infertile, but all of them; not just those who had not yet conceived, but those who had already conceived— that is, those whose wombs had already been opened. In closing their wombs, God is not therefore bringing about a new state, but rather returning the women to their original state. One can be punished with infertility only if one had already been made fertile.

There are, however, other texts that suggest something slightly different. When we meet Samson's mother, we are told not merely that she is infertile. The text reads, "His wife was barren and had borne no children" (Judg 13:2). This is ostensibly redundant: if she was barren, obviously she had borne no children.[122] But this may be importing our modern understandings of infertility back into the biblical world. We think of infertility as a permanent state. But as we have already seen, in the Hebrew Bible infertility is decidedly impermanent. The inability to conceive is dependent on divine (in)activity. Perhaps this description of Samson's mother, then, can be read not as redundant but as two separate statements: she is unable to conceive now; and her womb had not been opened previously.[123] This suggests that fertility and infertility are not lasting conditions but are rather constantly negotiated. One can be fertile and then be so no longer.

This is, in fact, precisely what we know to be the case with Leah. Her womb is opened by God, and she bears four sons: Reuben, Simeon, Levi, and Judah. At that point, however, we are told that "she stopped bearing" (Gen 29:35). She has done no wrong; nothing about her situation has changed in the slightest. She is simply unable to conceive. Her solution, "when Leah saw that she had stopped bearing" (Gen 30:9), is to give her maid, Zilpah, to Jacob as a concubine, so that more children can be born under her name. This is, of course, a well-known technique in the Bible—but it is otherwise known only in cases of explicit infertility: Sarah gives Hagar to Abraham (Gen 16:2), and Rachel gives Bilhah to Jacob (Gen 30:3). Leah thus acts as an infertile woman, despite having already borne four sons—she considers herself to be barren. Even more surprisingly perhaps, after Zilpah has given birth to Gad and Asher, Leah begins to conceive again, and produces Issachar, Zebulun, and Dinah. Leah is neither permanently fertile nor permanently infertile. It is quite possible, then, that when she "stops bearing," it would be appropriate in biblical terms—though strange to our modern ears—to say that "she was barren and she had borne four sons."[124]

It is commonly assumed that the word "barren" refers to someone who is, for whatever reason, biologically incapable of ever bearing children. Yet just as we have observed is the case in modern times, so too in the ancient world "barren" was always defined against the backdrop of the desire to bear children. Miriam is not infertile, because we are never told that she wants or tries to have children; Leah is infertile when she tries and fails to have children, despite the fact that she *already has* four sons.

ASSESSING THE ORIGINS OF INFERTILITY

Without the benefit of modern science—and often even with it— there can be no diagnosis of permanent infertility. The only way to know that one is "infertile," as a lasting condition, is to have lived an entire life attempting and failing to conceive.[125] This lack of certainty is found in the Bible in the aforementioned levirate law: though the woman might be assumed to be barren, her state is uncertain, and so she is required to remarry.[126]

Unsurprisingly, we also find a substantial catalogue of texts from around the ancient Near East that provide means for determining the fertility of women. There are physiognomic texts, those that attempt to determine a woman's potential fertility by her physical appearance: "If a woman's breasts are pointed, she cannot bear children"; "if her navel lies high, she cannot bear children";[127] if her eyes are different colors, then she will not give birth, but "if you see them of one color, then she will give birth."[128] There are various tests that can be undertaken: from Egypt, urinating on barley at night and checking the resulting state of the crop in the morning,[129] or coating a woman with beer and date flour and seeing whether she proceeds to vomit;[130] from Babylonia, inserting a wad of medicated wool into the vagina and checking its color three days later.[131] The most famous of such tests, originally Egyptian but taken up almost word for word into the Hippocratic medical texts of ancient Greece, reads as follows:

"Another recipe to distinguish a woman who will conceive from one who will not: You shall let a clove of garlic remain the whole night in her vagina until morning. If an odor is present in her mouth, she will conceive; if there is no odor in her mouth, she will not conceive, ever."[132] (Predictably, there are no such texts or tests for a man.) We can imagine that these tests were not perfectly accurate.

Common in the ancient world was the notion that certain plants or potions could be beneficial in the process of conception and pregnancy. These include, prominently, the "plant of birth," the object of the childless hero's quest in the Akkadian myth of Etana.[133] A remarkable pharmaceutical list of such plants contains two plants for "acquiring seed," one for "a woman who does not bear," and two for "a woman who does not get pregnant."[134] It is impossible to distinguish precisely the functions of these herbs; regardless of specific application, their very existence indicates that some problems with pregnancy could be handled without direct recourse to the deity. Nonherbal remedies were also available: "To make a not child-bearing woman pregnant: you flay an edible mouse, open it up, and fill it with myrrh; you dry it in the shade, crush it, and grind it up, and mix it with fat; you place it in her vagina, and she will become pregnant."[135] Alternatively, from Egypt, "You should fumigate her with spelt in her vagina until it ceases, to allow for her husband's seed to be received."[136] It seems reasonable to assume that a case of infertility that could be cured with herbs or other such treatments was not attributable to divine disfavor; even if these treatments were intended to manipulate the deity into opening the womb, it is hard to imagine that they could be used to avoid confronting sin or guilt.[137] These herbal techniques may provide the background for the story of Rachel's attempt to use the mandrake plant to improve her fertility.[138] It may also suggest that this narrative be read as a subtle

Israelite rebuke to just such medicinal treatments: the mandrakes are not efficacious for Rachel, and in the end it is God who opens her womb.[139]

Of course it was known that after a certain age pregnancy was unusual, if not in fact physically impossible.[140] It is this knowledge that lies behind the version of the Abraham and Sarah story in Genesis 17, where Sarah is described not as barren but merely as old: "Can a child be born to a man a hundred years old, or can Sarah bear a child at ninety?" (Gen 17:17). The implication, given how the story goes, is that only by a divine miracle could such a thing take place. An amusing parallel is found in a series of letters between the Pharaoh Rameses II and the Hittite king Hattušili. The Hittite king, relying on Egypt's renowned magicians, requested that some special herbs be sent on behalf of his sister so that she could become pregnant. Rameses's response is revealing: "It is said [in your first correspondence] that she is a fifty-year old. No, she is a sixty-year old! . . . No, for a woman who has completed sixty years, it is not possible to prepare medicines for her, so that she might still be caused to give birth."[141] It is not necessary to assume that the Egyptian understanding of fertility is exactly the same as that in the Bible. But it is noteworthy that there is an underlying assumption in Rameses's letter that—even without special herbs—it is possible for a fifty-year-old woman to become pregnant; and, moreover, that such a thing is impossible—even with special herbs—for a sixty-year-old. At a certain age, there is no more that human ingenuity can do.[142] However, Pharaoh offers to send the herbs and two of his best men to prepare them, because there is always the chance that the gods will intervene: "may the Sungod and the Stormgod give order that this enterprise succeeds."[143] This is the epistolary equivalent of the biblical narrative: Sarah has passed the age when pregnancy is known to occur; the only chance of it happening now is through divine intervention.[144]

There is an inherent similarity between the reliance on the deity when a woman is beyond the normal age of childbearing and the reliance on the deity when a woman is well within that normal age. That is, the inability to conceive is functionally identical regardless of what we would consider the "medical" rationale for such inability. And, conversely, conception is functionally the same regardless of the manner in which it occurs. Direct divine activity is required to "open the womb," whether a woman has had children before or not, whether she has even tried to become pregnant before or not. Every pregnancy, be it the first or the fifth, is ascribed to God's power. Sarah, who bears Isaac at ninety years old, says "God has brought me laughter" (Gen 21:6). When Leah, still in her relative youth, bears Issachar, her fifth son, she credits God: "God has given me my reward" (Gen 30:18). For her sixth, Asher, she says "God has given me a choice gift" (Gen 30:20). In the ancient Israelite view, God is involved in every human conception.

This is expressed most fully in the often misunderstood rite of circumcision. Though frequently thought to be a means of demarcating "in-groups" and "out-groups" on an ethno-societal level—Israelites being identifiable by circumcision, non-Israelites not—in fact circumcision is given a very different meaning in the biblical text.[145] In Genesis 17, God makes a promise to Abraham, which he describes as a "covenant": "I will make you exceedingly fertile, and make nations of you" (Gen 17:6). Abraham's sole responsibility for maintaining this covenant is to circumcise himself and his offspring, and for an explicitly stated reason: "This shall be the sign of the covenant" (Gen 17:11). The key word here is "sign." We find this word and this concept also famously at the end of the story of the Flood, where the rainbow "will serve as a sign of the covenant" (Gen 9:13). There too the "covenant" is a promise: "never again shall all flesh be cut off by the waters of a flood" (Gen 9:11). The sign of the rainbow works in a very particular manner: "When the bow is in the clouds, I will see it and remember the everlasting covenant" (Gen 9:16). The "sign" in the story of the Flood, then, is not for humans, but for God: it is a reminder of his covenantal obligations to the world. In an age when God is generally thought of as omnipresent, omnipotent, and omniscient, the idea of God requiring a physical reminder of a divine promise may seem strange. But the biblical God was none of those things, at least not all the time.

When this concept is transferred to the covenantal "sign" of circumcision, as the parallel language virtually demands, we come to understand that circumcision is not a marker for the Israelites to distinguish themselves from others, but rather a reminder to God, and a particularly appropriate (if graphic) one at that. Just as the rainbow reminds God to fulfill his promise not to destroy the world with rain, so circumcision reminds God to fulfill his promise to make Abraham's descendants fertile; it is, as Howard Eilberg-Schwartz put it, "the fruitful cut."[146] Just as God sees the rainbow whenever it rains, so too God sees the circumcised flesh of the Israelites—whenever they have intercourse. Of course, God would need no reminder if he had no role to play in the process. His role, as we have seen, is the opening of the womb—but not only the first time a couple attempts to conceive; every time the circumcised flesh is revealed during the procreative act. Again: without God's active—and repeated—intervention, the Bible proclaims, there can be no fertility.

When it is recognized that the default state of all women—at all times—is infertile, and that God needs to be reminded to open the womb every time an Israelite couple has intercourse in order to allow conception to occur, the idea that infertility should be regularly understood as divine punishment can hardly be maintained. In fact, the explanation suggested by the Hebrew Bible seems to be rather more banal, if somewhat more theologically difficult for the modern reader: infertility is the result not of divine punishment, but of divine inattention. That is, despite having created a system to jog the divine memory, God is still sometimes forgetful.

The need to get God's attention explains another element common to the stories of these women. When Rachel's womb is finally opened, the Bible declares that "God remembered Rachel" (Gen 30:22). The word used for "remember" here, *zakar*, is the same word used in the story of the Flood: God will "remember," *zakar*, the everlasting covenant. Hannah prays that God will "remember me and not forget your maidservant" (1 Sam 1:11). With Sarah, a close synonym is used, *paqad*: "The Lord took note of Sarah" (Gen 21:1). In every case, of course, circumcision has already taken place; yet God still has to further remember his obligation.

When all of the pieces are put together, it is clear that, from the perspective of these biblical authors, infertility is not a human shortcoming, but a divine one. The Hebrew Bible does present infertility as a religious phenomenon, to be sure. It is, however, not the religious phenomenon commonly assumed. With only the most uncommon exceptions (really exception, singular), God does not decree infertility. Those who have never borne children, who have never been able to conceive, have not been punished for any mysterious sin. They have done nothing wrong. It is not their actions that are at the root of their infertility; it is God's inaction.

From the nearly complete absence of information about these matriarchs to the mystery of conception itself to the final problem of why God would be inattentive, the issue of infertility in the Hebrew Bible revolves around gaps in human understanding. As the Bible pushes the mystery further and further away from humanity and into the realm of the divine, it hardly lessens it. Rather, it reveals that there is much we simply do not, or cannot, know about why a woman is unable to conceive. What the Bible does make clear, however, is that even when infertility is explicitly conceived of as a "religious" phenomenon, it cannot simply be considered the result of human sin. Divine punishment is not the only "religious" interpretation available; it is directly confronted in the Hebrew Bible by the very contrary understanding that infertile women are blameless and undeserving of their fate. In fact, direct divine intervention of any sort, whether as punishment or not, need not necessarily be behind every individual case of infertility.

CONCLUSION

From the ancient past to our own present, the inability to conceive has always been a source of anguish and confusion, a fundamental question of "why me?" The mystery of the ancient world remains in many ways our mystery today. The experience of infertility is one of gaps: the empty space in the home and the heart where the desired child would reside, and the open questions that seem impossible to answer. These are ever present. What makes the biblical text so powerful is that it replicates that sense of confusion and questioning. When we read the stories of these women, we are denied the information we desire. We long for an explanation, for a rationale, for an answer to the question of "why them?"

But such answers are not forthcoming—in this the biblical stories, so often invoked as the source of wisdom beyond human understanding, validates the lived experience of infertility. We grasp for answers, and the text we read as scripture tells us that our inability to find them is no fault of our own. The biblical text does not provide easy answers, but affirms that there are no easy answers.

The conclusion most often reached, the dominant interpretation, is a particularly painful and harsh one. The easy association

of infertility—as of any impairment—with divine displeasure is
an ancient one, and its biblical roots can hardly be denied. But it
is only an interpretation, one among many, and it is not necessarily the strongest. From the perspective of the suffering woman, it
is all too often unhelpful or even damaging, broadly accusatory
in a subtly insidious manner. The dominant voice is, consciously
or not (but strangely in either case), heard in the taunt of Peninnah. When the language of sin and punishment is associated
with infertility, we align ourselves with the "haves" against the
"have-nots," with the antagonist's taunt rather than with the protagonist's prayer.

As readers and as inhabitants of the lived world, we feel a constant need to fill the gaps left in the story and in our own stories.
We are readers of our own lives as much as we are readers of the
biblical text. The answers we provide will always be interpretations, attempts to make sense of the empty spaces. There is no
predetermined answer, neither in life nor in the various biblical
accounts. As we have outlined here, the stories of the matriarchs,
and the world from which they emerged, offer an alternative
reading: one that does not lay blame at the feet of the sufferer, nor
forces us to encounter a God who would intentionally cause the
emotional trauma of infertility. This explanation does not "solve"
the problem. It does not bring instant relief to the suffering. It
does, however, remove the social stigma of responsibility from
the infertile woman, and this is an important step. The stories of
Sarah, Rebekah, Rachel, Samson's mother, and Hannah do not
deny that this stigma is a social reality, in the culture from which
it emerged to the present. But at the intersection of depicting the
social experience of infertility and coming to terms with it theologically, we may find in these narratives a countervailing voice.

CHAPTER 2

The Blessing and the Curse

The first words that God says to humanity, according to Genesis, are "be fruitful and multiply" (Gen 1:28). These instructions are repeated: to Noah after the Flood (Gen 9:1, 7), and to Jacob when God changes his name to Israel (Gen 35:11). They appear also as a self-willed act of God: "I will make you very fruitful," Abraham is told (Gen 17:6). Even of Ishmael, who stands outside the line of the covenantal promise, God says, "I will make him very fruitful and multiply him greatly" (Gen 17:20).

For thousands of years, these words have been understood as a divine imperative to each and every individual: it is every person's responsibility to produce offspring according to God's will. (The common mistaken translation "go forth and multiply" has surely contributed to this interpretation.) This command, unlike so many in the Hebrew Bible, was given to all of humanity, not just to Israel—a distinction that appears to be emphasized by the fact that it is given both to Adam and then again to Noah, in other words, to the two "first men." According to the Mishna, the earliest codification of Jewish law, "A man must not abstain from 'be fruitful and multiply' unless he already has children."[1] This law was taken up and applied in midrash over the next eight centuries as a staple of rabbinic thought.[2] Clement of Alexandria, despite his clear approval of celibacy, also stated that "He has said 'increase,' and one must obey."[3] In Islam, reproduction is seen as a requirement, as the duty to multiply the followers of the faith beyond those of other faiths.[4]

"Be fruitful and multiply" is more than merely a command; it is a blessing: "God blessed them: 'Be fruitful and multiply'" (Gen 1:28; so too Gen 9:1; 17:20; 35:9). Isaac says to Jacob, "May El Shaddai bless you and make you fruitful and numerous" (Gen 28:3), a blessing that Jacob recalls later in life: "El Shaddai . . . blessed me and said to me, 'I will make you fruitful and multiply you'" (Gen 48:3–4). Even when the exact words are not used, the connection of blessing and fertility is found: "I will bestow my blessing upon you and make your descendants as numerous as the stars of heaven and the sands on the seashore" (Gen 22:17).

When the emphasis is put on the aspect of blessing, then it is all too easy to consider those who cannot procreate as cursed. "Barrenness was a curse," claims the authoritative *Encyclopedia Judaica*.[5] The *IVP Women's Bible Commentary* agrees, interpreting the notion of infertility as curse as the corollary to fertility as blessing.[6] The theme even dissolves into common imagery and parlance. Shakespeare's King Lear implores God to make Goneril's womb sterile.[7]

God's first words to humanity are thus something of a double-edged sword for those without offspring. If one chooses not to bear children, then one could be seen as violating a direct divine command, perhaps even the primary divine directive. If one is unable to bear children, one is considered cursed. This has practical implications for those members of communities, like the Christian "Replenish" movement, that especially focus on procreation as a religious responsibility.

In the previous chapter we decoupled infertility from sin by offering a reading of the narratives of barrenness in the Hebrew Bible. Here we want to think more carefully about the categories of blessing and curse, and specifically about this blessing of fertility: Is it accurate to state that the Bible demands, or even expects, that all humans procreate? Does it really envision infertility as a divine curse? Should we? Is there another way to read these texts?

INDIVIDUAL BODIES

Those initial words to humanity seem fairly unequivocal. And when that first man and woman are seen as not only prototypical but also archetypical—not just the first humans, but the models for all of humanity that followed—then it is logical enough that everyone, each of us living today, should be beholden to the same divine command. After all, the curses that are laid on Adam, Eve, and the serpent at the end of the story of the Garden of Eden were, it is assumed, meant to establish and explain everlasting conditions. The snake still has no legs. We remain banished from paradise. If the story of Adam and Eve is the origin of our present existence, then surely the command to procreate is an eternal one. The command to be fruitful is akin to the (Christian) concept of original sin: an aspect of the first human experience that is passed down, almost genetically, to every living person thereafter. The command to multiply, it would seem, is in our DNA.

If Genesis 1:28 were the only occurrence of this command/blessing in the Bible, there might be little else to say about it. That dominant interpretation would be difficult to challenge. As we have already noted, however, the command, and the concept, occur regularly, and provide us with the means of taking a quite different interpretive path.

The blessing of fruitfulness is issued not only to the first man and woman, as noted earlier, but again to Noah and the patriarchs. And there is something different about the command when it is delivered to everyone after Genesis 1—a difference of timing. When God speaks in Genesis 1:28, it follows directly on the creation of human beings, effectively at "birth," and certainly well before Cain and Abel and Seth are even remotely near entering the scene. Yet when God speaks the blessing the next time, to Noah, the timing could hardly be more different. Noah receives the divine word in his six hundred first year of life. He is hardly a youth. He already has three sons. His sons are themselves already a hundred years old. They have all just experienced the destruction of the Flood, and now, as they step out of the ark, "God blessed Noah and his sons, and said to them, 'Be fruitful and multiply'" (Gen 9:1). As a command, this is sensible enough for Noah's sons. We know that they have wives, who were also on the ark, but they have no children in the time of the Flood. But why should Noah also receive the command to be fertile? He has already done so—what's more, he will not have any further children after the Flood. How is Noah supposed to be fruitful and multiply?

When Abraham is told that God will make him very fruitful, Ishmael has already been born, though Isaac and Abraham's other lesser-known children (Gen 25:2) are yet to come. But when God tells Jacob to "be fruitful and multiply" (Gen 35:11), Jacob may well have looked around at his twelve sons and one daughter and thought, "More?" Jacob's procreative days were behind him; his youngest son, Benjamin, had just been born. There would be no more children in Jacob's future—there are only twelve tribes, after all. Jacob's favorite wife, Rachel, has just died, while Leah, Bilhah, and Zilpah will never be mentioned in the story again.[8] What, then, could God have intended by instructing Jacob to be fruitful and multiply?[9]

COMMAND OR BLESSING?

Here emerges the basic conflict between reading God's words according to their grammatical form, that is, as imperatives, and reading them according to their context, that is, as a blessing. If God's words are understood as a command, then we would have to conclude that both Noah and Jacob are guilty of disobeying the divine will.[10] Yet this is hardly fathomable. We would also have to believe that, when God spoke the exact same words to the fish of the seas in Genesis 1:22, a command was being issued to the animal world, that animals have the will to obey or disobey the divine will.[11] There are abundant reasons, therefore, for rejecting the common, if not universal, view that the words "be fruitful and multiply" should be taken as a divine imperative to procreate, one that can be either obeyed or disobeyed.[12]

If we are to read them as a blessing, however, then the question of obedience or disobedience is entirely moot. With a divine blessing, despite being couched in the imperative, the one obliged to act is in fact the speaker. This is the responsibility God assumes when he says to Abraham, "I will make you very fruitful." One cannot disobey this sort of blessing. If it is not fulfilled, the fault—as suggested on different grounds in the previous chapter—is with God, not with the blessing recipient. And yet the same problem exists: if the blessing of fertility is envisioned to be a promise of offspring, then why would God give it to Noah and Jacob, neither of whom would have another child?

In short, whether as a command or as a blessing, there is something fundamentally problematic about reading "be fruitful and multiply" as if it mapped squarely onto "procreate and have children."[13] To put it differently: "be fruitful and multiply" cannot be associated with, or restricted to, an individual, or an individual couple. It is not a blessing, or a command, that necessarily calls for any action on the part of the person to whom it is addressed. Nor, for that matter, can it be easily read as something passed down genetically ever since it was delivered to the first humans; if this were true, why would God need to repeat it? Why would a father bother to wish it upon his son?

We can best understand the import of this blessing in light of its functional parallel, expressed first and most famously in Genesis 12:2: "I will make of you a great nation, and I will bless you; I will make your name great." As we noted in the previous chapter, having a "great name" is dependent on having descendants to carry that name forward. This is the blessing God promises Abraham: offspring. There is also, however, the first clause of God's promise: to make Abraham into a great nation. Offspring are obviously necessary for this promise to come true. But it would be foolhardy to read the promise of Genesis 12 as related primarily to the question of whether Abraham and Sarah will have a son. That issue will be raised repeatedly, to be sure; but not here. Here the horizon is far more distant. No matter how many children Abraham may have in his lifetime, they will never be enough to be considered a great nation. No matter how many stories of their father they tell, they will never be able to make Abraham's name great. God's promise to Abraham of blessing, of offspring—like the promise of land that will come to pass only centuries later—is multigenerational. It anticipates nationhood, not fatherhood.

So too the blessing "be fruitful and multiply." Noah will have no more children; yet all of humanity will descend from him. Jacob will have no more children; yet he will be the father of the entire Israelite people. Abraham, for all his blessedness, has eight children in all. Jacob has thirteen, Ishmael has twelve, Noah has three, and Isaac has two. Even Adam and Eve have only three sons.[14] Despite the regularly voiced belief that God's words encourage a large family, it is not the number of children produced that is at stake in the divine blessing of fertility.[15] It is the people who, far in the future, will descend from those who are blessed. God takes the long view.[16]

THE SCOPE OF THE BLESSING

The individualism of the blessing, so often claimed, at least implicitly, by interpreters, is called into question perhaps most readily by the rest of God's words, which are often disconnected from the issue of fertility. God says to the first man and woman not only to be fruitful and multiply, but also to "fill the earth and subdue it" (Gen 1:28). Here again: no matter how many children they tried to produce, even though Adam lived to be eight hundred years old (Gen 5:4), there is no possible way for a single couple to "fill the earth"—especially as, in the end, they have only three children (one of whom is tragically erased from the story early on). There is no way for them, even with their sons, to subdue the earth. Noah and his sons, too, are told to "fill the earth" (Gen 9:1). There being only four of them, this would seem a tall task. In the cases both of Adam and Eve and of Noah and his sons, however, we know that the blessing ultimately did come to pass: the earth was filled with Adam's, and then with Noah's, offspring. But not in Adam's or Noah's lifetime. God's blessing, God's promise, was indeed fulfilled—so long as we correctly understand the timeframe for which it was intended.

Isaac blesses Jacob, hoping that God will make him fruitful and numerous; but he also goes on to wish that Jacob should "become an assembly of peoples." An assembly of peoples will eventually be called in Jacob's name: the twelve tribes of Israel. But Jacob's twelve sons are no assembly, not yet. It will take generations before they have multiplied to the point of deserving the title "tribe," or "people." Isaac knows how God's blessings work. And indeed, when God does bless Jacob as Isaac had hoped, he says, "A nation, yea, an assembly of nations, shall descend from you; kings shall issue from your loins" (Gen 35:11). Kings there will be—but not for nearly a thousand years.

We can thus reimagine what the divine blessing of fertility entails. It is not a hope that an individual will be fertile rather than infertile; it is not the hope for an abundance of successful pregnancies. It is, rather, a hope that, in the distant future, an individual's descendants will be numerous—"as numerous as the stars of heaven and the sands on the seashore" (Gen 22:17; a divine promise that is given, it should be noted, long after Isaac's birth).

Now it is undeniable that, in order for these patriarchal blessings to be fulfilled, it is necessary that the patriarchs have children of their own. To that end, fulfillment of the blessing does indeed have individual fertility as a prerequisite. But what is expected of these specific individuals is not therefore expected of everyone who came after them. The blessing was given to them in particular, and not, quite pointedly, to others. Those who claim that the blessing (or command) of fertility is universal—or those of us today who may feel ourselves implicated in it—may be ignoring the important detail of precisely to whom these words were addressed, and why.

The first two sets of addressees, Adam and Eve on the one hand and Noah and his sons on the other, obviously have to be fertile and produce children—they are the two sets of progenitors for all of humanity. If they didn't bear children, it would be an awfully short story. Abraham also has to be fertile, since God designates him to be the forefather of the Israelite people. Part of that role, however, entails the isolation of Abraham and his line of descent from everyone else on earth: the separation of Israel from the gentiles. Abraham must be blessed with long-term fertility (and therefore requires children of his own) in order that Israel become numerous enough to require noticing. Isaac's offspring will be "as numerous as the stars of heaven" (Gen 26:4); it would be reasonable to wonder why it was necessary to say this after the same promise had been made to Abraham. If the blessing of Abraham was transgenerational, surely Isaac would automatically be part of it. Yet it was necessary to highlight Isaac's blessing also, because Abraham had another son, Ishmael (the recipient of his own blessing, in fact). The lineage of the promise made by God is more restricted than the lineage of Abraham. The same situation obtains for Jacob: though ostensibly implicated in the blessings of both Abraham and Isaac, it was necessary for Jacob to receive his own blessing of fertility because he too had a rival through whom the promise would not be carried: Esau (who is also the progenitor of an entire nation, the Edomites).

The divine promise of becoming a great nation runs through only one of Abraham's two sons, only one of Isaac's two sons. The identity of the promise recipient is marked by the transmission of the blessing of fertility. Yes, the recipients of the blessing all must have children of their own. But this is precisely because the blessing is restricted to one person per generation. Jacob's children, unlike Abraham's or Isaac's, are all part of the promised line. Notably, God does not bless any one of them individually. They carry on Jacob's blessing collectively.

The most straightforward, and most often ignored, reason to believe that the blessing to be fruitful and multiply is not incumbent on every individual is that, according to the Bible, it was fulfilled long ago. In fact, it was fulfilled at least three times. The first blessing, at the moment of creation in Genesis 1, to "be fruitful and multiply and fill the earth," has been completed by the time of the Flood. It is then, we are told, that "the earth was filled"—albeit with violence (Gen 6:11).[17] The Flood represents a second attempt at creation, the first try having failed. That failure is clear to God only when the earth he had created and populated was full, when the blessing of fertility had resulted in violent chaos.

Thus Noah is required to start again, and thus Noah and his sons receive the same blessing of fertility: the end of the Flood is the equivalent of the end of creation, the moment when the wheels of time begin to spin forward (again). Just as Adam's descendants quickly multiplied and filled the earth, so too Noah's. This is the purpose of Genesis 10, known as the "Table of Nations." Here we hear of Noah's grandchildren: seven sons for

Jephet, four sons for Ham, and four for Shem, who stand as representatives for the entire extent of the known world for the biblical authors. "And from these the nations branched out over the earth after the Flood" (Gen 10:32). The completion of the Noahide blessing of fertility is signaled also in the next chapter, in the story of the Tower of Babel: "Thus the Lord scattered them from there over the face of the whole earth" (Gen 11:8). This story explains the existence of multiple nations with multiple languages, and the presence of people in every part of the world; that is, it assumes that the increase of humanity is complete, such that all that is left is its distribution across the planet.

The blessing "be fruitful and multiply" is not, therefore, one that is transmitted down through every generation because it was given to Adam and Eve and Noah. It is not a command from the past that pertains to the present; it is a blessing in the past that explains the present. There are people all over the world, and there have been for the entire span of human memory; this is because, the biblical authors are saying, God decreed fertility and the spread of humanity upon the first people (twice). The blessing of fertility is a historical explanation for a long-completed fact.

The same, though on a slightly smaller scale, is true for the divine blessing as given to the patriarchs. Here the issue is not one of filling the earth—those words are delivered exclusively to Adam and Eve and Noah—but rather of becoming a substantial nation among the others that already fill the earth. The carving out of space among the nations of the world for the people of Israel is at stake. And the fulfillment of this Israelite blessing is realized even more explicitly than those to Adam and Noah: in Genesis 47, Jacob and his descendants settle in Egypt, where "they were fruitful and increased greatly" (Gen 47:27). By the beginning of the book of Exodus, it was possible to say of the Israelites that "they were fruitful and prolific and they multiplied and grew greatly in strength, such that the earth"—here, cleverly, referring solely to the land of Egypt—"was filled with them" (Exod 1:7).[18] This is the word-for-word fulfillment of God's blessing upon Abraham, Isaac, and Jacob. They were not to multiply indefinitely, every single one of their descendants destined for abundant fertility until the end of time. They were to become a great nation; to be fertile until they could authentically carry the label of "the people of Israel." Israel comes into being as a nation in Egypt, at the juncture between the books of Genesis and Exodus. Pointedly, from that point forward, no *individual* in the Bible receives the blessing to "be fruitful and multiply" or even any variation on it—either by God or by another human (though the phrase will be used once more, albeit in a very different context, as we will see below).[19]

The blessing to be fruitful and multiply was neither timeless nor universal.[20] It has, in all of these instances, an end in sight; and in all of these instances, that end was long since achieved.[21] The last individual person to receive a divine promise to become a nation—and the last person to receive the divine blessing "be fruitful and multiply"—is Jacob, Israel. Everyone who comes afterward stands as part of the fulfillment of that promise and blessing. Individuals after Jacob—down to the present—are not expected, far less required, to become a nation. They are not required to multiply dramatically. They are, in fact, not required to multiply at all. Jacob's descendants collectively bear the burden of becoming a nation; but no individual among his descendants is obligated to contribute. All of Jacob's sons have children (they need to become tribes eventually)—but his daughter, Dinah, does not. She is not said to be barren, nor is she said to be punished for failing to fulfill God's word. She neither is fruitful nor multiplies, yet she is firmly part of the promised line. One need not be fertile to be blessed.

It is suggestive that Dinah, Jacob's only daughter, is also the only one of his children who has no offspring of her own. Was she infertile? Certainly the text never comes close to suggesting so. There is, of course, a tradition-historical concern behind the Bible's silence regarding Dinah's offspring: when Jacob's twelve sons and their offspring all represent the ancestors of the later tribes of Israel, what would Dinah's offspring be? There is no thirteenth tribe. It is, however, precisely in this historical and genealogical concern that we can see another avenue leading to the recognition that fertility is not decreed for all of humanity. It is patently not at stake for Dinah, as no tribe, no lineal descent, no inheritance of name or land, goes through her. And this is true, in the biblical model, of all women.

GENDER AND THE BLESSING OF FERTILITY

Property and title, in the ancient world and until quite recently, were passed down through the father. This claim is at the basis of innumerable biblical stories and laws, including the law of the levirate that we encountered in the previous chapter. The concern for lineage is a paternal one. Women may not inherit land, according to the Bible, except if a deceased father leaves behind only unmarried daughters and no sons; even then, however, the moment the daughters marry, the land becomes the possession of their husbands (Num 27:1–11; 36:1–12). If a man owns land, he passes it down to his son; in the rare instance that a woman owns land, she passes it to her husband.[22] The physical burden of childbirth falls on the woman; the legal burden falls on the man. To put it perhaps more painfully: the work of childbirth is the woman's, while the rewards belong to the man.[23]

This unequal division is represented most starkly in some of the least discussed passages of the Bible: genealogies. It is exceptionally rare for a woman, a mother, to be named in a biblical genealogy. In the list of Jacob's family that entered Egypt with him in Genesis 46, Leah and Zilpah and Rachel and Bilhah are indeed mentioned as the mothers of Jacob's children; but we are not told the names of his sons' wives—even when, as in the case of Judah's wife, we know her name from elsewhere. The number of persons tallied in Jacob's familial entourage does not include any of his sons' wives, though they could hardly have been left behind.[24] Most pointedly, the expansion of the first couple into an entire world is communicated largely through the genealogy of Genesis 5, where there is nary a woman in sight. Notice the remarkable transition from the emphatically equal recollection of creation—"Male and female he created them, and when they were created he blessed them and called them 'Human'" (Gen 5:2)—to the genealogy of their descendants: "When Adam had lived 130 years, he begot a son in his likeness after his image" (Gen 5:3). It is the man who has a son in his likeness—not the woman. And so through the rest of the genealogy. When humanity expands anew after the Flood in Genesis 10, there are again no women involved, or at least so the genealogy would have us believe. The genealogies in Genesis, like the blessing of fertility, are not about childbirth, though they take that outward form. They are about the transfer of name and land. They ignore women because women are effectively tools toward that entirely male end.[25]

When the blessing of fertility is understood not as an abstract encouragement toward childbirth for its own sake, but rather as having a specific goal in mind, we may better understand one of the more troubling phenomena regarding these blessings. To wit: with the exception of Genesis 1, to which we will return presently, the blessing to be fruitful and multiply is delivered exclusively to men.

Noah's sons are blessed—but not their wives. It would be one thing if these women were never mentioned; yet they are explicitly and repeatedly listed among the people with Noah on the ark: "Noah, with his sons, his wife, and his sons' wives, went into the ark" (Gen 7:7). Surely they too need to be blessed with fertility in order for the earth to be repopulated? When God speaks to Abraham in Genesis 17, there are three people under discussion: Abraham, Sarah, and Ishmael. God promises to make two of them very fruitful—not Abraham and Sarah, but Abraham and Ishmael. Jacob too receives the blessing, but none of the four mothers of his children.

One is tempted to cry foul: after all, there is no fertility without the woman to bear the child. The biblical authors' willful ignorance of women in the repeated speeches of "be fruitful and multiply" is undoubtedly representative of the overwhelmingly male perspective of the ancient authors. But recognizing this also allows for two important interpretive moves to take place. The first is to rightly see the blessing of fertility as embedded within and dependent on the systemically male social world that the Bible inhabits and re-presents. If "be fruitful and multiply" were a truly universal speech, it would be addressed equally to male and female (if not in fact weighted more heavily toward the female). It is not addressed equally, because it is not truly universal. Its goal is not childbirth, which is the realm of the female; its goal is political and ethnic establishment, which in the world of the Bible is a male project.

The second observation, which derives from the first, is that by reconfiguring "be fruitful and multiply" as a nation-building and predominantly male concept, we may conclude that women are released from any obligation or expectation that the divine word may entail. By virtue of the fact that it is almost always delivered to men rather than to their wives, the Bible has already effectively excluded women from the blessing's purview. When God's words are understood as directed toward a goal in which women in the Bible could simply not participate, this exclusion is reinforced. The rabbis of the Mishna recognized this principle: "The man is commanded with regard to being fruitful and multiplying, but not the woman."[26] Exclusion is often reason to claim injustice; in this case, however, it may well be reason to rejoice.[27] Women who choose not to have children are released from any divinely authorized expectation. Women who are unable to have children are freed from any feelings of religious guilt.[28]

EVE'S FERTILITY

We can turn now to the single exception to the otherwise entirely male blessing of fertility: the truly exceptional case of the first woman, Eve. She is indeed the only woman to be party to God's blessing "be fruitful and multiply." At the same time, Eve is also the only woman—in fact the only person, woman or man—to receive a curse associated with fertility.

It is natural to assume that an analogously paired binary exists in biblical thought: fertility:blessing::infertility:curse. And it is certainly true, as we will see below, that blessing and curse are regularly set in opposition this way. Yet for all the blessings of fertility that we find, to different individuals and in different forms, there are no equivalent curses of infertility. It is not that curses are on the whole less common—people are cursed throughout the Bible. Goliath curses David (1 Sam 17:43). Elijah curses the children who mock him (2 Kgs 2:24). The Israelites are instructed not to curse their leaders (Exod 22:27). Balak hires Balaam to curse Israel (Num 22:6). None of these has anything to do with infertility. Just as fathers often bless their sons with fertility, so too there are cases of fathers cursing their sons: Noah curses Canaan (Gen 9:25), Jacob curses Simeon and Levi (Gen 49:7). But these are curses of subservience and disinheritance—the analogy does not hold.

Although God threatens to curse some individuals—notably those who curse Abraham (Gen 12:3)—in practice the only individuals who directly receive a curse from God are the three characters in the Garden of Eden: the snake, Adam, and Eve. Here too there is an analogic break. In Genesis 1, the blessing "be fruitful and multiply" is spoken by God first to the animal kingdom, then to the newly created humans, male and female. All three are present in the Garden: the snake, Adam, and Eve. If infertility were the cursed equivalent of blessed fertility, then we might expect all three to be cursed thusly. But the snake is cursed with the removal of its legs and enmity toward humans; Adam is cursed with labor in the fields, with an unyielding land. Only Eve's curse has to do with fertility. Eve is singled out.

Traditionally, Eve's curse has been read as an elaboration on the blessing of fertility. "I will make most severe your pangs in childbearing; in pain shall you bear children" (Gen 3:16). This reading assumes that Eve's fertility has already been established, back at the moment of creation in Genesis 1:28.[29] But there is something problematic here, on a simple plot level. Before God banishes them, Adam and Eve are intended to live forever in the Garden of Eden. How, in that case, are they supposed to "fill the earth"? They are meant to eat only that fruit that they can readily pick from the trees of the garden; this hardly seems to count as "subduing" the earth. If, in fact, they are supposed to be reproducing, and if, as we know, human reproduction leads to the enormous population that we now see covering the planet, then how is it imagined that all of these people were to fit inside the confines of the Garden?

At issue here is the well-known conflict between the two accounts of creation in Genesis 1 and Genesis 2–3. The account in Genesis 1 envisions humanity, like the rest of the animal kingdom, as blessed with fertility—as expected to expand across the planet—from the very beginning. But not so according to Genesis 2–3. In the story of the Garden of Eden, Adam is created alone at first, expected to live in peaceful solitude in the Garden forever. The animals, and Eve, are created only when God realizes that Adam might be lonely. Adam and Eve are not instructed to procreate; she is there to provide not children but companionship. Had they not eaten from the tree in the center of the garden, Adam and Eve would have lived in an eternal state of childlessness.[30] The ramifications of this vision of the original human state will be treated at greater length in the next chapter. For now, however, we can concentrate on the fact that in the absence of any children in Eden—as far as we can tell, Cain and Abel were born only after the expulsion from the garden—the curse on Eve can hardly assume any previously given blessing of fertility.

How, then, might we read God's words in Genesis 3:16? Carol Meyers has controversially—but to our minds persuasively and correctly—argued that they mean not "I will make most severe your pangs in childbearing," but rather "I will make very great your toils and your pregnancies."[31] This rendering takes full account of the narrative setting: from a place where no work was needed of any kind, Eve will enter a world where, as a woman, she is expected to contribute substantially to the labors of the household. Note that the same is true of Adam, whose curse in Genesis 3:17 contains the same word: "Cursed be the ground because of you; by toil shall you eat of it." We have already observed that the language of human fertility is derived from agriculture; here we see that parallel in full flower. Adam, who to this point has had to do no work at all for his food, simply plucking fruit from the trees, now must work in the fields. The curse is not that he will have to labor harder for his food; it is that he will have to labor at all.

So too, *mutatis mutandis*, for Eve, who goes from a life without labor of any sort to one in which labor is required. From a paradise in which there was no expectation or even real possibility of offspring, she will enter a world where children will be needed to help work the ground, and to repopulate the earth; Eve will indeed become a mother, repeatedly. Her name, of course, explicitly refers to that role: "The man named his wife Eve, because she was the mother of all the living" (Gen 3:20). But she receives that name only after the curse. And, of course, she gives birth to her children, Cain and Abel and Seth, only after she and Adam have left the Garden entirely.

In its original context, Eve's curse is not that she will experience pain in childbirth. It is that she will be pregnant in the first place. It is not a curse *about* fertility. It is a curse *of* fertility.[32]

We may now take this interpretation and bring it to the larger canonical setting, in conversation with Genesis 1 rather than in contradiction with it. As we saw above, both man and woman are blessed with fertility in Genesis 1:28. As we also saw, however, that blessing, everywhere it appears thereafter, is given exclusively to men. Something changes between the blessing at creation in Genesis 1 and the blessing of Noah and his sons in Genesis 9; indeed, something changes between the equal-minded blessing of Genesis 1 and the exclusion of women from the genealogy of Genesis 5. The meaning of fertility itself has bifurcated: into a positively charged genealogical, hereditary, sociopolitical concept for men on the one hand, and a negatively charged physical obligation for women on the other. This split occurs precisely when God changes the female blessing of fertility into Eve's curse. From that point forward, women become mere tools of reproduction in the male-oriented biblical world, while men aggregate to themselves the rights of inheritance and family name. The equality of blessing and fertility envisioned in Genesis 1 is exclusive, temporally and spatially, to the Garden of Eden. Once humanity enters the real world, that equality breaks down into two very unequal parts: a continued blessing for men, and a curse for women.[33]

The biblical authors did not create this imbalance. They were, rather, quite accurately representing the world they knew, a world in which women were reduced to the status of property. To a certain extent, we might appreciate the fact that they described that imbalance as an undesired state; God's original creation, they tell us, was the picture of gender equality.[34] If responsibility is to lie anywhere, it is with the generations that subsequently took up the Bible and used it as a foundation on which to build even stronger supports for male dominance and female subservience.

THE CURSE AS GENERAL, NOT UNIVERSAL

Typically, infertility is seen as a curse—replicating Peninnah's claim that Yahweh closes the womb, and in combination with the perceived universality of "be fruitful and multiply." This is the standard religious model, in which infertility is reckoned as a disability and God as its cause. But if, in Genesis 3:16, female fertility is in fact the curse—with, at least in biblical terms, God explicitly stated as its origin—then this would seem to turn the standard religious model on its head. The problem is that we have created a society in which those who do not or cannot have children are judged in violation of the blessing of Genesis 1; those who do are suffering under the curse of Genesis 3.

The aspect of so many traditional readings of the Bible that causes the most problems is the notion of universality. As we have seen repeatedly, in this chapter and in the last, there are enough elements in the text suggesting otherwise to urge caution in this regard. Whether fertility is a blessing or a curse, or both, the Bible readily admits that there are women—righteous, blameless women—who are not fertile. The blessing in Genesis 1 and the curse in Genesis 3 are not spoken merely to individuals, to be sure, but neither are they spoken to every person who ever lived thereafter. Even after God blesses the first man and woman with fertility, not everyone in the narrative is fertile. Even after God curses the first woman with pregnancy, not every woman becomes pregnant.

That God's words to Eve in Genesis 3 are meant to apply to women in general, rather than to every individual woman, is clear from comparison with the curses leveled against the serpent and Adam. Part of the curse on the serpent is that there will be "enmity between you and the woman and between your offspring and hers" (Gen 3:15). If this curse were intended to be universal, there would be no accounting for those snakes that are perfectly harmless to humans, or for those humans who keep snakes as pets. Adam is told that "your food shall be the grasses of the field" (Gen 3:17). If universal, this would apparently prohibit any consumption of wild fruits, the sort of food that was available in the Garden, and would present a significant challenge for those on the Atkins diet. The curse, like the blessing, is descriptive rather than prescriptive. They are generalizations, not universalizations. The power of the former is explanatory; the power of the latter is all too frequently doctrinal.

It is problematic, then, to find any fault in one who is unable to conceive. In light of Genesis 3, infertile women cannot be seen as cursed—they are the very ones who do not participate in the cursed female state. Are they therefore blessed? As we will see below, this is a false dichotomy. Blessing and curse may be antonyms, but they are not exclusive options. It is probably enough to say simply that they are not cursed. Given how the infertile have been treated throughout history, right up to the present, even this is a significant step in the right direction.

Though it is possible to construct a rather broad narrative about the transition of fertility from blessing to curse, as we have here, we must also remember that the Bible need not always speak with a single voice. As we saw in the last chapter, the biblical authors and society put a very high value on childbirth; no doubt they did see fertility as a blessing (though we may continue to ask whether that value took any female perspective into account). But the author of Genesis 3 also described fertility as a curse. The experience of infertility is not a uniform one, and the Bible, read generously, does not demand that it be so. We are not restricted to walking the well-worn path of traditional interpretation. We can, in fact, take a starkly different and far more generous approach to infertility while still maintaining a link to authentic biblical concepts.

To this point we have tried to argue, from a variety of angles, that those texts that seem to impose fertility on women—the blessing of Genesis 1 and the curse of Genesis 3—do not in fact do so. We need not see every individual woman as implicated in the words addressed to Eve. Such a universalizing tendency reads blame and guilt into the mere existence of infertility (and, for that matter, fertility as well). The Bible, however, does not; rather, it recognizes that there are, within the class of women, individuals who do not have children. This is clear enough from the mere presence in the text of such women, and prominent ones: Dinah, Miriam, Deborah. But it is reinforced in another set of texts, passages that treat not individuals, but the nation of Israel as a whole.

CORPORATE BODIES

As we saw above, there is an implicit temporal boundedness to the blessing "be fruitful and multiply": it has its terminus in the expansion of humanity to fill the earth, accomplished (twice) already by the end of Genesis 11, and in the expansion of Abraham's family to become a nation, accomplished already by the beginning of the book of Exodus. We may well say the same for the curse on Eve: the multiplication of women's pregnancies was an obvious necessity once the first couple left the Garden, not only to fill the earth but, given the curse on Adam, to work the land as well. Yet by the end of the primeval history, the earth is certainly full, humans having been dispersed across its face. By the time of the Exodus, the Israelites are said to be two million people strong (Exod 12:37).[35] If the curse in Genesis 3 is read, as we suggested above, as the gendered bifurcation of the blessing in Genesis 1, then it stands to reason that once the male half of the blessing, "be fruitful and multiply," has reached its final stages, then so too should the female half, "I will make great your toils and your pregnancies."

The culmination of the individual blessing of fertility coincides, not coincidentally, with the narrative transition from the story of individual to the story of an entire people. This is marked in the text by a decisive shift in the meaning of the phrase "children of Israel": in Exodus 1:1, and in virtually every passage in Genesis, the phrase means, quite literally, the offspring of the patriarch Jacob; from Exodus 1:12 forward, it means the Israelite nation. The verse in which the transition takes place is Exodus 1:7: "The children of Israel were fruitful and prolific and they multiplied and grew greatly in strength, such that the earth was filled with them." Here the phrase can uniquely have both meanings—Jacob's children and the nation—in precisely the verse where the blessing of fertility is finally said to be fulfilled.

In the first part of this chapter, we have tried to show that, even before Exodus 1, the blessing (and curse) of fertility was not meant to be imposed on each and every individual, even within the family of the promised line (see the example of Dinah). Even if it were, however, the Bible firmly consigns that blessing to a period in the distant, even semimythical, past. Despite traditional attempts to see the patriarchal period as a model for the present, to apply the blessing of fertility laid on Abraham, Isaac, and Jacob to those who live millennia later, the biblical authors were under no illusion that the patriarchal period was anything like their present. It was, rather, more like the picture of a lifestyle long abandoned, a past to which there was no returning. Those biblical texts that depict the patriarchal past should be far less relevant to the modern reader than those that describe and illuminate the present, and even the future.

The demarcation between these two types of biblical passages comes with the revelation at Sinai. There the patriarchal past is left behind and Israel enters its present existence, as God imposes an entirely new set of laws upon them, governing their ethical and ritual behavior. The break with the patriarchal lifestyle was clear: the patriarchs, for example, were constantly building altars, erecting pillars, and planting cultic trees at spots all around Canaan—exactly the behavior that is expressly forbidden in Deuteronomy. These divine laws are intended to speak directly to the Bible's audience, as Deuteronomy makes clear: "I make this covenant, with its sanctions, not with you alone, but both with those who are standing here with us this day before the Lord our God and with those who are not with us here this day" (Deut 29:13–14). Even though the laws were given hundreds, even thousands of years ago, that moment of revelation is constantly renewed in every generation. Readers of the Bible, to the present, are not merely living in the aftermath of the revelation; we are intended to experience it for ourselves in the very act of reading. Thus when Moses says to the Israelites, "I have put before you life and death, blessing and curse—choose life" (Deut 30:19), generations of interpreters have correctly understood that we are the ones asked to make that choice.[36]

Our task, then, is to understand how the Bible envisions the existence of infertility in this present state, present both for the biblical authors and for us today. Is it, as so commonly thought, a curse? Is it an aberration? What are the expectations regarding fertility now that Israel has become a nation? These questions can be answered, perhaps somewhat surprisingly, not by examining how the Bible depicts the Israelites in its narrative present, but by looking at how it thinks Israel will be in the future.

THE FUTURE REVEALING THE PRESENT

There are three legal codes in the Hebrew Bible, and each one concludes with a forecast of Israel's future, should they choose to obey the laws (or not). Obedience brings blessing; disobedience brings curse. And the middle ground—the neutral state—is the ground we stand on, as we are faced with that same choice. That we live in neither the blessed nor the cursed state is clear from the way these are depicted. The blessings that will accrue to the obedient include the disappearance of all dangerous animals (Lev 26:6), lack of national debt (Deut 28:12), an end to all sickness (Exod 23:25), the awe of all other peoples (Deut 28:10), and the ability to win every battle fought (Lev 26:8). This all sounds lovely—but it is far from the world that ancient Israel inhabited, and far too from our own. Similarly, the curses that will befall the disobedient include a rush of wild beasts (Lev 26:22), rains of sand (Deut 28:24), incurable skin diseases (Deut 28:27), the inability to be satisfied by food (Lev 26:26), the failure of all crops (Deut 28:39–40), and a descent into cannibalism (Lev 26:29; Deut 28:53–57). Horrors indeed, but confined in our world mostly to horror movies.

God, through Moses, puts before us the choice of blessing or curse: two possible roads down which we can travel. Yet it is clear that we are, as readers, imagined to be on neither path. We, like the Israelites in the desert, stand at that fork in the road, at the intermediate stage. And from the choices before us we can understand more clearly where we stand. Many of the blessings and curses are presented as extremes on a spectrum. If the blessing brings the removal of all wild animals (Lev 26:6), and the curse brings a flood of them (Lev 26:22), then we know that the present state is somewhere between those two possibilities: we live in a time when there are some wild animals, but thankfully not too many.[37]

The blessing is that God "will open for you his bounteous store, the heavens, to provide rain for your land in season" (Deut 28:12). The curse is that "the skies above your head shall be copper . . . the Lord will make the rain of your land dust" (Deut 28:23–24). These extremes are somewhat different from those in the case of the wild animals, but they are closer to the question of fertility in which we are interested. The curse of drought is clear enough; but the blessing of rain is less straightforward. It does not promise continual rainfall, which, as we know from the Flood story, would be a curse in itself. Rather, the blessing of rain is that, when the rainy season comes, the rain will indeed fall on schedule. That is the extreme associated with the blessing; what, then, is envisioned as the present state? Not constant drought, nor perfectly regular rains, but rather precisely what we experience today, and what people have experienced forever: the hope, even the expectation, of rain in its season, but equally the knowledge and fear that sometimes the rain simply does not fall when it should. In the present world, sometimes misfortune comes to pass; this does not happen every time, but neither is it wholly unanticipated.

The blessing is that God "will remove sickness from your midst. . . . I will let you enjoy the full count of your days" (Exod 23:25–26). The curse is that God will "wreak misery upon you—consumption and fever, which cause the eyes to pine and the body to languish" (Lev 26:16); Yahweh will "strike you with the Egyptian inflammation, with hemorrhoids, boil-scars, and itch, from which you will never recover. The Lord will strike you with madness, blindness, and dismay . . . strange and lasting plagues, malignant and chronic diseases" (Deut 28:27–28, 59). The extremes are perfect health for the entire nation and devastating illness for the entire nation. What is the intermediate position?

Some health—perhaps, even, mostly health—but, inevitably, some sickness as well. "The full count of your days"—that this is a potential blessing reflects the truth that, at present, not everyone reaches the fullness of old age. Like the rains, there is a hope for the good, but also a recognition that there is also bad. Some day, perhaps, God will push the nation toward one end or the other; for now, however, we live in a world where there is some of each.

Now we come to fertility. The blessing of fertility is stated in a variety of different ways, each of which deserves some attention. In Deuteronomy, we read, "Blessed shall be the fruit of your womb" (28:4). This is not properly a blessing of fertility, but a blessing of the fertile: not that Israel's wombs will all produce offspring, but that those offspring that are produced will fare well.[38] Along similar lines is the language of Deuteronomy 28:11: "The Lord will give you astounding prosperity in the fruit of your womb." Here we can say that the point is not necessarily the quality of the offspring, but their quantity: in this blessed future, Israel, as a nation, will produce many children. In both cases, however, fertility itself is not at issue. These blessings are both about the fruit produced; fertility is about the initial planting of the seed. And neither of these blessings implies universal fertility.

Leviticus 26:9 uses familiar language: "I will make you fruitful and multiply you." This is what God said to Abraham, in the blessing that was fulfilled at the beginning of Exodus. Here, however, for the first and only time in the Bible, it is addressed not to an individual, but to the nation as a whole. How do we understand it in this new context? Given that the immediately preceding verses describe how Israel will never be attacked but will win every battle, it seems most likely that what is intended here is national expansion beyond Israel's traditional borders. Israel had achieved nationhood, the requisite population to fill the promised land, long ago; in the future, should it receive God's blessing, it will grow even beyond those boundaries. We may note, however, that the very concept of Israel as a nation being made fruitful and multiplying assumes that the nation has already come into existence—the individual blessing of fertility had to be fulfilled in order to transform it into a national blessing. And, finally, it should be pointed out again that even if the nation is expected to expand in that blessed future, there is no notion here of every single individual procreating.[39]

UNIVERSAL (IN)FERTILITY

That notion does occur, however, and quite explicitly. Exodus 23:26 states, "No woman in your land shall miscarry or be barren." Deuteronomy 7:14 says, "There shall be no barren male or female among you or among your livestock." In Israel's future, when the nation lives under the overarching blessing of God, there will be no infertility—we will come back to this in the next chapter. But here we note what such a statement means for the present: if the future will witness an absence of infertility, then the present we inhabit, by necessity, must be one in which there is infertility. Fertility is analogous to rain and health: it is the expected and hoped-for outcome—but it is not taken for granted, and its opposite is not unusual.[40]

In Deuteronomy 7:14, Israel's perfectly fertile state is contrasted explicitly with the rest of the world: "You shall be blessed above all other peoples." The present state of the world, as described by these biblical texts, is one in which infertility is a fact of life. One might be tempted to say, with universal fertility being the blessing, that infertility is therefore the curse, and that those individuals who suffer from it are somehow harbingers or exemplars of God's punishment.[41] Such an argument suffers, however, from a circumstance unique to the blessing of fertility in these passages. Simply put, there is no corresponding curse of infertility. Rain is paired with drought, health with sickness; but when we look for the text where fertility is paired with infertility, we search in vain.

Since we saw earlier that there are also no curses of infertility leveled against individuals, either by humans or by God, this absence may not seem so unexpected. Yet when set into the broader ancient Near Eastern context, it is more surprising. Curses of infertility are found across the ancient Near East: from Mesopotamia: "May Marduk take away his potency, destroy his seed";[42] from Egypt: "O ye gods, let not his seed germinate."[43] Infertility curses addressed to individuals appear in numerous contexts, from warnings against desecration of a text—"He who destroys this tablet, may Enki block up his canal with silt. May Ninhursag cut off his childbirth from his land"[44]—to military oaths: "Whoever should transgress these oaths . . . let his wives bear neither male nor female children."[45]

Most relevant for our current purposes are those curses that are found at the end of various treaties, as the suzerain adjures the vassal to obey the stipulations set forth in the text. These treaties form the generic background against which the legal structures in the Bible were composed: the laws required by God are the equivalent of the treaty stipulations demanded by the king, and just as disobedience against God's laws brings devastating punishment, so too does neglect of the treaty agreement.[46] With these parallels in mind, it is revealing that a Hittite treaty contains precisely the curse of infertility that we are lacking in the Bible: "If you . . . do not fulfill the words of this treaty, may the gods . . . blot you out . . . may your sons and your country have no seed."[47] Or, from another Hittite document: "If you transgress the oaths, then let your cattle, your sheep, and your human beings not give birth."[48] In an Akkadian treaty that has long been considered the potential literary model for Deuteronomy, we find the following: "May Betet-ili [an Assyrian goddess], the Lady of all creatures, put an end to birth-giving in your land."[49]

Israel's God threatens sickness, death, and destruction for disobeying the divinely given laws, for breaking the divinely or-
dained covenant treaty. But there is no threat of infertility. This
may well be because God does not want to destroy Israel forever,
but to force them to repent and return to obedience. National infertility would—as the Pharaoh of Exodus 1 well knew—eliminate
Israel within a single generation. God's hope for Israel's future,
despite its disobedience, may therefore stand behind the absence
of such a punishment. At the same time, however, the fact that
there is no curse of infertility anywhere in the Hebrew Bible
makes it difficult to equate infertility with curse. The Bible is
clear: even when fertility is put forward as a blessing, infertility
is still not a curse.

We may also note that the notion of fertility as a blessing is
often misunderstood. As we have seen, it is not individual fertility
per se that is considered blessed in these passages—it is universal fertility. The mixture of fertility and infertility that we know
today, that has existed for all of human history, is neither blessed
nor cursed—it is the unmarked state of humanity. Blessing, here
and everywhere in the Bible, is not abundance, but superabundance: not that a person should have a good lineage of descendants, but that he or she should become an entire nation; not that
an individual might avoid illness, but that a whole people might
be eternally healthy; not that a single person would be healed of
infertility, but that all of Israel would be perfectly fertile.

It is expected that, in this world at the crossroads of blessing
and curse, there will be some people who are infertile. That is
the state of things before God intervenes to change the course
of human history. The fact that the Bible envisions divine intervention bringing about universal fertility in the blessed future
dovetails neatly with the argument of the previous chapter: God
changes humans from infertile to fertile, and not the other way
around—there is no curse of infertility. God opens the womb.

The one exception to this general rule, the story of Abimelech in Genesis 20, nevertheless supports the larger point being made here. Yes, in this story God does appear to cause infertility. But, as noted briefly in the previous chapter, this is not a story about God causing an individual to become infertile. It is an entire community of women—"every womb of the household of Abimelech" (Gen 20:18). If this story were about a few women in Abimelech's household being infertile, God's hand would not be apparent—it is expected that there will be some barren women in every community. It is the universality of the condition—be it fertility or infertility—that is rare and representative of God's active intervention.

CONCLUSION

The ancient Babylonian epic of Atrahasis, from more than five hundred years before the earliest biblical texts, depicts the creation of humankind and its destruction in a flood, in a well-known parallel to the biblical account. After the Flood has passed, and humanity is set to begin again, the high god Enlil lays down some new rules to govern humanity, in order to ensure that the human population does not grow too loud or noisy and disturb his divine rest. The deity proclaims, "Let there be among the peoples women who bear and women who do not bear."[50] Leaving aside—for the moment—the notion of population control present in this ancient story, for our purposes here we may observe what this passage means for the Mesopotamian view of the existence of infertility in the world. Infertility is not conceived of here as an individual punishment—indeed, it has nothing to do with individuals at all. It is an aspect of the human community writ large: there are, in the world, some women who are unable to bear children. Crucially, this inalterable fact is chalked up to the decision of the gods at the moment of re-creation—at the moment when humanity entered its contemporary period, when life as we know it was organized and implemented. This story explains not some part of the past, but an aspect of the present. Not only is infertility not a curse or punishment in this story, it can even be read as a good: it is because infertility exists that humanity is allowed to continue on earth, that the anger of the gods is kept in check.[51]

There is no biblical equivalent of this last concept, but the general notion is quite close to what we have been suggesting here. The historical epoch that begins in both the Bible and Atrahasis at the conclusion of the Flood, and which is, for Israel, further refined at the end of the patriarchal period and in the revelation at Sinai, is the one in which we, the readers of these texts, find ourselves. The idea that, we have shown, can be carefully extracted from a close reading of the biblical material—that the presence of infertility in the human population is neither punishment nor curse nor in any way irregular—is stated quite directly in the Babylonian epic. And while it is certainly possible to find other perspectives in the Bible, this one cannot simply be discarded as a modern imposition on the text: it was present in the cultural milieu of the biblical authors nearly a millennium before they put pen to parchment.

Atrahasis, for its part, is not the only Mesopotamian text to express this idea. Even earlier is the text known as "Enki and Ninmaḫ," or, more descriptively, as "The Birth of Man," a Sumerian myth that has the right to be called the earliest creation story ever written down. In this tale, the god Enki creates man to assist the gods with the labor of caring for the earth, upon which he celebrates his newfound relaxation with drink. With him is another deity, Ninmaḫ, the high mother-goddess of the Mesopotamian pantheon, who challenges Enki: she will create a series of humans with various physical ailments, and Enki will try to find a place for them in his newly-created society. Thus the blind man is made to be a musician, the one with damaged feet is made to be a metalworker, the eunuch is made to stand in attendance on the king—and the woman who could not give birth is made to be a weaver.[52]

Like the epic of Atrahasis, this myth attributes the presence of infertile women in society to a primordial divine action. Again, there is no sense of curse or wrongdoing associated with infertility. Instead, there is a clear commitment to the integration of infertile women—along with all those who are physically impaired—into the broader human society. There is also the recognition, as in Atrahasis, that infertility has been a part of human life since the world came into being; that it is not only on the same level as other physical impairments but that all such impairments are as ancient and as part of the standard order as the fact that humans have to work the land. In the Bible, physical labor and fertility are correlated as the curses on Adam and Eve, respectively. In the Mesopotamian parallels, it is labor and infertility that are correlated: neither as a curse, but both as representative of the world we experience to this day.

It is all too common for the blessing and curse of Genesis 1 and 3 to be taken as informing the manner in which infertility (and fertility, for that matter) is to be treated in contemporary culture. Yet as we have argued here, those divine statements belong to an earlier epoch of human history. They are antediluvian. Even the echoes of that initial blessing that follow the Flood are, on the one hand, delivered only to men, and, on the other, come to an end when the blessing is explicitly stated to have been fulfilled, at the beginning of Exodus. The Bible's view is that we stand at a different moment in the history of God's creation. We are part of neither the primeval nor the patriarchal world; rather, we stand at Sinai, the fulfilled nation of Israel, constantly on the cusp of ascending into blessing or descending into curse.

Where we stand now is not of our own doing: God created humankind, God chose Abraham, God rescued Israel from Egypt, and God brought us to the edge of the promised land. This world that we inhabit, and the infertility that exists in it, are part of the divinely created order. We have not yet made the final choice that will shift the world into the promised state of blessing or the threatened state of curse. The infertility that we experience and see around us is not a curse. It is the way of the world, and it is as old as the world.

CHAPTER 3

Mother Zion and the Eschaton

In the sixth century BCE, as the Persian Empire achieved dominance over the Babylonians, the Israelites in exile in Babylon experienced a remarkable reversal in their fortunes. From the despair of utter defeat, a return to their ancestral home suddenly seemed imminent. This crucial historical moment was captured most incisively by a prophet whose name is now lost to us, who heralded God's renewed care for Israel, declaring in a voice of new hope, "Comfort, comfort, O my people." This prophet's words have been preserved as the continuation of the speeches attributed to the eighth-century prophet Isaiah, and are found in chapters 40 to 66 of the biblical book by the same name.[1] This prophet, known to scholarship as Deutero-Isaiah (though hereafter called simply Isaiah for the sake of simplicity), was responsible for the famous "Servant Songs." Yet he also gave voice to a different figure: Zion, the city of Jerusalem embodied in female, maternal form, and her experience of exile and impending restoration.

Isaiah uses a range of female imagery to personify Zion, but we are here concerned with one particular aspect: his depiction of exilic Zion as a barren mother.[2] Like the matriarchs of Genesis, Isaiah's Zion is defined by her infertility. The first, and almost the only, words that Isaiah puts in her mouth are about nothing else: "I was bereaved and barren, exiled and disdained" (Isa 49:21). The equation with the matriarchs is made clear in Isaiah 54:1, where Zion is addressed as "barren, who bore no child"—barren, 'aqara, the very word used of Sarah (Gen 11:30), Rebekah (Gen 25:21), and Rachel (Gen 29:31); bore no child, lo' yaldah, the precise phrase applied to Sarah (Gen 16:1) and Rachel (Gen 30:1).[3]

Zion is an infertile woman, subject to all the social detriment that such a state called forth in ancient Israel. And yet Isaiah does not condemn her, or even merely console her. Instead—in language that, given the cultural assumptions about barren women, must have been a shock to his audience[4]—the prophet encourages her to rejoice aloud: "Shout, O barren one, you who bore no child; shout aloud for joy, you who did not travail!" (Isa 54:1). The language remains shocking even today: what woman, unable to bear despite her deepest desires to do so, could imagine celebrating her condition? Yet this is precisely what Isaiah calls for.

The historical-theological message that the prophet proclaims here has been recognized by all commentators, and is obvious enough: Zion will celebrate the return of the exiles as a barren mother celebrates the birth of a child.[5] Isaiah uses the image of Zion as a barren mother in the service of depicting a gloriously reversed future state, a time when Israel will in fact be so full of people, so fertile in every sense, that her previously barren state will be but a distant memory. This much of the metaphor is clear. But there is the other half: not the historical situation that is being illuminated, but the infertility that is being invoked.[6] By alluding to the matriarchal stories through the metaphor of Mother Zion, Isaiah shines a new light on the traditions of the past. Yet, in accordance with Heisenberg's Uncertainty Principle, older traditions cannot be reexamined without fundamentally altering them. There is no perfect allusion, in which the received material is not changed by the very act of recalling it.[7] Isaiah is no exception to this rule. For our purposes, it is the reconfiguration of matriarchal infertility, and infertility in general, that is most in need of study.

Despite the familiarity of the basic concept—everyone understands the premise of motherhood—the metaphor is a complex one, with multiple moving parts. There is a temporal shift, from the present to the future, while there is simultaneously an explicit hearkening back to the ancient past. Time is collapsed. There is a change in status, from barren to fertile, and yet there remains the question of why the barrenness occurred in the first place. There is a change in emotional state, from bereaved to rejoicing; a change in social standing, from mocked to admired. Then we may ask, why this metaphor in particular? Reversal of fortune can be presented in any number of guises—what is the value of this imagery that it calls for such repeated insistence? How do the barren matriarchs undergird the prophetic vision for the nation, and how does the prophet reshape and reinterpret the matriarchal stories? What does motherhood mean on the national level? There need be no simple answer to these questions; metaphors are not reducible to singular meanings. But at the various axes along which these questions intersect we may discover new angles from which to understand the prophetic reimagining of infertility.

BARREN MOTHER ZION

The theme of matriarchal barrenness is almost entirely confined to Genesis. The matriarchs themselves are almost wholly absent from the rest of the Bible. It is thus telling—and remarkable—that Isaiah should choose to refer explicitly to Sarah, and to highlight in multiple passages the issue of her barrenness (and through Sarah, the barrenness of all the matriarchs of Israel). The choice was clearly not an obvious one, and for that reason deserves added attention.

In their original literary context, the stories of the matriarchs in Genesis are part of the ancient narratives of how the nation of Israel came into existence. They demonstrate the power of the divine will to bring about that which God had promised to Abraham. They depict a distant past, an earlier state of the people, before the defining national crisis of the enslavement in Egypt and the obligation to God that followed from the Exodus and the subsequent law giving in the wilderness. They establish, along with the rest of the Genesis stories, Israel's God-given right to the land of Canaan. But once Israel was firmly established in its homeland, once the nation had decisively come into being, once the need to assert that aspect of Israel's identity was no longer a pressing one, it might be natural for these stories to lose some of their original force. It is for this reason that these narratives are mentioned relatively infrequently in the later books of the Bible, while the Exodus remains a central reference point. Israel's obligation to God, the need to obey the divine will, was and remains a persistent topic, regardless of time or place; it is rather more difficult to convince readers and listeners to change their ways by recounting the long-completed fulfillment of an ancient promise.[8]

Although we have been focusing on them here, the matriarchs are relegated to distinctly supporting characters in the narrative of Genesis. Though they are inescapable parts of the story, to be sure, they serve a single purpose and then depart the stage. Once their sons are born and married, they are barely mentioned again, except perhaps to be buried (in which role they still serve the patriarchal purpose of establishing rights to the land). The beloved Rachel, whose attempt to bear children is described in such detail, dies upon bearing her last son, Benjamin. Her sister Leah simply disappears entirely, her death unmentioned and her burial related only in a later recollection by Jacob. The promise of land and progeny is given to the men—to Abraham, Isaac, Jacob,

even Ishmael—but not to the women. Moses recalls God's obligation to the patriarchs, but never mentions the matriarchs. The
nation is called Israel after Jacob, and the tribes are named for his
sons. The story of Genesis requires the matriarchs, but it is not
their story.

What's more, the matriarchs can be somewhat difficult models
for the infertile reader. Though they suffer, that suffering is inevitably relieved. This is not necessarily the case for most women
who might identify with the matriarchs. As each year passes
without successful conception and pregnancy, and as, with the
turn of each page, Sarah and Rebekah and Rachel successively
cease to be relevant exemplars, the matriarchal stories can come
to seem distant, even mocking. Their pain may be shared, but not
their eventual joy. No barren women in the biblical story remain
barren. The longevity of the matriarchs' delayed maternity can
serve to stifle and silence the pain felt by infertile readers. That
the matriarchs give birth so late in life means that the period of
uncertainty, and hope, extends well past the age of menopause.
At what point does the Bible allow us to voice our pain and despair, when Sarah and the others endured long into their old age?
In some ways the stories of the matriarchs silence those who
long to give expression to their despair and find the message of
the matriarchs oppressively hopeful.

REDEFINING INFERTILITY

Through a series of interpretive moves, Isaiah rectifies this situation and makes the matriarchal traditions newly applicable.
The prophet reimagines what it means to be barren. In depicting
Israel as an infertile mother, Isaiah must grapple with what exactly it means for a nation to have offspring (or not). A mother
sustains her children, provides them with shelter and food. In the
prophet's imagination, this is what Zion does for her inhabitants.

Those who dwell within her borders are her metaphorical offspring. This imagery again demands that Zion once had been fertile, before she was made barren: Israel could not have existed as a nation in the first place without people to constitute it.

If the establishment of Israel as a people in their land is to be equated with the fertility of Zion, then the definition of Zion's barrenness comes into focus: the absence of those people from Jerusalem's borders. And where did her children go? Here Isaiah binds his metaphor to history: they went into exile. The prophet rehearses the pentateuchal curses of Leviticus 26 and Deuteronomy 28. We have already seen that in these passages there is no direct counterpart to the blessings of national fertility; God never threatens to render Israel's populace infertile. What we find, rather, is the threat that, though children will be born, they will be slaughtered or led into exile: "Your sons and daughters shall be delivered to another people, while you look on; and your eyes shall strain for them constantly, but you shall be helpless. . . . Though you beget sons and daughters, they shall not remain with you, for they shall go into captivity" (Deut 28:32, 41).

The curses of Deuteronomy are relentless: there is no possibility offered for a return to God's favor. But by combining them with the theme of the barren matriarch, Isaiah provides just such a possibility, indeed even a certainty: "[My people] shall not bear children in vain . . . their offspring shall remain with them" (Isa 65:23). He has also radically reenvisioned both the matriarchal and the deuteronomic traditions by transforming the very definition of infertility itself. In Deuteronomy, the curse is one of fertility with a tragic ending; Isaiah renders this as barrenness. At the same time, the matriarchal traditions describing the inability to bear children are reimagined as the loss of children already born. For Isaiah, childlessness in all of its various configurations is a single phenomenon. This elision of categories has created consternation among interpreters, who puzzle over how a mother who had already born her children, now lost, could ask "who bore these for me?" (Isa 49:21).[9] Yet in precisely this way Isaiah connects the experience of loss with that of infertility: the return of offspring is akin to their initial birth, both equally unexpected and miraculous.

The prophet accomplishes this equation through the combination of particular words and images. He depicts Zion as saying, upon the return of her children, "Who bore these for me when I was bereaved and barren?" (Isa 49:21). Both terms here, "bereaved" and "barren," have deeply resonant nuances. The word translated "bereaved," *shekulah*, comes from a root, *shakal*, that is sometimes simply akin to "death," as in Jeremiah 15:7: "I will bereave, I will destroy my people." Often, it carries the more specific meaning "to render childless." This is what Rebekah says when instructing Jacob to flee from Esau, that she not lose (*'eshkal*) both of them in one day (Gen 27:45). It is what Jacob says when he unhappily agrees to send Benjamin off to Egypt: "If am to be bereaved (*shakolti*), I will be bereaved (*shakalti*)" (Gen 43:14). It is what wild beasts will do to the Israelite children according to the curses of Leviticus 26: "they shall bereave (*weshikk'lah*) you of your children" (Lev 26:22). Hosea, echoing the curses of Deuteronomy, says of Ephraim that "even if they rear their infants, I will bereave them (*weshikkaltim*) of all people" (Hos 9:12). Jeremiah prays that the wives of his enemies should be "bereaved (*shakkulot*)" (Jer 18:21).

While this common meaning comports well with Isaiah's depiction of Zion's offspring as having been killed and exiled, the word has a yet more specific meaning that relates it more closely to the notion of barrenness proper. This is the verb used for miscarriage: of flocks, as in Genesis 31:38 and Job 21:10; and, most notably, of Israel's inhabitants, in Exodus 23:26: "No woman in your land shall miscarry (*meshakkelah*) or be barren." Isaiah has chosen a nearly perfect word: one that captures both the inability to bear and the loss of those already born, and one that is thus suggestive of both the theme of matriarchal barrenness and the historical experience of exile.[10]

The second term in Isaiah 49:21, *galmudah*, translated as "barren," is rarer, but also entails multiple possible meanings.[11] Outside of Isaiah, it appears only in the book of Job, and there only three times. Once, it describes the wretchedness of those who taunt Job (thereby highlighting Job's even lower state) as "wasted (*galmud*) from want and hunger" (Job 30:3); here the word has the connotation of "empty." Elsewhere, Eliphaz reminds Job that "the company of the impious is desolate (*galmud*)" (Job 15:34), again with a meaning akin to "vacant." Most pointedly, when Job recalls in anguish the night of his birth, he wishes "may that night be desolate (*galmud*)" (Job 3:7). In Job's words we see the full extent of the term's nuances: that night should be emptied of all it bore, that is, of Job's birth—which is to say, Job's mother should have been emptied of all she bore. The emptiness of hunger, the emptiness of evil company, the emptiness of time and womb—perhaps all of these aspects are voiced by Isaiah's Mother Zion, by the city who was emptied of her inhabitants, her children.[12]

The emptiness of the land is equated with the emptiness of the womb, and in this way Isaiah is able to call on the tradition of the barren matriarch as a symbol for Israel's exiled condition. The prophet elides categories of childlessness that are often kept apart and differently valued, demonstrating their fundamental similarity. The past becomes present—and yet the past remains part of Israel's story, as Isaiah explicitly recalls Sarah as a model in his expectations for Zion's coming fruitfulness: "Look back to Abraham your father, and to Sarah who brought you forth" (Isa 51:2). This is followed by a recollection of the creation account: "Truly the Lord has comforted Zion. . . . He has made her wilderness like Eden, her desert like the garden of the Lord" (51:3). The change described here is from one of complete emptiness—

using the geographical terms for barren terrain, "wilderness" and "desert"—to one of utter fecundity, the abundant orchard from which all humanity emerged.[13]

The barren matriarch is thus figured as the world before Eden, that dry and desolate landscape depicted in Genesis 2:4b–5, and her eventual fertility as the first act of creation in which mankind was formed to populate the world.[14] The thrust of this imagery in Isaiah is intended to describe the return of Israel's exiles as a new creation, but it reflects a new reading of the matriarchal traditions. The fertility of Sarah is aligned with the fertility of Jerusalem via the language of tunneling through rock: Sarah is the stony ground from which, as if by a miracle, the waters of life burst forth, just as Jerusalem is sustained by the water channels dug into its ancient rock, just as the primordial world was watered by the rivers that flowed out of Eden (Gen 2:10–14).[15] Isaiah pointedly credits God with the act of hewing: "He has made her wilderness like Eden" (Isa 51:3), in line with the regular recognition that God is the one who opens the womb (see chapter 1). By this imagery the prophet reinforces his identification of bereavement with barrenness: the emptiness of the land after exile is so extreme that it may as well have never been populated in the first place; the absence of Zion's offspring is so deeply felt that, like Sarah, she may as well have never borne any children at all.

By eliding the categories of barren and bereaved, Isaiah broadens the traditions of the matriarchs, and opens up the possibility of speaking about childlessness in all of its various instantiations. We have noted how childless women today, regardless of root cause, tend to be lumped together under a single rubric. Isaiah seems to recognize and, in a way, take ownership of that phenomenon. Now not only those who are barren, but all those who have lost a child, can see themselves embodied in Israel's first mothers. Indeed the entire nation becomes mother. And just as the matriarchs did eventually bear offspring, so too the offspring of Mother Zion will return to her. The blurring of these distinctions is crystallized in Isaiah 66, where the prophet imagines the returning exiles not as the grown adults that their nearly fifty-year absence would suggest, but rather as newborns: "that you may suck from her breast . . . that you may draw from her bosom" (Isa 66:11).[16] We have returned to the beginning—Mother Zion will experience the joy that Sarah thought she would never know: "Who would have said to Abraham that Sarah would suckle children!" (Gen 21:7).[17]

THE ORIGINS OF ZION'S BARRENNESS

In the stories of Genesis, the matriarchs enter the scene already infertile—as we have seen, this is often how they are actually introduced into the narrative. They have no history before this. Yet the same could hardly be said about Mother Zion. Her history was lengthy and well known, elaborated in multiple diverse traditions—including, of course, those of the matriarchs themselves. It was thus impossible for Isaiah simply to take the beginnings of the matriarchal traditions as the starting point for his description of Zion. He had rather to explain how it was that Zion, once at the height of her glory, had fallen into despair. How was it possible for a mother to change from fertile to barren—and back again?

We have already encountered this phenomenon, in the story of Leah: she gave birth to four sons, then entered a period of infertility (in which she took the traditional path of offering her maidservant to her husband as a surrogate), and subsequently resumed childbearing. Although this story may stand as evidence that such changes in fertility were understood to occur, it provides little in the way of interpretive traction. No reason is given for Leah's sudden infertility, nor for her resumption of fertility. Though we may understand it in the way suggested in chapter 1—

as a sort of fluctuating of divine attention—this would hardly serve Isaiah's purposes.

Deutero-Isaiah is most famous, in scholarship on the history of Israelite religious thought, for his radical monotheism: the idea that God controls not only Israel but all nations and peoples. This notion is worked out historically in Isaiah's presentation of Babylon as an agent of God's wrath against Israel and of Cyrus the Great as the agent of divine mercy. Given Isaiah's depiction of all history as the direct involvement of God in human affairs, there could be little room for any divine inattention—quite the opposite. The barrenness of Mother Zion is equated, for Isaiah, with the anguish of exile, as the parallelism of Isaiah 49:21 makes abundantly clear: "I was bereaved and barren, exiled and disdained."[18] If the exile was the working out of God's wrath, then divine punishment must also lay behind the image of Jerusalem's barrenness. Again the word *shakal* is important: this is not only the term used by Zion to describe herself, but also the punishment that God decrees on Babylon: "Loss of children [*shekol*] and widowhood shall come upon you in full measure" (Isa 47:9). Equally pertinent is the condemnation of Sidon by the eight-century Isaiah: "Be ashamed, O Sidon! For the sea—this stronghold of the sea—declares, 'I am as one who has never labored, never given birth, never raised youths or reared maidens'" (Isa 23:4).

Isaiah seemingly affirms what we have seen as the dominant model for understanding infertility. In so doing, however, the prophet combines the common cultural view with the distinctly judgment-free matriarchal traditions, preserving neither in its previous state. For just as the matriarchal stories are now invested with an element of divine punishment, so too the notion of infertility as sin is leavened with the certain promise of future fertility. Perhaps the better narrative analogy is thus not Leah but the women of Abimelech's court. There we find infertility inflicted upon a population as punishment, as Isaiah suggests.

There too we find the eventual resumption of fertility, with Isaiah now playing the part of Abraham: the prophetic figure who announces that God has relented from his wrath.

The Abimelech intertext may also be particularly apposite because, as we saw earlier, it has the distinction of being the only tradition in which God inflicts infertility upon an entire population, that is, on a corporate rather than individual body. Isaiah's Mother Zion stands in an odd liminal position between the two bodily states: it is the incorporated nation that is being punished, but the nation is styled as an individual woman, Jerusalem. By playing between these two poles, Isaiah brings in aspects of each. If the nation as a whole is suffering, it must be the work of God: corporate infertility, unlike individual barrenness, can be the result only of divine curse. At the same time, when an individual woman is fertile, unlike when she is barren, it is equally attributable to the direct hand of God. Isaiah takes up those elements from each tradition that most forcefully express God's power in the world and combines them in a novel manner, one that, not coincidentally, reinforces his overarching theological position.

The ostensible responsibility, even guilt, that Isaiah's theological model—and his dependence on the curse formulations of Deuteronomy—would seem to impose on the infertile mother is potentially reinforced in his very choice of a female figure to personify Jerusalem. The choice may have been determined in part by grammar: in the gendered Semitic languages, cities are commonly feminine.[19] Thus Israel is often portrayed in a female role: frequently as a wife, famously in Hosea, or as "Daughter Zion," in Lamentations; the depiction of Israel as mother is far less common. Nevertheless, these three female types of Israel share certain features in their various biblical incarnations. When Zion is presented metaphorically as God's wife, it is as an unfaithful spouse who requires punishment, but who will be brought back into the divine household after she has learned her lesson. When presented as a daughter, it is as a rape victim, defiled and

ashamed (and, abhorrent as it seems to modern ears, at least potentially responsible for her condition; see Deut 22:23–24). In
both cases, the biblical authors imagine the worst possible social
condition for a woman in those respective positions.[20]

These analogs seem to support a sense of guilt on the part of
Mother Zion. Yet there are aspects of Isaiah's presentation that
provide a significant counterbalance. These come most prominently to the fore in Isaiah 54, the passage with which this chapter began. The verses describing Zion as barren are followed by
words of comfort: "Fear not, you shall not be shamed; do not
cringe, you shall not be disgraced" (Isa 54:4). We need not ask
what this shame is: we have explored already the experience of
the infertile woman in ancient Israel. But we may again note that
shame and disgrace are social terms, invoking the perception of
others, rather than anything inherent to the woman herself. The
prophet continues, "For you shall forget the reproach of your
youth, and remember no more the shame of your widowhood"
(Isa 54:4). The word for "disgrace" in the first half of the verse,
hapar, is a play on the same word Rachel uses of her infertile
shame, *herpah*—the word that Isaiah then uses to describe the
"shame" of widowhood. The language of disgrace is a hinge between the two unfortunate female states, a way of equating
them.[21] Yet widowhood is a decidedly guilt-free condition. The
closely drawn nature of this particular parallel implies that the
same guiltless qualities may be associated with infertility.[22]

We may wonder, however, what to make of the reference to
widowhood here. Although widows were vulnerable in Israelite
society—hence the regular association of widows with orphans
and resident aliens (see, e.g., Deut 24:17)—they were not typically
shamed.[23] Indeed, this is the only place in the entire Bible where
widowhood and shame are aligned.[24] In what scenario is widowhood a shameful proposition? The context provides the key:
widowhood is not being compared with barrenness; it is, rather,
being presented as an advanced state of barrenness. The contrast

drawn in this verse is between "youth" and "widowhood"—a contrast highlighted by the wordplay in Hebrew, *'alumayik* and *'almenutayik*, respectively—not different states, but the same state, simply further along the temporal plane. The widow in this imagery is the same barren woman as in the beginning of the passage, her shame having been continuous throughout her life.[25]

Widowhood in this passage, then, is not to be taken quite literally.[26] This is evident from the continuation of the passage, where we discover who Zion's husband is imagined to be (though we knew it already from the use of the metaphor elsewhere in Isaiah and throughout the Bible): "The Lord has called you back as a wife forlorn and forsaken" (Isa 54:6). If God is Zion's husband, then there can be no possibility of her being widowed in any literal sense, even in the world of the metaphor.[27] God, rather, has abandoned her, as she herself says in Isaiah 49:14: "The Lord has forsaken me, my Lord has forgotten me." Often, as in Hosea, the feminized Israel is rejected by her divine spouse because she has been unfaithful, worshipping other gods. It is somewhat of a surprise, then, to see no trace of that accusation here.[28]

Instead, we find that God takes all the blame on himself: "For a little while I forsook you. . . . In slight anger, for a moment, I hid my face from you" (Isa 54:7–8). But why would God do such a thing, if Zion did nothing to deserve it? We may find the answer in the social customs of ancient Israel: as we saw in the first chapter, an infertile wife was in constant jeopardy of being rejected by her husband, merely because she was unable to provide him with offspring.[29] Zion's barrenness, in this reading, is not the result of God's abandonment, but is rather the cause of it. The import of this imagery is enormous, for the emotion that Isaiah's God displays here is quite clearly regret, along with the promise never to repeat his behavior. This is commentary not only on the end of the exile, but also on the social practice underlying the metaphor. This sort of spousal abandonment may happen—but it is regrettable, and should be rectified. Part and parcel of the divine regret is the recognition—clear in its marked absence from the passage—that there is no guilt to be attributed to the barren wife.

And yet she is barren—what is to account for that? As we have seen, for Isaiah the notion of mere happenstance is unacceptable, especially with theological stakes this high. Here we recognize how the prophet creates a distinction between Zion and the Israelite people. By figuring Zion as mother and the inhabitants of Jerusalem as her offspring, they are read as separate entities. In such a circumstance, the question of where blame or guilt lies becomes complicated. The people of Jerusalem, the metaphorical offspring, are the ones who have gone into exile—they are the ones being punished, for their sins.[30] They have left their mother, Zion, behind to grieve her loss. It is her womb that has been emptied, but it is not because of what she did.[31] Those she carried within her have rebelled—against God, and perhaps also against her. She did no wrong; yet her body betrayed her. The prophet's message resounds throughout the ages.

REORIENTING THE MATRIARCHAL TRADITIONS

Isaiah redefines the notion of barrenness, takes up and complicates the question of sin and punishment, and in so doing opens the matriarchal traditions to a far broader base. He also reinvigorates the matriarchal stories by depicting his barren Mother Zion in a more fully realized way than the patriarchal narratives do for their female characters. There is, remarkably, more language of actual mothering here than in the matriarchal stories to which he alludes. Nowhere in Genesis do we hear of the matriarchs actually nursing their children—yet here is Zion, doing just that. Nowhere do the matriarchs physically hold their offspring—yet Mother Zion's children "shall be carried upon shoulders and dandled upon knees" (Isa 66:12). There is even a sense in which Zion is categorically different from her ancient models: though Rebekah struggles with the twins in her womb, and Rachel even dies in childbirth, Zion's labor is painless and instantaneous: "Before she labored she was delivered; before her pangs came, she bore a son. . . . Zion travailed and at once bore her children" (Isa 66:8).[32]

Here we see how Isaiah reorients the matriarchal traditions from their originally patriarchal context. By personifying Zion in their form, the prophet fleshes out their maternal experience in a way that Genesis never does. At the same time, Mother Zion takes on formerly patriarchal roles. She is the embodiment of the land, her inhabitants the long-ago promised progeny. It is now her offspring that constitute the fulfillment of God's blessing. The recollection of God's past promise to Abraham—"He was only one when I called him, but I blessed him and made him many" (Isa 51:2)—is to be fulfilled in the present via Zion: "Truly the Lord has comforted Zion" (Isa 51:3). It is the patriarchs who are said in Genesis to traverse the land, pitching their tents and establishing residency in Canaan—now it is to be Zion: "Enlarge the site of your tent, extend the size of your dwelling" (Isa 54:2).[33] In Genesis, it is Jacob to whom God says "you shall spread out to the west and the east, to the north and the south" (Gen 28:14)— now that same promise is addressed to barren Mother Zion: "You shall spread out to the right and the left" (Isa 54:3).[34] It is no coincidence that Isaiah also picks up on the blessing that is delivered not only to Abraham—"Your descendants shall seize the gates of their foes" (Gen 22:17)—but, notably, also to Rebekah, by her family: "May your offspring seize the gates of their foes" (Gen 24:60). Here that blessing is spoken to Zion: "Your offspring shall dispossess nations" (Isa 54:3). Rebekah is the only matriarch who is blessed this way, and notably it is by her kin, not by God; in

Isaiah, it is God who delivers this message, making it equivalent to those delivered to the patriarchs themselves.

Isaiah does not deny the patriarchs their role—rather, he corrects the imbalance inherent in the traditions of Genesis by giving the matriarchs their due credit. Jacob and his sons stand for Israel and its tribes in Genesis; in Isaiah, Zion is represented by Sarah, Rebekah, and Rachel. Zion is the barren matriarch, and the matriarchs are therefore Zion. The matriarchal narratives, the matriarchs themselves, are expanded to encompass more than just the barren, removed from their historical context, elevated to represent the entire nation of Israel.

Perhaps the most radical interpretive move that Isaiah undertakes is the temporal one. Essential to Isaiah's metaphor is the issue of at what point in the matriarchal narratives Israel is envisioned to now stand. In the previous chapter, we saw that the pentateuchal texts position Israel as standing before God at the mountain in the wilderness, faced with the choice of blessing or curse. From the perspective of Deutero-Isaiah, living at the end of the exile, that choice has already been made: the exile demonstrated that Israel had gone down the road of disobedience and curse. Zion was emptied of her inhabitants, her children carried off just as Deuteronomy had predicted. She was now barren and bereaved—Isaiah thus cleverly imagines Israel as embodying an even earlier point in her national history: not at Sinai, but back at the beginning, in the matriarchal period. And within that matriarchal narrative, Jerusalem is not in the throes of desperation, nor in the joy of childbearing, but at the edge between them. Her penetrating question—"Who bore these for me when I was bereaved and barren?" (Isa 49:21)—echoes the equally puzzled inquiry of Sarah: "Now that I am withered, am I to have enjoyment?" (Gen 18:12). Like Sarah when she doubted God's promise, Mother Zion is barren, but on the cusp of fertility. Isaiah himself represents the divine annunciation, the promise that Zion, though barren, will soon bear again.

Yet this promise remains firmly in the future, despite Isaiah's assurances that it will surely come to fruition. Like the possibility of a nation of perfect fertility held out by God in the wilderness, the fertility of Mother Zion in Isaiah has not yet arrived. Just as the blessings promised by God depict a world that is yet to come—a world without sickness, with divinely abundant agriculture, with Israelite dominance over all nations—so too Isaiah's prophecies are utopian: all the nations of the world will worship Yahweh (Isa 49:7), no harm will ever come to Israel (Isa 54:14), "the wolf and the lamb shall graze together" (Isa 65:25).[35] The prediction of Mother Zion's eventual fertility is part and parcel of this essentially eschatological picture.

What this means is that Mother Zion's infertility remains firmly rooted in the present. The matriarchs, living again as Israel's avatars, are returned to their barren state. We read and re-experience them not in the glory of their maternity, as the proud mothers of Israel, but rather in the anxious and uncertain period just before that. Isaiah reclaims the matriarchs as biblical stand-ins for childless women of all times. They are rendered perpetually barren in this world, their eventual fertility relegated to the world to come. The infertile woman of faith is permitted by the prophet to align herself fully not only with Israel's ancestral mothers, but with Mother Zion. She, like Sarah, Rebekah, and Leah, can be the embodiment of the nation, the symbolic representative of God's people in a time when the greatest crises may be behind us, but the perfected future is still yet to come.

Barren Mother Zion is exhorted by Isaiah to look joyously into the distance: "Shout, O barren one, you who bore no child; shout aloud for joy, you who did not travail" (Isa 54:1). Here the infertile mother is not only comforted, but celebrated. She may not bear offspring in this world, as the matriarchs of Genesis did. But in the world to come, her reward will be greater than those who shame her now: "Fear not, you shall not be shamed; do not cringe, you shall not be disgraced" (Isa 54:4). Isaiah subverts the social paradigm, transmutes the matriarchal narratives, and reconfigures infertility as a symbol of eschatological anticipation.

This reconfiguration affects not only the ancestral traditions of the matriarchs, which are now understood typologically, but also the experience of the infertile individual. Even if the dominant paradigm of sin and punishment for understanding barrenness is accepted—and though Isaiah may complicate it, it still stands at the center of his interpretation—it is no longer a cause for unending dismay. The pain of infertility is confined to this world; the social disgrace will be utterly forgotten in the world to come. The matriarchs are rehabilitated as models by fundamentally altering their story: the barren woman will experience the joy that Sarah, Rebekah, and Rachel all came to know, but not as they knew it. The matriarchs all pass quietly from the scene—not so the barren woman. The existence of the matriarchs effectively ended once they gave birth—the barren woman's maternal existence will be timeless, eternally gratifying. Isaiah uses the matriarchal narratives while going beyond them. Sarah claims that Yahweh has "restrained" (*'atsar*) her from bearing (Gen 16:2); Isaiah's God will never do so again: "Shall I who cause birth then restrain [*'atsar*]?" (Isa 66:9).[36] And yet the language used here still leaves that birth in the future: Zion is truly pushed to the very edge of fertility, but she remains ever poised on that edge.[37]

Isaiah, far more than Genesis, acutely recognizes the harsh reality of infertility: the unlikelihood, if not impossibility, of a miracle occurring in this lifetime. He makes no promises that cannot be kept, holds out no hope that will ultimately lead to even greater disappointment. By being set in the world to come, the future he envisions for the barren woman is ever available. His prophecies counsel acceptance, even of the shame that society inflicts, in the full security of a greater reward.

Deutero-Isaiah believed himself to be on the edge of time—like prophets before and since, he thought he was living in the period just before the world entered its final, permanent era. For him, the fertility of that period was to be realized in the return of the exiles, the metaphorical children returning to their barren and bereaved mother. By employing the metaphor of fertility to describe the eschaton, Isaiah opened the door for subsequent interpreters to consider anew how his prophecies would be fulfilled, not only for the nation, but for the individual. Isaiah created a chain of identity, from Zion to the matriarchs to the barren Israelite woman. Israel's exiles had returned; the matriarchs all bore offspring during their lives. The open question was that of the infertile individual: how would the barrenness of this world be addressed in the world to come? It is to these various renderings of (in)fertility in the eschaton that we now turn.

(IN)FERTILITY AND THE ESCHATON

The approaches to the question of what happens to barrenness in the eschaton are many and widely varied, and so we deal with them in two separate chapters. Here, we will look at those traditions that emerged primarily from readings of the Hebrew Bible: early postbiblical Jewish interpretations and rabbinic texts.[38] Even within this circumscribed corpus, there are distinctly different opinions expressed. Though it is impossible to provide comprehensive coverage, a selection of texts should demonstrate the point. The issues we are interested in examining through these various textual lenses, however, will remain constant: to wit, how do the writings of these later authors reimagine both the biblical material on which they are based, and what do their treatments suggest about the real-world phenomenon of infertility? Eschatological theories, though focused on the hereafter, serve as commentaries on the present: on the ideal state of humanity to which we aspire, and simultaneously on the distance between the reality we know and the perfected future we imagine.

Not surprisingly, there are postbiblical traditions that take up directly and make explicit Isaiah's implicit—though perfectly clear—association of Zion and the barren matriarchs. In a commentary on Psalm 113:9—"He sets the barren woman among her household as a happy mother of children"—the rabbis enumerated seven such women: "Sarah, Rebekah, Rachel, Leah, Manoah's wife, Hannah, and Zion." The two parts of the verse from Psalms are linked to two statements about each figure, one noting her barrenness, the other noting her eventual offspring. The rabbinic saying begins with Sarah, referring to Genesis 11:30 ("Sarai was barren") and Genesis 21:7: "Sarah would suckle children." It concludes with Zion: "The words 'He sets the barren woman among her household' apply to Zion: 'Shout, O barren one, that did not bear' (Isa 54:1); so do the words 'as a happy mother of children': 'You will say to yourself, "Who bore these for me?"'' (Isa 49:21)."[39] Not only are the parallels drawn here the same as those in Isaiah, but the structural distinction between the matriarchs and Zion is preserved: each of the matriarchal texts, naturally, refers to the successful achievement of fertility in the matriarch's lifetime; the reference to Zion stands out for being set in the future: "you will say to yourself."[40] As in Isaiah, Zion's fertility remains out of reach, though the types of the matriarchs endow it with a sense of certainty.

Similar is a rabbinic treatment of Isaiah 54:1 itself.[41]

R. Levi declared: Whenever Scripture says that something is not, it is implying that the converse will be. Thus Scripture says, "Sarai was barren, she had no child" (Gen 11:30);

afterwards she did have a child: "Sarah gave children suck" (Gen 21:7). Likewise, "Peninnah had children, but Hannah had not children" (1 Sam 1:2); afterwards Hannah did have children: "The Lord remembered Hannah and she conceived, and bore three sons and two daughters" (1 Sam 2:21). Finally, "She is Zion, there is none that careth for her" (Jer 30:17); but then one will come who does care: "And a redeemer will come to Zion." (Isa 59:20)[42]

The same phenomenon obtains here: the matriarchal reversal is in the past, but that of Zion is in the future.

MOVING BEYOND ISAIAH

Although these rabbinic statements look very much like pure distillations of Isaiah's message, there is an important difference that is perhaps not discernible to the naked eye. For Isaiah—as for most prophets, to this day—the remarkable events anticipated are understood to be imminent. Isaiah believed that the return of the exilic community would usher in the new and lasting era of Jerusalem's glory. Not so for the rabbis, living in the wake of the destruction of Jerusalem in 70 CE. Although there were some who searched for signs of the messiah's advent in their own times, the more common position—especially after the spectacular failure of the messianic Bar Kochba rebellion in 132–36 CE— was to link the arrival of the eschatological era with the complete repentance and obedience of the Jewish people.[43] In other words, the utopian vision of Israel's restoration was grounded not in historical events but in an equally utopian vision of complete adherence to rabbinic law.

At the same time, the nature of that eschatological restoration changed as well. Isaiah envisioned a perfected world of complete obedience to Yahweh, but it was still very much the same world. Over six centuries later, the rabbis could no longer imagine the continuation of the world that they knew, even in a perfected state. They envisioned, rather—as always, in a variety of forms—a radically new existence. It could be, in line with their apocalyptically minded predecessors, a world rising from the ashes of global destruction; it could be a world that is completely at peace; it could, of course, be a world located in the heavens—or a heaven descending upon the earth. It was not, in any case, the result of a mere change in political authority in Mesopotamia, as it was for Isaiah. There must be a decisive break with reality.

These two changes in the rabbinic concept of Israel's restoration—the loss of imminence and the untethering from reality—require a slightly different reading, therefore, of the metaphorical barren Mother Zion. She does not look ahead to a surprising revelation of her own fertility amid an otherwise recognizable world. Her fertility will come as part of a universal change of state, a complete overhaul of earthly existence. For the infertile woman who takes Mother Zion as a model, a similar message is implied. Eventual fertility is assured: but it will be part of a sweeping change of reality as a whole.

What does this eschatological vision imply about the infertility the rabbis, and we, see in this world? By continuing to use Isaiah's metaphor of barren Zion, the rabbis take earthly infertility as a synecdoche for the premessianic world. Universal infertility would mean the end of humanity; but the infertility of the individual serves as a symbol for everyone, as an indication that the world to come has not yet come. Barrenness, in this sense, is not only symbol but symptom: the archetypical side effect of the world's corrupted state.

INFERTILITY AND THE NEW JERUSALEM

The sharp distinction between this world and the next is typified in postbiblical thought by a concept that has strong ties to the Zion texts of Isaiah that we have been examining here: the notion of the New Jerusalem.[44] This notion is familiar to Christians from the book of Revelation and from Galatians, where Paul uses Hagar and Sarah—note the matriarchal references—as a basis for contrasting the "present Jerusalem" with "the Jerusalem above" (Gal 4:25–26). The apostle here takes up an idea found with some regularity in early noncanonical Jewish writings, as far back as the mid-second century BCE.[45] Most notable, as many have recognized, is the parallel with the first-century CE apocalyptic text known as *2 Baruch*. God admonishes Baruch for thinking that the devastated earthly Jerusalem is the same as that described in—note the citation—Isaiah 49:16: "On the palms of my hands I have carved you." No, says God: "It is not this building that is in your midst now; it is that which will be revealed, with me, that was already prepared from the moment that I decided to create Paradise" (*2 Bar.* 4:3).

The citation of Isaiah is not mere chance, nor is the reference to Eden, another feature of Isaiah's Jerusalem imagery. It was Isaiah, after all, who wrote, "I am about to create a new heaven and a new earth; the former things shall not be remembered, they shall never come to mind" (Isa 65:17). The concept of a truly new Jerusalem—as opposed to one that is merely restored to its former glory—seems to disentangle the threads of barrenness and bereavement that Isaiah twisted together so beautifully.[46] Bereavement, and unexpected return, requires continuity from past to present. Barrenness and subsequent fertility, however, represent the emergence of something new. Given the need to abandon the former on practical and historical grounds, the latter was elevated.

The image of the new Jerusalem reflects back on that of the infertile mother on which it is based. She will not merely become like those fertile women she sees around her. She will become something fully different: as Isaiah says, "the children of the wife forlorn shall outnumber those of the espoused" (Isa 54:1). The interpretive tradition promises a truly new beginning: not relief from pain—in which the pain has ceased but is never forgotten—but the complete eradication of the past, a return, as Isaiah suggests, to the Edenic innocence of harsh reality.

As the text from *2 Baruch* quoted above indicates, it was imagined that the heavenly Jerusalem not only differs from the earthly one, but that it has existed since Creation: "that was already prepared from the moment that I decided to create Paradise."[47] There exists, in heaven, the platonic ideal form of Jerusalem: not destroyed as the present one, but completely preserved; not barren, but fertile. By analogy, it may be argued that what is true of barren Mother Zion is true of those women who represent her. If infertility is a symbol of this depraved world, set between that which was created before the world and that which is to follow the passing of the world we know, then the fertile body attained at the eschaton is not merely new, it is also old. The body that seems to fail at its intended task is but a corruption of the body God intended. Just as Jerusalem will be not replenished but truly replaced in the world to come, so too the infertile womb will be replaced by one that exceeds any possible earthly comprehension. By this logic the barren woman—in contrast to the ancient understanding examined in chapter 1—was, like Mother Zion, created fertile, at least in heaven. We may not see that form before us, but it exists nonetheless, and it will be established for eternity when the time is right.

The mention of the New Jerusalem in *2 Baruch* continues with God's listing of the brief moments in which the heavenly city was revealed to humanity: to "Adam before he sinned," to "Abraham in the night between the portions of the victims" (i.e., Gen 15), to "Moses on Mount Sinai when I showed him the likeness of the tabernacle and all its vessels" (*2 Bar.* 4:3–5). These were but fleeting visions—the heavenly Jerusalem making a momentary visit to earth, but not to be confused with any earthly reality. Through this lens we may consider also the matriarchal narratives: could they also be but passing moments in which the eschatological future was experienced on earth? Not precisely, for the historical reality of the matriarchs was never in question in Jewish tradition, and their offspring were, of course, necessary for the existence of Israel. But once the basic distinction between infertility/Mother Zion/reality and fertility/New Jerusalem/eschaton is in place, and the parallels between Zion and the matriarchs made explicit, the meaning—if not the historical reality—of the matriarchal traditions is opened to new interpretations.

MOVING BEYOND THE MATRIARCHS

Even as the reality of the matriarchs was never in doubt, their utility for the interpreter changed over time. As we have already seen, the matriarchal traditions were, already in Isaiah, unmoored from their original context and used to promote a vision of a renewed future. In the rabbinic texts quoted above, we can see this process continuing and going even further. The matriarchs have really become types for Zion: the rabbis in these texts are focused on Zion, and on the certainty of her eventual restoration, while the matriarchs are used only as past parallels, as proof texts. The result of this interpretive treatment is that the matriarchal traditions are distanced from reality—not from the past, but from the present reality that the rabbis and their readers experienced. The matriarchs belong to a time unlike the one we know; the miracles they experienced, like the miracle of Zion's restoration that Isaiah prophesied, are the stuff of legend. In our time, as Isaiah hinted, the matriarchs are insufficient models. The realistic model is Zion, the one who remains barren, and will remain so in this world, but who looks ahead to a promised future.

The way in which the matriarchs were abandoned as models for the fertility of barren women in rabbinic interpretation is underscored by the way in which the eschatological healing of the infertile is depicted in one particular tradition. "You will find that the Holy One, blessed be he, anticipated in this world through the agency of the righteous everything that he will do in the hereafter." There follows from this introductory statement a series of prophetic acts associated with Elijah and Elisha that parallel God's acts to come in the eschaton: the resurrection of the dead, the stopping of the rains, the blessing of those who have little, and this: "God remembers barren women, and Elisha remembers barren women."[48] The divine remembrance of the infertile, by being explicitly introduced as what God "will do in the hereafter," cannot refer to the matriarchs, but rather is a reading of Isaiah 54:1, "Shout, O barren one." What is fascinating here is that the earthly parallel invoked is not that of Sarah, Rebekah, and Rachel, but rather of Elisha's encounter with the Shunammite woman in 2 Kings 4.

The presence of the prophetic interlocutor here is important, as a commentary on the way such miracles happen, and happened, in this world. With the matriarchs as models, the barren woman might well hope that God would directly intervene, even if silently, and make her fertile as he did those five women of the ancient past. Here we are told not only that the reversal of infertility is reserved for the world to come, but that its historical parallel is not the matriarchs but the prophetic act of Elisha; that is, those hoping for a taste of the next world in this one are bound to be frustrated. For it is a commonplace in rabbinic tradition that prophecy, at least in its biblical form, had long ago come to an end.[49] The divine spirit that empowered Elijah and Elisha had left Israel. The force of this rabbinic text is to clearly locate any future reversal of barrenness in the world to come, both in its explicit statement of God's eschatological acts, as well as in its conscious ignorance of the matriarchal traditions and their replacement with a now impossible prophetic miracle.

ESCHATOLOGICAL FERTILITY

As we saw in chapter 2, and in Isaiah as well, the rabbinic traditions are firm in the recognition that infertility is a real part of our world, and that the miracles of the matriarchs are consigned to a part of history that is utterly different and distant from our own times, if not in fact a sort of alternate reality in themselves. But as we can also see, the traditions hold out hope, even certainty, for the future, in the world to come, when God will "remember the barren woman." The question, therefore, is what form that divine remembrance will take.

The direct analogy to the matriarchal traditions would suggest the simplest answer: in the world to come, the infertile woman will be made fertile, and will bear as did Sarah.[50] Sarah's miraculous fertility is the model for that of all barren women. As a midrash puts it, imagining both mythic past and distant future: "All barren women everywhere in the world were remembered together with Sarah and were with child at the same time she was; and when she gave birth to a child, all of them gave birth to children at the same time she did." Indeed, Sarah's healing stands for eschatological healing of all types: "When Sarah bore her child, every blind man in the world was given sight; every cripple was made straight; every mute was given speech; and every madman healed of his madness."[51]

In this imagined future, the world to come is, essentially, the same as this one, a continuation of life as we know it but without the misfortunes with which we are all too familiar. It is very much like what the authors of the pentateuchal blessings had in mind: the elimination of all irregularities, from the climatic to the physical. In this view, infertility is taken as an unfortunate chance occurrence, due, perhaps, as argued in the first chapter, to divine inattention; it is this that will be corrected in the new era. Thus there is a rabbinic tradition that in the world to come there will be in the New Jerusalem a tree the leaves of which will cure barrenness.[52] No longer will Rachel have to bargain for her mandrakes: as in Eden, God will provide a new sort of tree of life. This vision is paradisiacal, but it is decidedly our world that is imagined—just with better and more universally accessible health care.

This minority view comes into conflict with the postbiblical belief that there will be a marked caesura between this world and the next. The world to come, in most traditions, will be utterly unlike anything we know. In light of the altered concept of infertility that emerges from Isaiah's prophecies—the linking of the barren woman with the New Jerusalem, and the concomitant recognition that the barrenness we see around us is the antithesis of what we can expect in the future—alternative possibilities for the future of the infertile woman were proposed.

One such alternative—admittedly a minority opinion—is that, in the world to come, "woman is destined to bear a child every day."[53] This is perhaps one of the clearest indications that the Talmud was written by men. What the statement may have in mind is the tradition that in the eschatological era childbirth will be painless, as Isaiah says of Zion: "before she labored, she was delivered; before her pangs came, she bore a son" (Isa 66:7). Regardless, the radical difference between the imagined future and our world could hardly be clearer here. What is physically impossible now will become the norm. What, according to conventional readings of the biblical text, women most want—offspring—will be given them in superabundance. This statement goes well beyond the pentateuchal blessings, which imagine only perfect regularity within the biological systems we are familiar with. Daily birth is like daily rain: it sounds good when there is none, but in practice it would be a bit complicated. An infinitely expansive world is imagined here, to accommodate births at such a rate. At the same time, there is some continuity with this world that must lie at the heart of this image: these children must grow up, and presumably have children of their own.[54] As different as a world with daily birth sounds, it remains rooted in the recognizable desires of the present: if offspring are a blessing, if they bring joy and support and the preservation of one's name, then the more the better. The mechanisms have changed, but the desire remains the same.

ESCHATOLOGICAL INFERTILITY

Quite different is the other, more common, alternative future for the barren woman. In the Talmud we find a clear expression of the radical difference between this world and the next. "The world to come is not like this world. In the world to come there is no eating, no drinking, no procreation, no business negotiations, no jealousy, no hatred, and no competition."[55] Here we have a depiction of a future in which the very foundations of human existence—eating, drinking, and procreation—are entirely absent. In this vision the barren will not become fertile, but in fact the reverse: the fertile will become barren. More accurately, perhaps, the category of barrenness will be eliminated altogether, for there can be no infertility without the desire for children. The very desires that, in our world, can be the cause of so much pain, will cease to exist in the world to come.

And yet the barren woman is promised divine remembrance—what form will that take, if not offspring? The Talmud continues: "The righteous sit with their crowns upon their heads, enjoying the splendor of the Divine Presence." The company of God is elevated over even the birth of a child as the ultimate human goal, to be fulfilled in the world to come. We can hear in this the echoes of Isaiah, who envisioned God as bringing abandoned Zion back into the divine household. And again we can see the sequestering of the matriarchal as formally distinct from those of Mother Zion, even as they serve as typological forebears.

We see this at work in a later rabbinic text, one that enumerates the classic seven barren women, from Sarah to Zion, and describes the reward given to each as being akin, through homiletical interpretation, to one of the seven days of creation. For each woman, it is her son that represents her reward—until we reach the seventh day and the seventh woman, Zion. Here, instead of adducing a verse that speaks of her offspring—of which there are enough from Isaiah to choose from—the text cites a verse that speaks of God's presence: " 'This is my resting place forever' (Ps 132:14); therefore Isaiah said 'Shout, O barren one who did not bear' (Isa 54:1)."[56] God's in-dwelling in Zion is the structural parallel to the matriarchs' sons, picking up the tradition that, in the world to come, it is the divine presence that will be the reward for the barren mother.

It is hard not to read in these texts an allusion to the relationship between Mother Zion and Eden. As we saw already, there was in Isaiah some tension in this comparison: Zion's fertility does not map precisely onto the childless state of Adam and Eve in the primordial orchard. Here, however, that tension is alleviated. The world to come is imagined as truly Edenic, as a place where, prior to God's curse on Eve, there was no fertility, but neither was their infertility—there was simply no thought of or desire for children. The barren woman will, in the world to come, return to Eve's original state of perfect contentedness, even without a child.

In the vision of a future without procreation, a real shift has occurred in the relative evaluation of fertility and infertility. No longer is the eventual fertility of the matriarchs the appropriate model for the eschatological era, with their barrenness, as in Isaiah, serving as the prototype of this imperfect world. Quite the opposite: the "barren one who does not bear" is now the type for the world to come. She no longer need seek to become something other: it is the rest of humanity that longs to become like her.

On the basis of this vision there is a wonderful midrash about Hannah and her prayer for a child. In this midrash, Hannah says the following to God:

> Master of the universe, there is a host above, and there is a host below. The host above do not eat, nor drink, nor procreate, nor die, but they live forever; and the host below eat, drink, procreate, and die. Now I do not know of what host I am, whether I am of the one above or the one below. If I am of the host above, I should not be eating, nor drinking, nor possibly bearing children, nor dying, for I should live forever, just as the host above live forever. But if I am of the host below, then not only should I be eating and drinking, but I should be bearing children and eventually dying, even as the host below eat, and drink, and procreate, and die.[57]

Hannah articulates perfectly the difference between this world and the next, between reality and aspiration. She brings a challenge before God: if these two planes are truly separate, then let them be consistent in their distinctions. Ironically, the lack of procreation in the world to come is used as an argument for complete fertility in this world. At the same time, however, Hannah expresses precisely the alignment of infertility and eschaton that we have been examining here. It is not in her desired fertility that she sees the future world; in fact, her desire for offspring tethers her unquestionably to the earthly realm. It is her barrenness that renders her potentially already part of the heavenly host, already a resident of that perfected world of the future. It is in her lack of children that she represents the world to come.

In every iteration of this eschatological vision, it is clear that the ancient association of infertility and sin has been effaced.

Those who cannot bear are not being punished; they are, rather, glimpses of humanity's eventual state. The early postbiblical text Wisdom of Solomon cleanly severs infertility and sin: "Blessed is the barren woman who is undefiled, who has not entered into a sinful union; she will have fruit when God examines souls" (Wisd. of Sol. 3.13). It is not that a barren woman cannot sin—indeed she can, and she would bear the same punishment as anyone else who disobeys God. But her barrenness is not equated with her sin: if she is pure, she will receive her just rewards in spite of her barrenness. Infertility plays no part in the divine judgment. There are echoes here of the tradition common to both Judaism and Christianity that it is better to be bodily impaired than to be spiritually deficient.[58] The negative social evaluation of the impairment, as something undesired, is maintained, but it is rendered theologically neutral.

The Wisdom of Solomon makes a parallel claim about eunuchs: "Blessed is the eunuch whose hands have done no lawless deed, and who has not devised wicked things against the Lord; for special favor will be shown him for his faithfulness and a place of great delight in the temple of the Lord" (Wisd. of Sol. 3:14). Here the author alludes to Isaiah, who also held out hope to the faithful eunuch: "As for the eunuchs who keep my sabbaths, who have chosen what I desire and hold fast to my covenant, I will give them, in my house and within my walls, a monument and a name better than sons or daughters; I will give them an everlasting name which shall not perish" (Isa 56:4–5). In both texts, the eunuch, who cannot bear children, is promised a heavenly reward, and in both texts that reward is a place beside God and the eternal fame of a virtuous life. It is only in the Wisdom of Solomon, however, that we find this promise directly alongside the blessing of the virtuous barren woman. This text draws an analogy for us: the reward of the eunuch is the blessing not of offspring but of divine memory; this, too, is the "fruit" that the barren woman will receive "when God examines souls." The play on "fruit" here—so often a term for offspring, but here a notice of their absence—consciously undoes the common alignment of divine blessing and progeny. As the text goes on to say, "Better than [sinful fertility] is childlessness with virtue, for in the memory of virtue is immortality" (Wisd. of Sol. 4.1). Those who suffer a life of infertility can still strive for a virtuous life, with the heavenly rewards that accrue as a result. That reward is the very "name" that, in the earlier biblical traditions, was tied so closely to having children. No longer is it dependent on the physical production of offspring; now it is a divine reward for a life—barren or not—well lived.

One step beyond even this is the first-century CE allegorical interpretation of Philo. If, for the author of the Wisdom of Solomon, barrenness is compatible with virtue, for Philo it is practically identical.[59] Philo identifies Isaac with pure happiness, and says that Sarah, his mother, could have given birth to such joy only from a state of barrenness. She is, in her barren state, the embodiment of human virtue: "For indeed virtue is barren as regards all that is bad, but shows herself a fruitful mother of the good."[60] Philo draws a remarkable parallel between barrenness and virginity, which, in light of the Greek philosophical tradition he wrote from, was seen as the highest state of purity: "they have spurned the pleasures of the body and desire no mortal offspring but those immortal children which only the soul that is dear to God can bring to the birth unaided because the Father has sown in her spiritual rays enabling her to behold the verities of wisdom."[61] Akin to this virginal purity is infertility: "when [a woman, here discussing Zion in Isa 54:1] has become barren . . . she is transformed into a pure virgin."[62] Whereas Isaiah elided the categories of barren and bereaved, accepting that both are tragic misfortunes, Philo elides the categories of barrenness and virginity, treating both as wonderful virtues. The infertile woman may not be so by choice, but intention is subordinated to function: she, like those who refrain from procreation, achieves "a state of availability and receptivity which results in spiritual fruit."[63] That fruit is not human offspring, but, as the Wisdom of Solomon and the Talmud agree, the reward of virtue, of the divine presence.

Sin and punishment have been replaced by their polar opposites, virtue and reward. The barren woman embodies these ideals, and stands as a model of the eschatological future—even as she desires, in this world, to be fertile.

CONCLUSION

The Isaianic and postbiblical Jewish traditions provide a lens through which the matriarchal traditions, and infertility as a whole, can be reassessed. Their value lies not only in the various conclusions that they reach, but in the very fact of their interpretive approach in the first place. The texts of the Hebrew Bible are not single-minded in their presentation of infertility; even those that might have had a particular meaning at one point in history bear within them quite different meanings for later readers. Neither Isaiah nor the rabbis—nor we—are beholden to the dominant understanding of the Bible; there are, embedded within these ancient texts and the cultures from which they emerged, other possibilities.

Once we have attuned ourselves to hear these quieter voices in the text, those that have been drowned out by tradition or convention, we can ask what lessons they have to impart. From Isaiah to Philo to the rabbis, from the matriarchs to Mother Zion, the infertile woman is taken up as a potent symbol for the advent of the eschatological era. In some texts barrenness is accepted as a misfortune, while in others it is practically glorified; in all of them, it is a blameless condition, and one that is directly connected with hopes for, and certainty of, a transformed future. In this light infertility is distanced from any negative characterization; even if one might not desire to be infertile, there is some dignity in representing Mother Zion, God's beloved spouse, or for anticipating in this world the rewards of the next. If we think back to the standard presentations of barrenness that we saw in the first chapter, we can appreciate just how far the interpretive tradition, biblical and postbiblical, has moved the discussion. Infertility was a state of utter shame, from which the matriarchs were desperate to escape. From Isaiah through the later traditions we have examined here, infertility became not only an accepted aspect of reality, but one that embodies the world to come, either by radical transformation or, more radically, by the very essence of being barren.

Central to all of the traditions discussed in this chapter is the distance, be it small or great, between the present and the future, between this world and the world to come. In every transformation of infertility, and even in those texts that see childlessness as a feature of the eschatological age, there is the persistent recognition that barrenness is a very real feature of human existence. Indeed, were it not so, it could hardly serve the symbolic function that is routinely attached to it. Unlike the matriarchal stories on which they are based, and even more unlike the disparate ancient Near Eastern prayers and incantations, there is no sense in these traditions that infertility is avoidable or treatable in this world. Rather, they provide a variety of possible avenues for coming to terms with the inescapable fact of infertility.

When viewed globally, there is in that very variety an admission—even as each tradition promises a certain outcome—of deep uncertainty. The world to come has not been revealed to us; we are left to guess as to its specific contours. Those guesses, in their many differences, reflect the many different ideals of the interpreters who produce them. Thus paralleling the known in this world—the given of infertility—is the unknown of the world to come. In the first chapter, we observed that at the heart of every ancient conception of infertility was a fundamental lack of knowledge, a gap that was filled with various theories of divine involvement, or lack thereof, in the process of childbirth. That lack of knowledge has not disappeared, but has instead been re-configured. No more is understood about infertility in this world than previously, but the interpretive traditions have come to terms with it; there is no longer a struggle to diagnose its origins. Now the gap in our understanding has been pushed forward, from the unknown into the truly unknowable.

And yet every one of these traditions is, individually, certain of two things: that the barren woman is blameless, and that she will be particularly blessed in the world to come. The effect of these traditions in the social realm is important. For an audi-ence still accustomed to the dominant view of infertility as an unadulterated negative, as a condition deserving of shame, Isa-iah's call for the barren women to shout with joy could not but call for momentary pause. The later traditions that valorize the barren woman would require even more radical readjustment of previously-held beliefs and assumptions. From Isaiah onward, the barren woman is treated not as one to be shamed, but one to be honored—for her relationship with Mother Zion, for her position with regard to the world to come, and, overall, for her bearing in her body, on our behalf, the symbolic corruption of our common earthly existence.

CHAPTER 4

The Son of God and the Conception of the New Age

Sometime toward the end of the third decade of what is now called the Common Era, a relatively young man began to prophesy. His message was striking and sharp, reminiscent of the condemnation-tinged exhortations so characteristic of the biblical prophets of old. John the Baptizer, as the author of Mark calls him, is introduced only as a powerful voice. He is the fulfillment of Isaiah's prophecies of desert wanderers. His message? That people should repent and return. His version of baptism was an interior epiphany marked by confession and ritual cleansing; John evangelized a "baptism of repentance for the forgiveness of sins." But there was more. According to Mark, he proclaimed the coming of another, "more powerful" than he, one so great that he was unworthy even "to stoop down and untie the thong of his sandals" (Mark 1:7).

Many, perhaps thousands, went to hear John preach. They were swept up in the excitement, and lowered down into the waters of the River Jordan. Among them was Joshua (Jesus) of Nazareth. Jesus, like many disaffected young men of his time, was drawn to the charismatic figure of John the Baptizer. He went out to the river as part of the inquisitive throng and was baptized there like so many others. His arrival was unremarkable but, as he came out of the water, he saw the heavens "torn open" and the "Spirit descending like a dove on him. A voice came from heaven, 'You are my Son, the Beloved, with you I am well pleased' " (Mark 1:10–11).

This is the opening of the Gospel of Mark. What did it mean to Mark and his audience to start here? In keeping with the genres of biblical historiography and Hellenistic biography, Matthew and Luke start with the cradle. The virgin birth is the dominant model for thinking about Jesus's birth, yet Mark begins here, unassumingly positioned on the banks of the River Jordan. The event that sparked the missionary activity that changed the world was a ritual experienced by hundreds. There is no infancy story here, no description of education, of familial comforts or deprivation, of socialization, or of influence; there is only the voice that beckons Jesus to the river and the voice that acclaims him at his baptism. While Mark never discusses infertility, his portrait of the Holy Family is of interest to us precisely because it is not predicated on biology. As we tease out the significance of the baptism and Jesus's divine sonship, we shall see a model of parenting accessible to everyone and, crucially, divorced from individual procreation and procreative abilities. This has ramifications for our conversation about infertility because, as we have already seen, any vision of the family untethered from biology reconfigures parenthood in such a way that it can include those without biological offspring.

In explaining the structural curiosities in Mark, New Testament scholars have argued that the compact form of Jesus's life before his final week on earth is due to the tradition history of the account. Prior to the composition of Mark, Jesus traditions had begun with accounts of the passion. From there the Jesus story had mushroomed, gathering to itself stories of healing, parabolic sayings, and instructional set pieces. The bare-bones story of the crucifixion was fleshed out with the history of a man who ate with sinners, healed the sick, battled demons, and tra-versed ancient Palestine with a cohort of eager but foolish dis-ciples. This historical explanation of the form of Mark's Gospel makes a great deal of sense, but it cannot account for the abrupt-ness of Mark's opening: the sudden and staccato appearance of John the Baptist, the voice in the wilderness, and a story that be-gan not with birth, but with baptism. Why did our author begin here, thirty years after Jesus entered the world? What about the baptism communicated the mystery of Jesus's identity and mission?

Traditional scholarly interpretations have, correctly, lighted upon the allusions to the Hebrew Bible in the scene.[1] The refer-ence to a beloved son harkens back to Isaac, Abraham's miracle child, who is called the beloved son in Genesis 22.[2] It might sug-gest to the reader that Jesus will tread in the sacrificial footsteps of Isaac. The potential allusion to Psalm 2:7 ("you are my son"), one of the royal Davidic psalms, adds monarchic undertones, and the proposed gesture to Isaiah 42:1 ("with you I am well pleased") and the descent of the spirit in the form of the dove might sug-gest that Jesus is possessed by the Spirit of God or endowed with special abilities.[3]

Given that the phrase "son of God" in Mark 1:1 is almost cer-tainly a secondary addition to the text by a later scribe, this is the first place in the Gospel at which Jesus can be said to be called God's son.[4] And what of the dove that descends on the head of Jesus? Is the bird signifying a potent and real change in Jesus, or is it a crescendoing metaphor? What kind of sonship does Mark describe?

As with most biblical texts, this evocative scene is the sub-ject of scholarly debate and disagreement. The narrative context might suggest that Mark sees Isaiah 61:1–2 as providing the pro-phetic context for the baptism scene: "The Spirit of the Lord is upon me, because he has anointed me; he has sent me to preach glad tidings to the poor, to heal the broken in heart, to proclaim

liberty to the captives, and recovery of sight to the blind; to declare the acceptable year of the Lord, and the day of recompense;
to comfort all that mourn."[5] Certainly Isaiah's prophecy can be
seen as receiving fulfillment in the descent of the Spirit on Jesus
and in Jesus's healing ministry. If Mark is alluding to Isaiah then
we might interpret Jesus as a kind of prophetic messiah. The evidence does not end here, however. To this biblical allusion we
can add the significance of descending birds in Greek mythology.
Noting the lack of Jewish parallels for the Holy Spirit taking the
form of the dove, Edward Dixon suggests that the baptism should
be understood in the context of Greek deities descending to the
earthly realm in the form of birds. He argues that as the dove
enters into (*eis auton*) Jesus, audiences familiar with these stories
would have understood that the baptism made Jesus divine.[6]

The focal point of the scene, when it comes to Jesus's identity,
is the heavenly voice that proclaims Jesus's beloved sonship.[7] As
already noted, the proclamation is widely recognized as drawing upon the monarchic poetry of Psalm 2 and Isaiah's language
of suffering in servitude. The pulling together of language and
imagery of service, suffering, and reign suggests a nuanced portrait of Mark's messiah as part suffering prophet and part royal
monarch. It's a paradox that will preoccupy much of the evangelist's work. But whether Mark's Jesus should be more properly
described as king, prophet, messiah, or all three, the language of
sonship is not exhausted by any of these descriptions.

Interpreting the language of kinship in Mark, and the phrase
"You are my son" in particular, is complicated by the variety
of uses to which kinship was put in the ancient world. Honorific
language of divine sonship was accorded to Israelite monarchs,
the expected messiah, priests, Roman emperors, and God's chosen people.[8] It was not just the case that kinship in general was
fluid and "fictive"; it was the case that the language of sonship,
in particular, was often used to describe nonbiological relationships. Yet as tempting as it may be to divorce the "metaphorical"

application of sonship titles to kings and elites from the biological relationship between "natural" parent and child, this delineation is undercut by familial relationships and by fictive kinship in general. The unofficial and official adoption and incorporation of genetically unrelated individuals into the family meant that the distinction between biological and nonbiological was not so rigidly drawn. Even if Mark *had* intended his readers to think of the election of kings or a messiah, the application of sonship language carried with it overtures of more mundane parenting. Calling a monarch the son of a deity drew upon and was a part of the program of fictive kinship that underwrote familial patterns in the ancient world. In this respect, divine kingship and divine kinship were remarkably similar.

The interpretation of the baptismal scene in Mark is loaded with theological weight, as it appears to define and describe the identity and divine sonship of Jesus. While many potential solutions to the baptismal identity problem have been proposed, it seems impossible that language of sonship excludes a larger social matrix in which families were made and not begotten. It is to this matrix—the role of self-conscious and publicized adoption in the ancient world—that we now turn. What we will see as we consider ideologies of adoption in the ancient world is that adoption was not automatically and intrinsically inferior to biological parenting. The issue was complicated, but the robust ideology of adoption in the Greco-Roman world in general generated a robust theology of adoption among the writers of the New Testament.

THE IDEOLOGY OF ADOPTION IN THE ROMAN WORLD

For whatever reason, the Romans, and Roman aristocrats in particular, did not favor large families, despite the high rates of infant mortality, which might in theory encourage extra procreation in compensation. As a result, prominent Roman families were often left without heirs. On the level of individual families, the solution to this predicament was adoption. Adoption in the Roman world was not about child welfare or about constructing a charitable foster system. While the rescuing of abandoned infants was romanticized in Greek mythology, Roman adoption was concerned with the transference of property, wealth, and status. It ensured the continuation of the familial line.[9]

Like natural sons, and in distinction to children born out of wedlock, adopted sons were legal heirs. Their position was bolstered and established by law. We should note that biology alone was not enough to establish a legal claim. Octavian, later to become Caesar Augustus, was Julius Caesar's adopted son and legal heir despite the fact that Caesar had fathered an illegitimate child with Cleopatra. Illegitimate children had no rights to financial support or inheritance, but adopted sons did. In Roman thinking, legal rights outmatched genetic code.

Fundamentally, adoption was about stability and continuity, especially in the upper echelons of Roman society. Nowhere is this more clearly seen than in imperial practices of adoption. In imperial succession, adoption played a particularly important role in legitimizing dynastic succession and the transmission of imperial rights and powers.[10] In fact, adoption encapsulated the longing for stability and continuity; in the words of Clifford Ando, "[For the Romans] the desire at all levels of the population to see stability in the history of the empire was expressed first and foremost by the fiction of dynastic continuity on the throne."[11]

While the Senate was important in assigning priesthoods and public offices, and the army was often the source of authority or *auctoritas* for those who would be emperor, the status of the successor to a deceased emperor was secured and "consolidated through heredity, either natural or adoptive."[12] In other words, adoption was one of the primary sources of authority for the transmission of imperial power.

To a modern reader, adoptive metaphors can seem somehow concessionary: a flimsy patch for a practical problem. Whatever opinions are openly professed in modern society, the common insistence on distinguishing "adopted children" from "[biological] children" in descriptions of families reinforces the idea that biological parenting is natural, default, and somehow preferable. The same cannot be said of the situation in the ancient world, in which some authors theorized that adoption guaranteed a better caliber of offspring. According to Cassius Dio in his *Roman History*, Hadrian's adoption offers a meritocratic ideal: "Now there is a distinction between natural and adopted sons: for a begotten son becomes whatever kind of person seems appropriate to the heavenly powers, but a man takes an adopted son to himself through a deliberate selection. The result is that, through natural processes, a man is often given a deformed and incompetent son, but through a process of judgment, one of sound body and mind is certain to be chosen."[13] This view of adoption was by no means shared by all, but it would be a mistake to see it as an exclusively positive take on an intrinsically negative situation.[14] Simultaneously, however, adoption contained its own power. Adopted sons commanded the same legal rights as legitimately born biological heirs, but they had a decided advantage in being selected for their charisma and character.[15] We should take seriously the claims of Cassius Dio and others and recognize that, for some, adoption was idealized as a mode of succession. It always depended upon and utilized the language of dynasty and biological reproduction, but it was nonetheless treated as something positive in its own right.

Despite Cassius Dio's rosy picture of adoption, there was still some tension between "natural" and "made" offspring. Adoption as it was understood and articulated in the Roman world utilized

the same concepts of dynastic succession and ancestral genealogies embedded in "natural" kinship. Adopted sons were cast as
part of natural genealogies and ancestral traditions. To use the
language of Clifford Ando and Michael Peppard, the "grammar"
of succession was fundamentally the same for those sons "made"
through adoption and for those who were "begotten" through
biology. To an extent, therefore, the ideology of adoption reinforced the ideology of natural procreation.

Adoption was linked to *pietas* or piety, a term that connoted
not merely religious piety but something more akin to rever-
ence.[16] As *pietas* was displayed toward all those in superior positions of authority—fathers and gods alike—it carried with it res-
onances of obedience and respect. The adopted son was the good
child. Or, to put it another way, the beloved son.

For a ritual about status, the process itself was relatively de-
void of pomp and circumstance.[17] And adoption in the ancient
world was not limited to the imperial family. It was a relatively
standard means by which heirs were designated and thus was
common among property-owning classes and as a feature of estate planning. Exceptional examples of adoption clarify this. For
instance, a famous Egyptian papyrus composed during the reign
of Rameses XI (1107–1078 BCE) records the will of a certain Nebnefer who, having no other children, adopted his wife Rennefer
in order to ensure that she gained control of his estate at his
death.[18] He was apparently concerned that, had he not done so,
his grabby siblings would attempt to challenge his wishes. In her
own will his wife adopted the three children of a female slave in
their household. An ancient Egyptian reader might have assumed
that Nebnefer was their father,[19] and perhaps also that the slave
woman was brought into the household as a surrogate.[20] In any
case, to avoid the legal problems, the woman first freed the children, then adopted them, and subsequently married the eldest
daughter to one of her brothers, Padiu. Rennefer also adopted

Padiu, so that he became both her son (and legal heir) and her son-in-law. This unconventional arrangement demonstrates both the expediency of adoption and its malleability.

An important facet of adoption, stated in the papyrus, is that the three children had always treated Nebnefer's wife well: "They have not done evil against me, rather they have acted well towards me." There is, as in Greco-Roman law, an element of character assessment and moral evaluation that contributes to the selection of heirs and their formal adoption. Adopted children are in some sense proven quantities.

Knowledge of imperial adoptions was disseminated via architecture, sculptures, official texts, religious festivals, and other public events. Coins, in particular, were issued in order to naturalize adopted sons, acknowledge marriage, and establish the deification process. Public games were arranged to celebrate and announce imperial adoptions.[21] Jewish contemporaries of Mark and the Apostles, such as Philo and Josephus, make clear their familiarity with the structures and significance of imperial adoption. It is easy, therefore, to imagine that Mark and Mark's audience would have been familiar not only with the process of adoption in general, but also with the significance of imperial adoption in particular.

READING THE MARKAN JESUS AS DIVINELY ADOPTED SON

For our reading of the baptism scene in the Gospel of Mark, this means that we should resist the temptation to see adoptionism as negative and lowly. Traditional treatments of Markan Christology have seen Mark as a misplaced half step on the path to Nicea. Mark does not really think Jesus is God, he just thinks he's a very special guy selected out of the masses to serve as God's figurative child. The real question here, though, is this: does Mark think that Jesus is God's son? In some ways the answer is obvious: yes, of course he does. Mark clearly states as much on no fewer than three occasions: by divine voices at the baptism and transfiguration and by the Roman centurion at the cross.

The relationship between Mark's claims about the divine sonship of Jesus and the broader, better-known claims of the Emperor Augustus (who was known as "Lord") are open to interpretation. Mark can be read as reinscribing and yet augmenting the dominant cultural ideology of Roman imperial sonship.[22] By supplying a dove in the place of an eagle, Mark disavows the militaristic connotations of imperial power. In this reading, Jesus is the antiemperor who conquers with peace. Perhaps, however, Mark is less subversive and adapts imperial power in a way that serves merely to make divine sonship a common cultural reference for his audience. It is difficult to pin down the motivations of the author.

What is *not* being subverted in Mark, however, is the process of adoption itself. For Mark, and for Mark's audience, adoption was real parenthood. It was the model (in Mark at least) for Jesus's relationship with God. And it became, among later Christian authors like Paul, the model for humanity's relationship with God. Adoption is not concessionary here, it is divine.

THE INFANCY NARRATIVES

When it comes to the holiness of the traditional family, many Christians return to the image in the stable: an image of the Son of God born to a virgin in a lowly manger. It is familiar, reassuring, and inspiring. And the iconographic force of the Madonna and the infant has left an undeniable and lasting imprint on our world as the exemplar of motherly love. In scholarship and even in public debates in chat rooms and airport lounges the virginity of Mary is a subject of debate. But this conversation neglects another interesting aspect of the birth of Jesus. Looking at the birth of Jesus in its ancient context we will see that the Holy Family is one that is engineered through spiritual intervention and outside of the parameters of "normal" procreation. This is, of course, because Jesus's birth is miraculous; but it is miraculous in ways that are familiar and replicable in our own time.

If Mark sets the sonship of Jesus in an imperial key, Matthew and Luke follow what is, in many ways, the more familiar ancient script. Jesus is born of a human female after being overcome by a divine power. Stories of lascivious deities seducing or raping beautiful women were common in antiquity. Zeus famously transformed himself into a swan in order to ravish the beautiful Leda. She was not his only conquest, and the products of his unions—Perseus, Heracles, and Helen of Troy, to name but a few—are exclamations that punctuate Greek mythology. Ancient Greeks and Romans were well aware of stories of deities procreating with humans.

Ancient Jews also heard tales of celestial unions. The casual reader of Genesis 6 might miss the reference to the sons of gods (*b'ne elohim*) taking human women as their wives and producing exceedingly tall and heroic offspring (*nephilim*), but it is there. And in the Second Temple period speculation about the afterlife exploded with developed theories about the fate of these angelic beings who had transgressed the divine order, shared sacred and special knowledge with the humans, and were ultimately punished for their disobedience. These rebellious angels—the forerunners of the Christian theology of Lucifer, the fallen angel—were abominable. While Greeks and Romans loved to claim that they were descended from gods, there is no evidence that Jews did the same. So far as we know, Jews did not make boastful claims to nephilistic ancestry.[23]

Out of this murky world of transgressive human and divine comingling emerged the Matthean and Lukan infancy narratives.

Even the most reluctant nativity play attendee knows the story: Mary is visited by angels, conceives, travels with chaste husband Joseph to Bethlehem, and there gives birth to a child. There are numerous differences between the versions of the story told by Matthew and Luke. Matthew's genealogy begins with Abraham, has Jesus visited by Magi, and consistently focuses on Jesus's kingship and the parallels between the birth of Moses and the birth of Jesus. Luke favors shepherds, angels, and adds a more complicated familial backstory. What both authors agree on, however, is that Jesus was not conceived through sexual intercourse. Matthew and Luke both assume the existence of a virgin birth, even though it is nowhere referred to in the rest of the Gospels or elsewhere in the New Testament.[24]

According to both Matthew and Luke, Mary was betrothed to Joseph when she conceived Jesus. As a social status, betrothal was one that under ordinary conditions would have granted Joseph sexual privileges. That being the case, both evangelists are clear that Joseph and Mary had not had sexual relations. In Matthew, Joseph's angry response and resolution to have her "quietly put away" is evidence that he is convinced that the child is not his. Luke's version is slightly more straightforward. Even before we meet Mary she is twice described in Luke 1:27 as a *parthenos*, or "virgin." When the angel visits her to announce her impending pregnancy, she inquires how it is possible that she could conceive a child given that she does not "know" a man (Luke 1:34).

In biblical scholarship, the historicity of Mary's virginity is something of an interpretive crux. In the past century a great deal of exegetical angst has surrounded the citation of Isaiah provided by Matthew and assumed by Luke. As Matthew 1:22–23 has it, "All this took place to fulfill what had been spoken by the Lord through the prophet: 'Look, the virgin shall conceive and bear a son, and they shall name him Emmanuel,' which means, 'God is with us.'" The citation is from the Septuagint of Isaiah 7:14 and is problematic because of the different valences that the Greek and Hebrew terms used to denote the woman in the prophecy. The Greek *parthenos*, or virgin, is a translation of *'almah*, or maiden. The Septuagintal version gives a specificity to the sexual status of the young woman that is not found in the original Hebrew. The author of Isaiah never envisioned a virgin birth, and there has been no shortage of gleeful commentators eager to point out the origins of the mistranslation.

For our purposes the question is moot. The translational "error" (if it can, in fact, be called an error, rather than just a warning about the perils of dealing with texts in translation) calls into question the nature of prophecy and the extent to which the Bible is screened from such errors by some unseen divine hand. The message that Matthew wishes to convey is fundamentally the same—that Mary had not had sex when she conceived and that the prophets had foretold the birth of Jesus. If the Septuagint had not rendered *'almah* as "virgin," might the evangelists have selected another motif or theme for their introduction? Possibly; but we never will know, and there is no way to interpret texts that were never written. The important point for our purposes is that Matthew and Luke believe it. The birth of the Son of God took place outside the parameters of ordinary human reproduction.

THE HOLY FAMILY IN MATTHEW

In Matthew, the focus is fixed on Joseph. Matthew begins his Gospel with a genealogy that traces the ancestry of Jesus back, through Joseph, to David and Abraham, the father of the Jewish people. The beginning of Jesus's story, therefore, is in a genealogy grounded in a nonbiological (human) parent. A criticism raised by savvy students of the Gospel of Matthew is how Matthew can "have it both ways."[25] How is it that the evangelist can be so clear that Jesus is not the biological offspring of Joseph and yet begin his account with a genealogy that assumes that Jesus *was* Joseph's child? This quibble over the lineage is, for our purposes, precisely the point. The claim that Jesus is both Son of God *and* Son of David rests on untidy claims about dual patrilineage, and both claims play an essential role in establishing the way that Jesus is both messiah and God. We cannot set aside the importance of the relationship with Joseph, because it is only through Joseph (Matt 1:16, 20) that Jesus can claim to be "Son of David."[26]

Joseph's role is maximized throughout the Matthean infancy narrative. It is to Joseph that divine revelations are given. Joseph is alerted to the divine origins of the child in a dream and is instructed to relocate the family, first to Egypt to avoid Herod's slaughter of the Innocents, and finally to Nazareth. While we might assume, on the basis of the Gospel of Luke, that Mary had received her own divine revelations, especially upon realizing that she was pregnant, Matthew does not mention this. Instead he preserves the same structure found in the story of Abraham and Sarah, in which the male head of the household communicates with divine intermediaries and notifies his wife of the divine plan. Matthew's focus on Joseph indicates that while Joseph is very much not the biological father, he is not the emasculated cuckold either.

In reconciling divine and human parentage, the majority of commentators have assumed that Jesus was Joseph's son by adoption or—to use quasi-modern terminology—his stepson.[27] By marrying Mary, Joseph adopted Jesus and raised him as his own (Matt 1:24–25). It was, after all, Joseph who circumcised Jesus and presented him in the Temple (Luke 2:21–24) and taught him a vocation (Matt 13:55). The majority of scholars have made recourse to Jewish parallels in order to render this arrangement intelligible.[28] Yigal Levin has argued that the appropriate context within which to evaluate Joseph's paternal role is the Roman practice of adoption, outlined above.

Certainly the complexity and flexibility of Roman adoption fits with the unusual constitution of the Holy Family. In the ancient world the complexity of familial relations and exceptional families was openly acknowledged and handled with some sophistication. In portraiture and coinage we find a distinctly Roman blended family. Gaius and Lucius, adopted sons of Augustus, were the biological sons of Agrippa, himself a man of status and standing. That Agrippa was also depicted on coinage was potentially confusing. In portraiture, Agrippa's role was subtly minimized, but the unconventional arrangement meant that Gaius and Lucius effectively had two fathers—in ideology as well as reality.[29]

In Matthew, the good news of Mary's conception is announced to Joseph via a dream. This is a theme in Matthew: Joseph is directed to leave for Egypt in a dream, and Pilate's wife realizes the importance of Jesus in the same way. We are given no information about how Mary herself received this news. If we infer that Mary also learns about her condition in a dream, it is worth noting the special relationship between dreams and extraordinary births. Inscriptions from temples dedicated to Asclepius, the Greek god of healing, reveal that dream incubation (the practice by which supplicants would sleep in the temple overnight in the hope that the deity would send them a dream promising healing) was a means for securing offspring as well as healing.[30] And inscriptions found in the temple complex report on the efficacy of these dreams.

One interesting feature of these practices is that dream incubation and attempts to secure healing often took place without the presence of the husband or father at night. We can infer from the inscriptions that the women conceived naturally as the result of sexual intercourse, but the disconnect is suggestive. The husband is the biological father, but the night spent apart from him and in the company of the potent deity complicates the picture. Many of the dreams recorded by supplicants to the deity are suggestive not of "fruitfulness" but of sex. A woman named Agameda of Ceos recorded that "she slept in the Temple for offspring and saw a dream. It seemed to her in her sleep that a serpent lay on her belly. And thereupon five children were born to her."[31] The almost stereotypically Freudian dream evokes much more than divine healing; it invokes the idea of insemination. The procreative powers of the dream world lingered in the cultural subconscious for centuries, even being cited in legal judgments determining fatherhood.[32] It is possible—even though Mary herself is not the recipient of the dream in the narrative—that Matthew is utilizing that connection to provide a biological context for the miraculous conception while still maintaining his well-established focus on the role of Joseph.

Whatever miraculous mechanisms lie behind the virgin birth, Matthew is clear on several points: that Jesus was conceived apart from sexual intercourse, and that Joseph is the father of Jesus in some very real sense. The paradox is more striking to modern readers accustomed to the hard and fast rules of daytime television paternity tests and DNA. But even as Matthew labors to construct a vision of Jesus's conception and paternity that makes Jesus unquestionably both Son of God and Son of David, he undercuts that vision from the start.

The male-dominated genealogy with which Matthew opens his Gospel is broken up by the mention of four women. The inclusion of women can be explained by virtue of the fact that Mary is the instrumental tie between Jesus and God, but Matthew's choices raise a few proverbial eyebrows. The women mentioned are Tamar (Matt 1:3), who disguises herself and plays the prostitute with her father-in-law, Judah; Rahab (1:5a), the prostitute who facilitates the fall of Jericho; Bathsheba (1:6), the "widow of Uriah," who committed adultery with David; and Ruth (1:5b), David's grandmother, who snuck into Boaz's room at night and "uncovered his feet." All of these women have more than a hint of sexual scandal about them.

Two explanations have been commonly offered for the presence of these women in Matthew's genealogy. The first is that the women are representatives of the Gentiles, insofar as Rahab was from Jericho and Ruth was from Moab.[33] According to this interpretation, Matthew is foreshadowing the mission to the Gentiles and does not offer the genealogy in order to offer commentary on Mary's role. And yet, if Matthew does not mean to create an analogy between Mary and the other women, why does he include Mary in the genealogy in Matthew 1:16? Surely it would be better to leave her out of it.

The second explanation is that these unusual women serve as parallels for the unusual circumstances of Jesus's birth. Later opponents of Christianity would suggest that Jesus was the son of a Roman soldier.[34] Perhaps Matthew is responding to charges like these. And yet, if Matthew's intent is to exculpate Mary, why introduce prostitutes by way of comparison?

The waters are murky here. The lofty royal genealogy Matthew creates for Jesus is subtly undercut by the sexual histories of the prostitutes named in the account.[35] Matthew's insistence on Mary's virginity is offset by a structure that aligns her with prostitutes. It is here that we need to look further, beyond conception and generation to conduct and appearance.

Even apart from the socially awkward position of being pregnant out of wedlock, Mary's conduct would have struck ancient audiences as peculiar. In the final weeks of her pregnancy she cavorted around ancient Palestine with her fiancé. It was not necessary for her to journey to Bethlehem with Joseph, and ancient social conventions would have frowned upon it.[36] It would have been difficult for Mary and Joseph to sustain a public narrative of unimpeachable purity when they were behaving in such a way. As Francois Bovon notes with respect to Luke's version, "The shocking character of the pregnant bride-to-be who travels with her fiancé should not be smoothed over."[37]

The miracle of the virgin birth is that Mary conceived apart from sexual relations and as a result of the creative power of God. The scandal of the infancy narratives is that even apart from her condition, Mary did not behave in a manner that was—to external viewers—virtuous. The contrast is between the appearance of sexual scandal and the reality of circumstances in which Mary became pregnant. Ethics do not directly map onto social expectations and representation here. The contrast is doubtless familiar to those experiencing social discrimination for being childfree. Angst, misinterpretation, and speculation plague those who confront infertility and work through the issues of using medical intervention to become pregnant.

THE HOLY FAMILY IN LUKE

Theologians posit a strong divide between the extraordinary conception of Jesus and normal procreation. The birth of Jesus—which takes place apart from sexual intercourse and utilizes, according to ancient medical theory, the womb of a young woman to house the infant—is not supposed to be taken as a model for human beings. We need to ask, however, if Luke sees the distinction so clearly.

Luke's story begins with Mary's family and with the conception and birth of John the Baptist. We find ourselves in the midst of a familiar tale: John's parents—Zechariah and Elizabeth—are an aging childless couple. They are explicitly described as "righteous before God" and as "living blamelessly according to all the commandments and regulations of the Lord." Despite their righteousness they have "no children, because Elizabeth was barren, and both were getting on in years" (Luke 1:5–6). It is as if Luke has placed us plumb in the middle of the patriarchal stories.[38] Only, in Luke the righteousness of the barren patriarchal-style family is explicit in a way that it is not in Genesis. The double phrasing "barren . . . both advanced in years" recalls the description of Abraham and Sarah (Gen 11:30, 17:17, 18:11). Even the linguistic style of Luke's infancy narratives is reminiscent of the patriarchal narratives; his turn of phrase evokes Septuagintal style as easily as "once upon a time" deposits its reader in the world of fairy tale.

It is into this landscape of miraculous and divinely announced births that Luke places the annunciation of the birth of Jesus. The very structure of the Lukan infancy narrative presses the similarities between the conceptions and births of John (the Baptist) and Jesus further. A succession of scenes teases out the parallels between Mary and Zechariah: angels announce the miraculous birth (to John's father Zechariah, 1:5–25, and to Mary, 1:26–28) and the male infants are born, circumcised, and named (1:57–80//2:1–21) in a similar manner. The annunciation scenes, in particular, mimic one another: first, the angel appears and the human receives the angel with fear. The angel then delivers a tightly structured message that addresses the recipient by name/title, announces the conception, names the son, and predicts the son's future accomplishment. Finally, the recipient responds with incredulity, offering an at least halfhearted objection, and receives a sign as a guarantee.

The annunciations more closely parallel one another than do the births, circumcisions, and namings of the two infants. In other words, as they grow up they grow differently. But their conceptions are presented in near-identical forms, and both annunciations emulate the literary conventions of the angelic announcements of births to barren women in the Septuagint. Numerous scholars have indicated that these parallels suggest that there is something special about the birth of the hero. This is no ordinary birth, and this is no ordinary child. Isaac (Gen 17), Samson (Judg 13), John the Baptist (Luke 1), and Jesus (Luke 1) are all exceptional figures in biblical history. At the same time, and approaching these annunciation scenes from the perspective of exemplarity, Luke is grouping the virgin birth with the exceptional conceptions of barren women. If there are births that prophesy those of Jesus, they are the hard-fought, angst-ridden, and long-awaited miraculous births of the Hebrew Bible's matriarchs. If there are women whose experiences foreshadow and mimic that of the Virgin Mary, they are the infertile women who become pregnant through divine intervention.

While the annunciation to Mary parallels the divine interventions in the lives of the barren in the Hebrew Bible and the angelic intervention in the lives of Elizabeth and Zechariah, there are differences too. Mary's response to the angel's announcement is favorably contrasted to that of Zechariah. Having clarified that she will become pregnant despite being a virgin, she states, "Here I am, the servant (*doulos*) of the Lord, let it be with me according to your word" (1:38).

Traditionally, and appropriately, Mary's response is compared to that of Hannah. When Eli the priest confirms that Hannah will indeed bear a son, she responds, "Let your servant (*doulos*, in the Septuagint) find favor in your sight" (1 Sam 1:18). Later in the story, when Hannah returns to the Temple, she utters a prayer of exultation similar to Mary's Magnificat in Luke 1:46–55. The parallels are noteworthy.

Once again, we should note that Luke places the virgin birth into the larger framework of exceptional births, rendering it special but of a kind. Mary is distinguished in the sense that she is a virgin, but Luke constantly reminds us that she is not so different from Sarah, Rachel, Hannah, and Elizabeth. In Luke's story she is part of a cohort of women whose pregnancies illustrate the power of God.

As secure as the parallels to Hannah are, we should reflect further on the significance of the term "servant" to the audience of Luke. Mary calls herself the "*doulos* of the Lord," a word often rendered in translation as "handmaid." In the Septuagint, Hannah also uses the term in her exchange with Eli. The term *doulos* literally means a slave or bondswoman.[39] While it carries connotations of service, it means legal enslavement and is the word Paul uses for the antithesis of freedom in 1 Corinthians 7:21. The service of Mary is voluntary, in that she assents to the angelic proclamation, but the language used to describe this service invokes the larger cultural context of slavery, and women's slavery in particular.

In the ancient world slaves were assumed to provide sexual service to their masters.[40] They lay, in many respects, outside of the world of sexual ethics and moral conduct. Slaves could not be judged immoral or unchaste because they did not have free will and thus did not have the freedom to make sexual decisions. Domestic slaves were vulnerable to sexual violence, and there was no terminology to divorce the sexually available domestic slave from the household help. The same reality is envisioned in ancient papyri and in biblical descriptions of slavery. As we have already seen, when slaves were used as surrogates or proxy wives for the purposes of producing heirs, they assumed the role of wife. The horrifying reality of exploitation in the ancient world assumed that female slaves were sexually available. And the sexual exploitation of slaves was not, in the Roman world at least, conceived of as a means of acquiring legitimate offspring. While they could serve as legitimate wet nurses, they were not ordinarily surrogates.[41] While efforts were sometimes made to prevent slaves from becoming pregnant, the practical consequence of this reality was the production of offspring, offspring who were discarded or enslaved.

That Luke has Mary describe herself as a *doulos* creates a paradox. She is at once a virgin and the self-proclaimed *doulos* of God. The annunciation scene is reminiscent of God's actions in the lives of the barren, but Mary is no Sarah or Elizabeth. She is, instead, cast in the role of Hagar. She is the slave girl, the vessel, the mechanism by which God's son would be born. If we tug the allusive loop taut against the tapestry of biblical allusions and economies of procreation, we find ourselves wondering about the characterizations of the various actors. Mary becomes pregnant at the behest of the omnipotent God, the creative powers of whom are directly referred to in Luke 1:37 ("For nothing will be impossible with God"), and through the intervention of the Holy Spirit/power of God (1:35). Luke does not want us to see Mary as the bride of God. She is the favored vessel chosen to carry his Son; she plays the role of the surrogate or handmaiden. If there is a human context within which we can understand the birth of Jesus, it is the context of infertility.

For Luke and his readers the stories of barrenness, of sterility, and of divine intervention created a context in which the exceptional birth of Jesus could be understood. They were the births and the families that formed natural analogues to the exceptional birth of Jesus. Mary was not a victim of coercive sexual exploitation, but her role is that of the surrogate girl.

This raises an interesting question with respect to assumptions about Mary's role, status, and fertility. Generally, the miraculous element of Mary's pregnancy is thought to begin and end with immaculate conception. In the world of the story, Mary is understood to be a fertile young woman who has not previously had sex. But should Mary's fertility automatically be assumed? This is a miraculous event that parallels miraculous births in the patriarchal stories: her fertility, often assumed by modern readers, is by no means assured. Alternatively, and if we read Mary as the surrogate who produces the child as a response to divine intervention, who is the infertile wife supplanted by Mary? Perhaps Mary fulfills both roles: the barren wife and the surrogate. The tension between these roles and the miraculous intervention that obscures our ability to speak in concrete terms about Mary's innate fertility blurs the boundaries between fertile and infertile. This presents a counterreading to the dominant view of fertility in the family.

THE AESTHETICS OF THE VIRGIN BIRTH

Western tradition has exalted Mary as the maternal figure par excellence; her image almost never appears outside of the context of motherhood. The cultural distortions of the female form and the modern media's overwhelming postpartum pressure to "snap back into place" pale into insignificance next to the glossy and calm portraits of Mary with the Christ child. Mere moments after giving birth she is shown upright, invigorated, and clean. Her body is scrubbed by a corporeal imagination that will not allow her—unlike her own mother, Anne—to appear disheveled.

It is not the pain and gore of labor and delivery that is the problem. Christian artists have never shied away from slavishly reproducing the distended body of Jesus. To adopt the words of Jennifer Glancy, we have no problem with the crown of thorns, but recoil in horror at the thought of the crowning head of the infant Jesus.[42] In Mary, the realities of the pain of childbirth are erased from our visual memory.

This Renaissance photoshop has theological backing. Mary is depicted as calm and pain-free because Mary conceived and gave birth apart from sin. She did not feel pain because she was not encumbered by the curse visited upon Eve in Genesis 3:16. We have already noted how the holistic experience of having children was theologically fragmented into blessing and curse in the Hebrew Bible: men were able to claim God's blessing of progeny while women toiled under the curse of pregnancy. This inequitable division of labor not only encumbered women with the painful reminders of primordial sin; it parsed this particular pain as punishment. Woman's pain was her just deserts.

As time passed, the pain experienced by individual women during childbirth was explicitly associated with their own moral condition. Even before second-century Christians told stories about the painlessness of the birth of Jesus, biblical commentators like Josephus were describing Moses's mother giving birth without pain.[43] By the rabbinic period the correlation between pain in childbirth and individual righteousness was set, so that Rabbi Judah could say of the birth of Moses, "As the conception was painless so was the bearing painless. From this we learn that righteous women were not included in the decree upon Eve."[44]

The legacy of the painless and idealized childbirth experienced by Mary has left a subtle but discernible impact on childbirthing practices to this day. Since the nineteenth century, pain has been recast as a medical problem that should be treated with anesthesia, yet with respect to childbirth a more subtle discourse has emerged. Concerns to alleviate pain are offset by fears of danger to the infant and the feeling that the pain and knowledge acquired through pain during childbirth have value.[45]

The idea that childbirth is a natural and intrinsic part of the woman's experience of the world is emphasized in certain women-centered theories of birthing. Glancy cites Elisabeth Bing, one of the early advocates for the Lamaze method of childbearing in the United States, who bemoans a medical profession that seeks to minimize pain. Bing writes, "There is nothing accepted anymore by the medical profession that childbirth is part of a women's life, of her inner experience, or of her development. Even with regard to the pain—there is no satisfaction achieved because the woman does not have to work for anything. We've minimized the sense of achievement one obtains when mastering a difficult experience."[46]

When the idealized, painless, stress-free, and sinless experience of Mary enters into this debate, things grow even more complicated. Mary's presumably pain-free experience of giving birth inevitably reinforces the idea that sin and pain are inextricably linked. When religious interests are interwoven with debates about pain relief, the ability of the individual woman to conquer pain without external medical intervention becomes a moral issue. The language of "accomplishment" and "achievement" mingles with ancient characterizations of heroes as immune to pain and religious portraits of Mary as unaffected by childbirth.

Each side of this debate has in view women's health and best interests and seeks to preserve some cherished part of the female experience. But both sides assume, or state explicitly, that childbirth is indeed that cherished part of the female experience. And while the traditional painless birth suggests that pain is associated with original sin, natural birth advocates today seem to think that there is something cleansing in the pain, something manifestly positive. Both, through different means, reinforce the master narrative of childbirth being a fundamental female experience. Once again we must ask, what does it mean to take Mary as model here? She is at once barren wife, surrogate, the one who carries the burden, and the one who feels no pain. Mary as everywoman rather than aspirational type of motherhood perhaps better encompasses the experiences of both fertile and infertile women. The tensions in her roles break down the iconography of Mary as mother and allow for a variety of maternal experiences detached from a single biological path.

JOHANNINE PATRIARCHY

If the mechanics of divine generation are shrouded in a veil of pneumatic mystery in Matthew and Luke, they are utterly otherworldly in the Gospel of John. There is no birth in John. There is not even the assumption of birth. The generation of the Son, the "word made flesh," takes place in the much-debated "beginning" either before or at the commencement of time itself (John 1:1). While John dedicates some space to the relationship between the word and God—it is *with* God, it *is* God—and even the word's role in creation, "all things were made through him," there is no description of the nuts and bolts of the incarnation other than the powerfully oblique passive: "and the word was made flesh and dwelt among us" (1:14).

Throughout, the Gospel itself is strangely bereft of references to mothers or the procreative abilities of women. The term "mother" (*mētēr*) is used only of "the mother of Jesus" and figuratively by Nicodemus. There is a tension in the way that Jesus's mother is presented. On one hand she is defined exclusively in terms of her maternal relationship. Despite the superabundance of Marys in the Gospel of John (the mother of James, Mary Magdalene, and Mary the wife of Clopas), the mother of Jesus is unnamed. She appears as his mother only at traditional family events: weddings (2:1–11), deathbeds (19:25–27), and road trips (2:1–12). She is not a source of advice or consolation, nor does she appear to have any special knowledge about Jesus's mission (2:1–11). While the Fourth Evangelist does not go so far as to portray Jesus as sending her away (cf. Mark 5), the Patristic tradition that portrays Mary as possessing special knowledge is notably absent from the New Testament.

Where John deviates from the Synoptics is in the crucifixion dialogue scene. As Jesus hangs on the cross he looks down and notes the presence of his mother and "the disciple whom he loved." When Jesus sees them there, "he said to his mother, 'Woman, here is your son.' Then to his disciple, 'Here is your mother.' And from that hour the disciple took her into his own home" (19:26–27). The scene is of both practical and theological importance. The comingling of Jesus's biological and pedagogical families represents a view—found also in Paul and the Synoptics—that Christian families are malleable and expansive. At the same time it is utterly practical. At this stage of the Gospel of John, Joseph the carpenter is no longer in view. We might infer that Mary is widowed or otherwise financially vulnerable. By, in a sense, bequeathing her to her new son, Jesus is providing for her after his death. And we can infer, from the note that the disciple *does* take her into his home, that she becomes a part of his family and that he provides for her financially.

In many ways the scene is a narrative evocation of the biblical theme of caring for widows and orphans. Mary is now financially secure and provided for. But while some passages portray care of the widows as a form of almsgiving and many interpreters label this practice "charity," it is clear that John has something more personal in mind. If this scene is, as most scholars have agreed, about care for others, then the model for that care is most properly seen as familial, not charitable. Jesus binds his mother and his disciple to one another, and in doing so unshackles familial ties from biological foundations.

The exemplary nature of this event is further amplified by the ambiguity that surrounds the identity of the "Beloved Disciple." Who is this person whom Jesus loves? Over the course of the past two thousand years scholars have been divided over the identity of this enigmatic figure.[47] Scholarly opinion tends to favor either John the evangelist or Peter the fisherman. Popular theories have lighted upon Mary Magdalene, who plays a larger role in the Gospel of John than in the Synoptics. But the text is fundamentally unclear. One alternative theory posits that the "Beloved Disciple" is a representation of ideal disciples in general. According to this view, the process of ruminating on the identity of the Beloved Disciple encourages reflection on the ideals of discipleship and, in turn, promotes good behavior by audience members. The idea that the Beloved Disciple is an exemplar is not mutually exclusive with other theories about the identity of this individual. It is possible, indeed it is *likely*, that the Beloved Disciple is a moral exemplar even if it is also a historical person.

What the exemplarity of the Beloved Disciple would mean for the audience is that the "family" is more amorphous than is conventionally understood. It is not physical, natural ties that bind members of John's community; it is the assumption of familial relationships. To an extent, as already discussed, all parenting relationships in the ancient world required moments of assent: the moment at which the midwife decided the infant was viable, when the father picked it up from the ground, or when a Roman male designated a particular adult his heir. The idea that families were made, not generated, was a principle more familiar to ancient audiences than today.

In this way, the scene from the cross is a narrative representation of the family of believers, a theme to which we will return in the next chapter. The point for now is that the descent from preexistent consubstantiality with God to incarnation and crucifixion bypasses biological, but not spiritual, birth. The Jesus follower born again from above is a part of a community, and while John demurs on issues of the family, where he invokes family as a model for believers he does so seriously.

In the waning hours of Jesus's life, John recasts motherhood as potentially, if not primarily, nonbiological. The disciple enters into a family, but so too does Jesus's mother, who gains the social standing and benefits of motherhood without biological ties. This, in turn, provides a model for those women who are unable to bear children at all—they are childless just as Jesus's mother is rendered childless by his death, and this text shows the way toward a new and heightened valuation of that childless state. This model of parenting, a model that reappears in numerous early church descriptions of the family, leans toward a family of believers and a notion of motherhood as nonbiological and families as predicated on duty, not DNA.

CONCLUSION: CONCEPTION AND DIVINE IDENTITY

In Christian tradition there is a tension between the exceptionality of Christ and the exemplarity of Jesus. On one hand, ethics, belief, perspective, conduct, and comportment are all firmly rooted in the person of Christ. Jesus tells his disciples to "follow" him and to "go and do likewise." Unisex bracelets ask "What would Jesus do?" Jesus is the model, the exemplar, and the moral touchstone. On the other, Jesus is set apart, his birth the monumental break in theological history that inaugurates a new era of salvation and challenges ancient metaphysics. This is no ordinary birth, and it is not described as one. Some would argue that his birth is exceptional, rather than exemplary, and that the unusual way in which the Messiah is born is not something to be imitated. Herein lies the rub: as the Savior of the world, everything about Jesus—his death, his gender, and his provincial identity—is of great theological import. The divine sonship of Jesus is *at the very least* a way to think about reproduction and parenthood.

In the history of scholarship, the task of describing the ways in which Jesus was conceived of as God has been overshadowed by the weighty intellectual and doctrinal commitments of scholars. Encumbered by and bound to the doctrinal assertions of the councils of Nicea and Chalcedon, scholars have worked within a framework in which parenthood and fatherhood are explicitly tied to biology. Religious commitment to a Christology that stresses the uniqueness of Jesus's position as divine son and the necessity of ontological sonship has framed discussions of the conception of Jesus and the nature of his sonship.

For Mark, the author of our earliest Gospel, life begins at baptism. Prior to the call of the desolate voice in the wilderness and the sudden appearance of Jesus at the River Jordan, we know nothing of Jesus. His occupation, parents, familial background, occupation, and social status are nowhere described for us. They are, for the author of Mark, apparently unimportant. It is at this moment, on this day, that Jesus becomes the beloved Son of God. If Mark circumvents the problem of the birth of Jesus, he does not escape the problem of how Jesus is the child of God. The imagery of the baptism, as we have seen, draws upon ancient understandings of adoption. If God acquires children via adoption, we can reasonably infer that, if Jesus is the "son of God," God was unwilling to or incapable of reproducing using ordinary channels.

Divine sterility may be inferable only from Mark, but reproductive issues lie at the heart of the openings of the four canonical gospels. All of the evangelists are at pains to describe the genesis of the Savior. In producing a narrative of how God became man they labor under pressure from the dictates of logic and monotheism and within the narrow constraints of ancient philosophy. These parameters produce myths of origins that are atypical and "unnatural." Yet even if the reasons for the unusual mechanics of divine sonship can be understood in light of intellectual commitments to divine transcendence, we find ourselves led to the inescapable conclusion that the genesis of Jesus is a case of either nonbiological parenting or assisted reproduction. According to traditional models of parenthood, even if humanity is created in the image of God, it should not re-create itself in the manner of God.

Regardless of the skepticism of Roman critics like Celsus, who joked that Jesus was the son of a Roman soldier,[48] or of rabbinic commentators who named the soldier Tiberius Julius Abdes

Panthera,[49] Matthew, Luke, and most early Christians were convinced that Jesus was conceived apart from sex. The mechanics of this conception go undissected in the canonical New Testament. Even Luke, the most medically inclined of our evangelists, does not hazard a guess at the scientific processes that led to this birth. Nor does he have to; miraculous events defy explanation. But they raise tangled issues for modern Christians who live in an age in which conception can take place without sex, women can serve as surrogates to those who are procreatively challenged, and reproduction can be divorced from "traditional family" units. The vast majority of handbooks and guides for Christian readers encourage their audiences to eschew medical technology.

Even in a system that privileges Jesus as the "only-begotten," natural, and biological Son of God, adoption is not devalued and discarded. The family found in the Gospel of John is one that is constructed at the foot of the cross. Parents and children find themselves in the Christian community. By the time we turn to the Epistles of Paul it is clear that the relative value he assigns to biological and adoptive relationships is starkly different from our own. Paul presents followers of Jesus as adopted children of God and as co-heirs with Christ. Even when the birth of the Christ child is set to one side, it is not "normal" parenting but adoption that becomes the focal metaphor of Paul's message. If human relationships are modeled on heavenly patterns, then the relationship that breaches the earthly-heavenly divide is adoption. If biological parenting and adoptive parenting must be weighed in a theological balance, we cannot forget that the God of Christian soteriology is the deity that sacrifices his biological child *for* his adopted children.[50]

CHAPTER 5

Chastity, Marriage, and Gender in the Christian Family

There was trouble in Corinth, it seems. Confusion abounded over who belonged to whom, how to settle differences, and how life should be organized. Paul had arrived in Achea in 51 CE, fearful and trembling. When he moved on from Corinth to Ephesus a year and a half later he left a dedicated cluster of Jesus followers. They were having problems with the details. By the time rumors of discord reached Paul in Ephesus a handful of years later there was a laundry list of problems, ranging from men sleeping with their stepmothers to eating food dedicated to idols to valuing some members of the community more highly than others.

Among these was the issue of marriage.[1] The Corinthians had written to Paul that "it is well for a man not to touch a woman" (1 Cor 7:1). As familiar as we are with marital problems, it might seem strange that marriage itself was the subject of controversy. And yet it was. In chapter 7 Paul responds to the Corinthians, stating that while "it is better for them [the unmarried and widows] to remain [single]" (7:8), "if they are not practicing self-control, let them marry" (7:9a).[2] In other words, marriage was permissible for those for whom abstinence was simply too hard.

Paul further explains, "But because of cases of sexual immorality, each man should have his own wife and each woman her own husband. The husband should give to his wife her conjugal rights, and likewise the wife to her husband. For the wife does not have authority over her own body, but the husband does; likewise the husband does not have authority over his own body, but the wife does" (1 Cor 7:1–5). From the outset, therefore, Paul is clear that he does not see marriage as innately wrong, as his correspondents in Corinthians do. But Paul does not ground this presentation of marriage in either procreation or the natural order. There is no reference to children or childbearing, and he does not make recourse to the Garden of Eden, to Adam and Eve, or to divine commands to procreate. Marriage may not be wrong, but it is not a self-evident good either.

The key to Paul's understanding of marriage is in the first clause: it is "because of sexual immorality" (*porneia*) that each person should have a spouse.[3] It is presumably for this reason that each man and woman should permit his or her spouse conjugal rights. The issue, quite clearly, is sex, and the effects of sexual deprivation.[4] Paul is concerned that members of the Way, eager to practice the principles of self-denial that are preferred, might inadvertently lead themselves and their spouses into graver danger.

This much is made clear in the following sentences, in which Paul goes on to say that they should "not deprive one another except perhaps by agreement for a set time, to devote yourselves to prayer, and then come together again, so that Satan may not tempt you because of your lack of self-control (*enkrateia*)" (1 Cor 7:5).[5] The introduction of Satan and temptation makes Paul's overarching point. There is danger in sexual self-restraint.[6] Paul's theory about monogamy is, as he himself puts it, a "concession, not [a] command" (1 Cor 7:6).[7] The ability to be sexually abstinent is a "gift from God" (1 Cor 7:7), but Paul is aware that not everyone has received it.[8] Those out of practice and lacking the divinely given faculty of self-control should not attempt anything extraordinary. To put this in the terms of modern bodily self-denial: Paul is afraid that fasting may give way to overindulgence. Even if fasting is the cultural ideal, a balanced diet is preferable to gluttony.

Paul's view of marriage as a "concession" may come as a shock to modern Christians. Nowhere in 1 Corinthians does he invoke the idyll of Eden as a prototype for male-female relationships. There is no primordial dyad to which we should aspire. Marriage is a concession for the lusty, and while he repeatedly states that marriage is "not a sin" (1 Cor 7:28), neither is it necessarily a blessing. Celibacy is to be preferred.[9]

Paul's ambivalent attitude to marriage has ramifications for his—and our—understandings of procreation and fertility. Without sex there can be no procreation, and without marriage there can be (for Paul) no legitimate sex. That Paul here encourages his communities to eschew marriage and focus on God means that he devalues procreation and childbearing. When we consider that Paul *is* interested in the *family* of believers, his lack of attention to parenthood becomes especially noteworthy. It places him in tension with modern Christian views of parenthood as the cornerstone of the family and in line with Jesus's teaching about leaving one's biological family behind in order to receive a new divine family. While it is possible to value both procreation and childlessness, it is also true that you cannot devalue them both. If Paul downplays marriage and procreation he implicitly prefers celibacy and childlessness.

In struggling to interpret Paul's argument, many have argued that Paul's instructions about marriage are only temporary. Paul, like other members of the first generation of Jesus followers, believed that Christ would soon return to gather the faithful and judge the living and the dead.[10] His reluctance to endorse marriage stems from an increased focus on the eschaton and the knowledge that any marriage will be short-lived. To an extent this argument is present in the part of this passage that pertains to a life lived in perpetual virginity. Paul writes,

> Yet those who marry will experience distress in this life, and I would spare you that. I mean, brothers and sisters, the appointed time has grown short; from now on, let even those who have wives be as though they had none, and those who mourn as though they were not mourning, and those who rejoice as though they were not rejoicing, and those who buy as though they had no possessions, and those who deal with the world as though they had no dealings with it. For the present form of this world is passing away. (1 Cor 7:28–31)

The eschatological doomsday clock sounds loudly. The world is passing away, and ties to the world—be they marriage or possessions—will be an impediment to the faithful Christian. Paul is encouraging Christians to live as if the present world is temporary, and avoiding marriage is part of this larger lifestyle of having "no dealings with the world." In this way, Paul is part of a larger apocalyptic tradition—also found in Mark 13—in which familial ties will be a hindrance in the final days.[11] In Mark 13, those who are pregnant or nursing will be at a disadvantage when it comes to escaping the disasters of the end times. Perhaps Mark means that traveling with a young infant or while pregnant would be difficult and slow.[12] Paul may utilize a similar idea, or perhaps he means something more straightforward: that watching one's family members suffer and perhaps even die would be unspeakably difficult for members of the community.

The problem with these explanations is that they do not account for why Paul groups family (both marriage and mourning) with possessions. Material possessions would be destroyed at the end of time as a temporal and temporary accessory of earthly life. Does Paul view the biological family in the same way? It is certainly possible, in which case we can hardly say that, even in the absence of impending judgment, Paul would suddenly be *pro-*marriage.

Ultimately, the problem with the "Paul-only-wrote-this-because-the-end-of-the-world-was-nigh" argument is that it utilizes historical criticism in a rather selective way. It is one thing to acknowledge that Paul's timetable for the end of the world was off. But Paul's arguments about marriage are not grounded solely in his mistake about the imminence of Judgment Day. His argument is more robust than a misjudged apocalypse; there is a sustained thesis about the preferential status of the unmarried and the chaste. Paul's statements about celibacy cannot be swept under the numinous carpeting of the eschaton.

One reason that Paul's arguments elicit these kinds of exegetical contortions is that his statements about marriage have seemed untenable to generations of Christian readers.[13] Christian readers tend to equate marriage with the family in a way that ancient readers did not.[14] Roman Catholics see marriage as a cosmic building block: the sacrament of marriage mirrors the relationship of God to Israel and Christ to the Church. The majority of Christian readers of Paul have been married and have, understandably, prized those marriages highly. The notion that settling down is actually a form of "settling" is difficult to stomach.

In addition, Paul's statements about sex are foreign to modern secular readers.[15] Twenty-first-century Westerners tend to see human sexuality not only as natural and good, but also as a necessary prerequisite for a healthy lifestyle. The rise of feminism, sex-positivism, and the gay rights movement took human sexuality out of the shadows and into the public arena. Parallel (yet ideologically distinctive) theological movements that praised human sexuality within marriage as divinely originating and natural repositioned sex as a human good. While some might argue that polyamory is more biologically natural than monogamy, the right to love and be loved is idealized. It is naturalized. We assume that sex is a natural and basic human right.

It is easy to devolve into stereotypes of prudish Christianity, morally licentious modernism, or debauched paganism, but the array of approaches to sex is both broad and cluttered. The way that we evaluate and embrace human sexuality is peculiar to our own time. While there have been religions, cultures, epochs, and societies that have held views of sexuality vastly different from stereotypes of both modern Western "openness" and Victorian Christian repression, they are all highly individual. When it comes to cultural attitudes to sex and sexuality, there are many fish in the sea.

For those invested in what the Bible has to say about sex, it is easy and tempting to latch onto points of continuity between Paul's view of sexuality and our own. But if we want to understand Paul's argument we need to understand him in his own ancient context. Why is it that Paul views sexual self-restraint as superior to marriage? What sets of values, ideals, and assumptions render his argument intelligible? Is there a context in which Paul's views on marriage and concomitant views on procreation make sense?

SEX, CHASTITY, MARRIAGE, AND PROCREATION IN THE ANCIENT WORLD

Our views of sex and marriage in the ancient world are tangled in popular and academic stereotypes about the "Greeks" and the "Romans" and "Christian" prudishness versus "Pagan" hedonism. These caricatures of ancient sexual practices and values are held in tension with the history of sexuality in the past two thousand years. When it comes to sex, marriage, and procreation, we have our own ideals and value systems. These systems—which can vary wildly from one another—intersect with science, politics, and religion, but we, like ancient peoples, view our own perspective as good and natural. It is difficult to peel back the lacquered assumptions.

In introductory textbooks to the ancient world, the Greeks are often characterized as debauched hedonists. Plato's *Symposium*, with Socrates's speech about the merits of young boys, has bequeathed to the Greeks a reputation as pederasts. This reputation is cemented in the term "Greek Love," but misses the diversity of opinion. The Greeks loved widely.

Next to the Greeks, the Romans can appear only to be straight-laced family reformers. It is true that the Romans were deeply concerned with female purity and male sexual continence; they even passed laws to promote marriage and the family. But, again, this characterization misses the depth and texture of the Roman social world. Caricatures do not peek behind curtains or venture into brothels, and, once we do, it is clear that sex was as omnipresent in the Roman world as it was in the Greek. But, just as with the Greeks, sexual mores varied, and their evaluation was contingent upon who was involved and what they were doing. A married man having sex with a slave or a prostitute was unremarkable and ethically irrelevant. Slaves were nonpersons, culturally stripped of honor and—to the Romans—incapable of being shamed. For that same man to have sex with a married woman who was not his wife, however, made him guilty of adultery, a crime punishable by death.

In addition to the academic caricatures that lumber across our stage, there is the specter of modern assumptions. Most modern people, whether Christian, Jew, Hindu, or atheist, regard sexual desire as a natural impulse. While psychology recognizes and pathologizes hypersexuality, and social and legal conventions regulate that desire, most people view at least heterosexual sex within marriage as the product of natural biological impulses. In addition, most religious traditions and people view these impulses and their expression as good, healthy, and beneficial.

While it may be true that our own sexual codes accurately represent biological facts and/or spiritual truths, it is also the case that sexual codes vary and shift over time and our valuation of sexual practices also shifts. The same biological event can be evaluated in many different ways. The pheromones and hormones that course through our veins as sexual desire can and have been interpreted as natural and good, as demonic and sinful, or as the product of an excess of wine. For our purposes it is important to recognize that even if an ancient person experienced the same flush of desire as we do, he or she may have interpreted that sensation in a manifestly different manner.

MARRIAGE, SEX, AND PROCREATION

The world into which Paul was born was a heady, bustling, vibrant world. It was a world in which the seedy underbelly was constantly exposed. Between the idealized virtue of the civilized world displayed on Roman coins and the private domain of the aristocratic household, death, torture, disease, nudity, and sex were on full display. Sex was cheap, so cheap that prostitution played the part that masturbation does today.

Against this backdrop stood marriage, an institution idealized in Roman society as a sign of order and civilization. It was through marriage that a man's legacy and virtue were secured. Simultaneously marriage was—for the senatorial classes at least—a means of acquiring status and power. Marriage solidified social ties and political alliances.

Girls were often engaged or married as young as eight or nine, but some doctors were of the opinion that these girls were simply too young for procreation. The ancient gynecologist Soranus argued that a girl should remain a virgin until she her body was ready for procreation, that is, when menstruation began around the age of fourteen.[16] Both sex too early and sex too late could cause problems. In the case of the latter, women who remained virgins until late in life could suffer problems: in the absence of sexual activity, the neck of the womb could become flabby or the woman could suffer from the "disease of virgins."[17] For women sex was fraught with danger.

SEX

Sex today is viewed as natural, but even for men ancient writers were more ambivalent about its place in the natural order.[18] While manliness was associated with virility, respectable Roman authors also equated manliness with sexual self-control (*sophrosyne*). The true man was the one who could control his appetites for sex, wine, and food and retain composure in those circumstances that provoked lust, anger, grief, or pain. This interest in and focus on self-control and composure included the ability to abstain from sex, or, as *Seinfeld* would put it, being "master of your domain."

This broad cultural valuation of sexual self-restraint had scientific underpinnings. Second-century Roman medics saw sexual desire as related to bodily constitution. The human body was a mixture of natural elements kept in check by the appropriate balance of moisture, dryness, heat, and cold. The emphasis here was on balance. Health was a form of harmony.[19] Just as in the modern world we talk of "burning desire," ancient physiological theory linked sexual desire and even sexual faculties to heat. The association could explain the heightened appetites of the adolescent male. Young bodies were warm and moist and over time became dry. Sexual appetites were mapped onto the inevitable progress from hot-headed and moist young person to desiccated corpse. The gradual loss of heat and moisture led to the evaporation of sexual desire.[20]

Heat was not only naturally present in the young but could be produced by food and drink.[21] Wine, the ubiquitous beverage of the ancient world, heated the blood, thereby stirring the passions. Wine was healthy for older people, whose bodies had grown cold, but could be dangerous for the young, whose bubbling blood threatened to overflow at any moment. It was not for nothing that it was known as "Aphrodite's milk."[22] As heat grew in the body, blood and pneuma coagulated in the testes to form *sperma*, which was released only during sexual acts. If it was not expunged, the body burned with unexpended and distracting heat, but when it was released it left the body depleted. As a result, keeping the body in check was paramount.

THE ROMANS AND PROCREATION

While the virtuous wife, the *matrona*, was an idealized figure in the Roman world, pregnancy was a source of danger.[23] Gynecological health in general was a source of danger for women. Some medics, such as Herophilus, believed that menstruation was always harmful to health, while others saw it as problematic chiefly in cases where women experienced severe pain and discomfort.[24] A number of physicians, for example Soranus, noticed that both premenstrual girls and women who no longer menstruated were actually in excellent health. This led him to the conclusion that menstruation contributed to procreation but not to general health.

Pregnancy, too, was a dangerous and difficult affair. Even though the ancient Greeks conceived of childbirth as the primary purpose and function of women, they recognized—more clearly than we do today—the inherent risks attached to the birth pro-

cess. Pregnancy was, in the words of the popular ancient gynecologist Soranus, not good but useful.[25]

Even though marriage, and sex within marriage, was concerned with securing legal heirs, upper-class Romans were not
inclined to produce large families. We saw in the previous chapter that adoption was a common practice among the Roman elite.
This may strike some as strange: how is it that aristocratic Romans found themselves so frequently bereft of children? One
reason was simply the child mortality rate: as many as a third of
children died before the age of five. But this can hardly account
for the particularly low childbirth rate of upper-class Romans.

There seems to be more to it than just the harshness of life
in the antibiotic-free world. The low birth rates are difficult to
explain in either cultural or biological terms. Why would the
Romans desire small families, and even if they did, how would
they have been able to limit the growth of their families without
abstaining from sexual intercourse almost entirely?

Some have argued that the Romans must have developed effective means of contraception and abortion to maintain their
small families.[26] But even if we can understand *how* Romans kept
their families so small, we still have to understand *why* they
wanted to. The idea of an ancient society that consciously practiced widespread under-procreation both undermines every cultural stereotype of the religious preindustrial world and calls into
question our contemporary narratives about the decline of childbearing and its connection to secularization and feminism.

A romantic view of the situation might assume that the danger inherent in pregnancy was one reason the Romans avoided
large families. But the risks associated with childbirth were likely
to have been balanced by the financial, professional, and political rewards of reproduction. The Roman imperial period saw
the introduction and development of the *lex Iulia*, the cornerstone of Roman sexual policy. The *lex Iulia* criminalized adultery

and the violation of any respectable woman (virgin, married, or widowed) among Roman citizens.[27] Less innovative, but equally proscriptive, was the complex web of legislation supporting marriage and procreation. In 17 BCE Emperor Augustus quoted the censor Quintus Caecilius Metellus Macedonius to the Roman Senate: "If we could survive without a wife, citizens of Rome, all of us would do without that nuisance; but since nature has so decreed that we cannot manage comfortably with them nor live in any way without them, we must plan for our lasting preservation rather than for our temporary pleasure."[28] In addition to supplying the foundations of both Roman legislation and the modern saying "can't live with 'em, can't live without 'em," the quotation betrays the ancient view that unmarried life was more desirable and comfortable for men. In a world in which slaves could provide all the creature comforts necessary for bodily health and flourishing, and friends could supply the social stimulation, wives could be a willful bother.

Augustus's legislation provided a system of rewards for good family men and punishments for dedicated bachelors.[29] He assessed heavier taxes on unmarried men and women and supplied financial and professional incentives for those who married and produced more than three children. The dearth of women among the noble classes hampered the ambitions of many, and so, with the exception of the most elevated senatorial class, he permitted anyone to marry freedwomen and declared any resulting children to be legitimate. Those who declined to have children were barred from certain areas of professional life and, if they never married at all, were de facto disinherited.

The Julian laws are a fascinating innovation in Roman history. While they were not uniformly implemented and targeted aristocrats, it is nonetheless remarkable that it was necessary to coax and cajole men into marriage and families. And yet even these tangible benefits were not enough for some. There is ample evidence to suggest that some men exploited loopholes in the

legislation by marrying young girls incapable of producing offspring or by engaging in quickie marriages and divorces for the
sake of career advancement. While many married for political
gain, there were others who seemed resistant. Augustus supplies
us with at least one rationale, but the aversion to procreation
was not always rooted in a dislike for matrimony. The Augustan
poet Propertius wrote the following to his older, deeply cherished wife:

> Why should I beget children for national victories?
> There will be no soldier of my blood!
> You alone give me joy, Cynthia
> Let me alone please you.
> Our love will mean far more than fatherhood[30]

Propertius's poetry may be the judicious statement of a younger
lover to his older beloved, but in the utterance he reveals a dis-
satisfaction with the commingling of patriotic procreation with
love. The production of children for the benefit of the state, espoused by Augustus, remains a feature of the discourse of reproductive duty to this day. By rejecting it, Propertius was both
countercultural and crafting a notion of ruinous *amor* that divorced adoration from issue. It is not for nothing that he is seen
as the father of modern notions of love.[31]

Whether either Propertius or Augustus can be seen as a typical Roman male is open for debate; what is clear from our sources
is that among men there was an ambivalent relationship toward
marriage and procreation.

SEX, NATURE, AND SELF-CONTROL

Sex in the ancient world was intimately bound up with notions
of civilization and order. Just as today sexually transgressive behavior is sometimes described as animalistic, carnal, or base, the
Romans looked down on those societies that endorsed rampant

sexuality between freeborn adults. At the same time, however, many philosophical groups espoused a lifestyle lived in accordance with nature. Nature, in this case, rarely meant hedonism. It meant a life lived properly in accordance with the natural laws that governed the universe.

Writing in the Roman period, in the aftermath of imperial legislation supporting marriage and childbearing, Plutarch compared Romans unfavorably with animals. He noted, "In the first place, [animals] do not wait for laws against celibacy or late wedlock, as did the citizens of Lycurgus and Solon, nor fear loss of civil rights because of childlessness, nor pursue the honours of the *ius trium liberorum*, as many Romans do when they marry and beget children, not that they may have heirs, but that they may inherit."[32] Ordinarily we might suppose that a life lived in accordance with reason would be far preferable to a life lived in accordance with nature, but Plutarch is here indicting the Romans for procreating for political and financial advantage. He judges them for marrying solely for the purpose of accessing their inheritance and for having children so that they could become eligible for certain ranks.

He goes on to contrast the wanton pleasure-seeking conduct of human beings with the practical ambitions of animals, writing, "In the next place, the male [animal] does not consort with the female during all seasons, for the end and aim is not pleasure, but procreation and the begetting of offspring."[33] The contrast Plutarch sets up is between human beings who have sex only for pleasure and marry only for personal gain, and animals for which sex is only for procreation. The Romans do not fare well here.

Even as Augustus and Plutarch viewed the attitudes of the Romans to reproduction as unnatural and antistate, there were philosophical and practical reasons to avoid it. *Sophrosyne*, or self-mastery, was a cardinal virtue for the Stoics and a cultural commonplace in the Roman world. While *sophrosyne* encompassed everything from moderation of food to the control of anger, one primary focus was on the regulation of sexual desire and passion. The base effulgence of attraction and embarrassingly emotive displays of lust manifested by teenagers and the *kinadoi* (womanish men) were effeminizing.[34] As Dio puts it, "He who cannot bridle his anger, often over some trivial matter, who cannot cut off his lust for shameful pleasures, who cannot ignore physical pain . . . is he not surprisingly unmanly, less a man even than a woman or a eunuch?"[35]

The tension between sexual performance and conquest as a sign of virility and excessive sexual indulgence as gauchely womanly is palpable. The underperforming male would seek medical treatments to improve his virility, but the glutton for sexual satiety risked a descent into irrational femininity. At the perimeter of the camp of the properly masculine *vir* (the true man) lurked uncontrolled barbarous femininity. Contrary to what we might expect, the man who indulged in *too* much sex was more slut than stud.

The ability to abstain from sexual relations was a sign of masculinity and self-control, but the effects were, as already discussed, tangible. The costly psychosomatic expenditures of sex could adversely affect men who wielded political and military power. In his description of the Roman Republic, the historian Polybius tells a story about the famous Roman general Scipio's time in Carthage. While there, some well-meaning locals brought a beautiful young girl to the notorious womanizer in an attempt to curry favor. Scipio responded that if he were in a private position he would be very welcome to accept the girl, but that as a general he should not. By this Polybius understands Scipio to mean that in times of rest and relaxation these entertainments are fine, but in times of great activity "[sexual activity] is an impediment to the mind and the body alike."[36]

Scipio's rationale here is a practical implementation of the loftier discussions of Plato on the ascent of the soul. In his discussion of the relationship between the soul and the body, Plato is clear that bodily pleasures are capable of seducing the soul from its proper contemplative pursuit. Excessive quantities of food, drink, and sex can render the soul sluggish and docile. Rather than pursuing the Good or the Platonic forms, the postcoital soul reclines languidly in the material realm, content to wallow in the corporeal husk of the body. The sedative effects of sex so clearly apparent to later medics like Galen threatened to lull the soul into a perpetual slumber, a dormant soul sleeping far from beauty.

The Greco-Roman interest in self-control as physically beneficial operates in two registers, or, better, in dual explanatory keys. For the military man, sex dulls the mind and distracts the person. For the philosopher, sex is the soporific drug that leads the soul away from its proper task. Incarnations of this perspective can be found in the practices of ascetic philosophers and communities in which sexual abstinence was highly valued. Abstinence as a way of life was not purely theoretical. Philosophers developed a reputation for practicing what they preached. Clitophon, the hero of the Hellenistic romance novel *Leucippe and Clitophon*, boasts of his supposed self-restraint while marooned abroad by saying, "Throughout our exile we have behaved like philosophers. . . . If men have a maidenhead, I have kept it with Leucippe up to the present."[37] While early Stoics like Zeno and Chrysippus may have seen properly moderated *eros* as sometimes beneficial, late popular conversation turned philosophy and celibacy into synonyms.[38]

SEXUAL CONTINENCE AND INFERTILITY

The well-known and eminently respectable Stoic philosopher Musonius Rufus reportedly stated that those "who are not wanton or immoral are bound to consider sexual intercourse justified only when it occurs in marriage and is indulged in for the purpose of begetting children, since that is lawful, but unjust and unlawful when it is mere pleasure-seeking, even in marriage."[39] His words are not only severe, they are innovatively austere in their prescriptions. For Musonius Rufus the problem is not the lost seed (the *pneuma*) of Pythagorean physicians; it is the lawfulness of the act itself. In and of itself pleasure was neither good nor lawful.

Musonius Rufus is firmer than his contemporaries on issues of sex within marriage, but his rigid statement laid the groundwork for codified personal behavior that degraded nonprocreative sex. Sex for pleasure, even in the context of marriage, was considered fornication. Marriages in which the woman was sterile or had no potential to produce issue were unlawful. To an extent this same logic was present in Roman society more broadly. Roman censuses inquired of members of the equestrian and senatorial classes whether or not they had married for the purpose of creating children (*liberorum procreandorum causa*). Aristotle had suggested that fifty was the upper limit for the production of children in the male, as those produced by older men he believed to be weak.[40] Subsequent Augustan law codified a similar argument. The terms of Augustan marriage laws encouraged men to remarry up until the age of sixty and women to the age of fifty. The rationale was one of procreative abilities. Valerius Maximus relays the details of a case brought before Augustus himself, in which an elderly woman named Septicia of Ariminum married a *senex* (old man) in a similar stage of her life. When she died she left her estate to her husband, disinheriting estranged sons from an earlier marriage. Augustus ruled that her will be nullified because the marriage had not taken place for the purposes of producing offspring. Her husband was even obliged to return the dowry. While many Roman writers noted the merits of companionship in old age, there was certainly a sense that younger wives were to be preferred.

A similar line of reasoning is expressed in the writings of Jewish authors. Philo remarks that "the end of marriage [is] not pleasure but the offspring of legitimate children."[41] This idea led him to the conclusion that a man should and would abstain from intercourse with a barren wife. Philo reprimands those who have sex with barren women because they are "ploughing a hard and stony soil" and thus "waste their seed." Philo understands the sensitivities of divorcing a woman *because* she is barren, but has nothing but contempt for those men who marry women who are known to be barren. He compares them to goats and labels them "enemies of nature."[42]

This line of thought reappears in rabbinic literature in which one (albeit minority) opinion maintains that sterile women are like prostitutes and that sex with sterile women is akin to promiscuity.[43] "A common priest must not marry a sterile woman unless he already has a wife and children. R. Judah says, 'Even though he already has a wife and children he must not marry a sterile woman for she is the harlot mentioned in the Torah' (Lev 21:7)" (*m. Yeb.* 6:5). It is interesting that the Mishnah equates barrenness with wantonness. For both Philo and the rabbinic authors, marriage with barren women is prostitution cloaked in a mantle of respectability. The conceptual association of the inability to procreate with unchecked sexual immorality is present also in the Roman writer Juvenal, who wryly observed that natural eunuchs could cuckold a man with no tangible consequences.[44] With procreation out of the picture, all manner of infidelity could proceed under the radar. Sex for pleasure and without consequences was possible only for the infertile.

In a homily on sex written some two centuries later, John Chrysostom would extend the same logic to the ill-fated people of Sodom and Gomorrah. In his analysis of the scorched earth of the cities, Chrysostom argues, "truly the very nature of the punishment was a pattern of the nature of the sin. Even as they devised a barren intercourse, not having for its end the procreation of children, so did God bring on them such a punishment as made the womb of the land ever barren and destitute of all fruits." Chrysostom plays on the ancient linguistic and conceptual association of agricultural and gynecological fruitfulness. His argument, a reflection of the ancient legal premise of the *lex talionis*, draws out the idea that sex that does not have procreation in mind is "barren" and that, just as certain forms of sex are immoral for their sterile nature, so too marriage to those who were incapable of conceiving was deeply problematic.

What these authors hold in common is a perspective that links nonprocreative sex to lawless conduct. There is something unseemly, unnatural, and illicit in "barren sex." And in the legal and moral repugnance toward marriages between the infertile or the aged, the lines between chastity and continence are blurred. Sex with an infertile spouse becomes profane.

PAUL AMONG HIS PEERS

Setting Paul in the context of his Greek and Roman peers is instructive for our understanding of his views of marriage. His ambivalent position on marriage is countercultural, but in a way intelligible to those familiar with Greek philosophy and medically derived theories of sexuality. In preferring celibacy to marriage, Paul took a position similar to that of the later Stoics. His concern that some could not tolerate self-imposed abstinence for long and would need release echoed the sentiment of ancient medics and Romans in general, for whom an excess of blood-boiled *sperma* required a legitimate outlet. In selecting marital affairs over liaisons with prostitutes, Paul wove together biblical ethics and Roman practicality. If there was something striking about Paul's instructions, it was insistence upon the avoidance of prostitutes, but otherwise his countercultural preference for celibacy was recognizable and intelligible to those familiar with Stoic sexual ethics or Jewish asceticism.[45]

The distractive and debilitating effects of sex, well known to Plato, help us interpret Paul's concerns about the anxiety-inducing powers of matrimony. In his catena of arguments for the preferential option of celibacy in 1 Corinthians 7, he writes, "I want you to be free from anxieties. The unmarried man is anxious about the affairs of the Lord, how to please the Lord; but the married man is anxious about the affairs of the world, how to please his wife, and his interests are divided. And the unmarried woman and the virgin are anxious about the affairs of the Lord, so that they may be holy in body and spirit; but the married woman is anxious about the affairs of the world, how to please her husband" (1 Cor 7:32–34). The tension between the focus on the sublime and the concerns of this world, which underwrites Plato's idea of the soul weighed down by the affairs of the world, supplies the logic for Paul's argument. Here, concern for one's spouse is not a metaphor for or a reflection of God's love for his people or Church; it is one of the worldly things that will perish. The divided interests of the Christian threaten to tear him or her away from God.

Paul's apparent implicit equation of marriage with "the affairs of the world" stands in tension with the overarching concern he has in 1 Corinthians 7 for communal responsibilities and care for the other. Given that Paul conceives of the Corinthian community as one body of which they are individually members, it is strange that Paul eschews union here. There is, for him, something particularly problematic about the personal relationships between married couples. To participate properly in the community of believers is to be a part of the body of the now heavenly Christ; matrimonial conjugation is divisive and worldly.

Paul's instructions have had a controversial legacy in the history of Christianity. Even today the relative statuses of celibacy and marriage are contested. In the chinks of Paul's reticence about marriage we can detect something of interest for us. Procreation is not in and of itself important enough to require engaging in sexual intercourse. The preferential course for a follower of Jesus is celibacy, and with this realignment of the relative status of marriage there necessarily follows a demotion of the importance of natural childbearing. Paul will go on, in the remainder of his epistles, to focus on the concrete and tightly knit family of his community. They are, in his words, one body. It is not that Paul advocates for singular isolated bachelorhood; he proposes a model of family and union with God that exists outside of the structures of biological procreation. The unity of the fraternal community—the *family* of believers—is of paramount importance.

Paul's words and ideas here could be read as a strong counterbalance to the master narrative of infertility. When he advocates for sex as release, he softens some of the harsh anti-nonprocreative-sex notions of his time, even as he works from their general principles. Paul systematically works to sever sex, marriage, and procreation from one another. In doing so he allows for distinctive valuations of each. These are valuations that do not directly overlap with our own definitions. Simultaneously, he lays the groundwork for models of parenting in which spiritual ties bind more strongly than biological ones. By the time we reach the Gospel of Mark, Jesus tells his followers that he does not recognize his biological relatives (Mark 3:31–35) and urges them to abandon their own families in anticipation of a divine family (Mark 10:29–30). And by the second century, Christians are wrestling—in the literary imaginary at least—with the practical ramifications of Christian women eschewing marriage and romantic partners for life in the Jesus movement.[46]

Paul's successors wrestled with his prescriptions regarding marriage. Some embraced the freedom and preached celibacy as the divine life while others channeled the path to salvation through the birth canal. If 1 Timothy saw childbearing as the path

to female salvation, the fictional *Acts of Paul and Thecla* narrates
how the heroic Thecla abandoned her fiancé for a celibate (though
eroticized) life with Paul. It suggests that "the only way to keep
the flesh pure and experience the resurrection and eternal life is
to remain virginal and celibate."[47] The dispute over Paul's legacy
and the debates over the proper interpretation of his words were
as heated as any ancient Roman contestation over monetary inheritance. Each party and author claimed the right to interpret
Paul's words.

A variety of opinions emerged. Of those engaged in the emerg-
ing discussion over the role of sex and marriage in the Christian
community, only the Pastorals achieved canonical status. Their
view that salvation for women could be found only through
childbearing was penned in the name of Paul, but they were only
one articulation of how sex relates to salvation. Dissident voices
can be heard and, in many ways, better represent the religious
climate that bred monasticism, martyrdom, and voluntary celibacy. While many examples can be adduced here, we will focus
on but one: the presentation of celibacy and its location in physical infirmity in the *Acts of Peter*.

ACTS OF PETER

In the second century CE, an unknown author composed a story
that relays the traditions about Peter's activities after the end of
the canonical Acts of the Apostles until his death in Rome.[48] As
a whole, the *Acts of Peter* is oriented toward chastity and sexual
continence. He persuades the wives and concubines of key individuals to withhold sexual favors from their partners. In fact, we
could reasonably make the argument that it is Peter's teachings
on sexual continence and on sexual hierarchies that lead to his
death. In this respect, the Peter of the *Acts of Peter* stands very

much in the tradition of Pauline rejection of marriage and exhortation to sexual self-restraint.

One of the more troubling portions of the *Acts of Peter* is found in the story of Peter's daughter, which, in modern editions, opens the narrative. The scene begins with Peter healing those brought to him by the crowd. One of the bystanders asks Peter why—given that he has dedicated so much time to curing the sick—he has not helped his "virgin daughter, who has grown up beautiful and believed in the name of God?" and "is quite paralysed on one side, and lies there stretched out in the corner helpless." Peter smiles and responds that it is clear to God why her body is not well, but that in order to demonstrate God's power he would (temporarily) heal her. To the amazement of the crowd he instructs his daughter to arise and walk around, before instructing her to "return to [her] infirmity," adding, "this is profitable for you and for me."

Peter provides some context for the girl's condition and mentions that when she was born he was told in a vision that she would be a great trial for Peter and that if her body were healthy she would "harm many souls." At this point the manuscript starts to fragment, but when we pick up again Peter continues with a story about the girl's youth.[49] When she was ten years old, a man called Ptolemy saw her bathing and desired to take her as a wife. His servants brought her to his house and laid her in the doorway, but Peter and his wife perceived that this had happened, went to Ptolemy's house, and discovered the girl there, paralyzed on one side. And from that day onward the girl was unable to move.

As for Ptolemy, he cried until he turned blind, after which he decided to hang himself. He was interrupted by a bright light that chided him on the proper treatment of virgins and told him to go to Peter for further instructions. Upon being received by

Peter, his eyesight (both of the flesh and the soul, we are told) was restored. The text is opaque, but we can safely infer that he spent the remainder of his life in service to God. In his will he bequeathed to the girl a portion of land, which Peter then sold, distributing the funds to the poor.

The episode is troubling to readers who find Peter's treatment of his daughter disarming. As a story with biblical pretensions, it is styled with scriptural motifs. The categories of disability employed in the text—blind (Ptolemy), lame (Peter's daughter)—draw upon the Hebrew Bible's trilogy of impairments: the blind, the deaf, and the lame.[50] The blinding and subsequent healing of Ptolemy is reminiscent of Paul's Damascus road experience as told in the canonical Acts of the Apostles. The charitable donation in Ptolemy's will suggests an additional allusion to the story of Tobit, who, like Ptolemy, is blinded in an unusual fashion and longs to die, only to have his vision restored in connection with almsgiving.[51]

Some have found the punishment of Ptolemy himself problematic, because Ptolemy is intent on marrying, rather than seducing, the girl. That he encounters the girl as she bathes may gesture toward the story of Susannah in Daniel. Perhaps the author wants us to see Ptolemy as similarly motivated by lust. The fact that, at ten, the girl is too young to procreate would support this reading.

Whatever our interpretation of Ptolemy's fate, we are still left with the girl's condition. In the history of scholarship, the girl's condition has been interpreted chiefly as an illustration of the perils of lust and undesirability of marriage. It is read alongside another story of a young virgin that is also treated as part of the lost first section of the *Acts of Peter*.[52] In this narrative a gardener asks Peter to pray for the very best for his daughter, only to have her drop dead. The gardener, "distrustful" of this "divine blessing," asks Peter to have her raised from the dead, only to have the girl elope with a false Christian several days later. In this reading it is better for a young girl to be dead or disabled than used as a sexual vessel and (we can assume) damned.

The rhetorical power of these exhortations to celibacy turns on the conventional horrors of the alternatives. The stories are treated as moral tales, the thrust of which is articulated by a horrifying predicament. We are invited to dwell on the lowliness of Peter's daughter's condition. She is described as "helpless" and physically marginalized, being shuffled off to the side and lying "in the corner." But even this, the author implies, is not as dire as the fate that awaits those who choose lust—even the socially acceptable sexual practices encoded in marriage—over virginity.

For our purposes, it is possible to push farther than the ancient convention of using bodily disfigurement to convey ethics. We should note, in the first place, the way the conventional association of beauty and ability is undercut in the narration of the story. In the ancient world, and even today, beauty and ablebodiedness were linked on a fundamental level. Not so in the story of Peter's daughter. She is identified as beautiful prior to her healing. It is certainly not the case that the girl is rendered ugly by virtue of being paralyzed. She is beautiful when she is able-bodied and she is beautiful when she is paralyzed. Paradoxically, her condition is not metaphorically disfiguring.

The fact that she is explicitly described as beautiful should direct us to enquire further about the mechanics of the paralysis and the manner in which it renders her sexually unavailable. The onlooker who remarks on her beauty also describes her as physically "helpless." She is now perpetually reclining and stretched out. Envisioning the scene from a modern perspective, we might wonder if she is not, in fact, more vulnerable than ever, given that it would be impossible for her to resist unwanted sexual advances. And yet this reading is not supported by the logical progression of the story. Why, then, is Peter certain that her paralysis makes the girl and others around her safe given that she remains physically attractive?

The paralysis itself holds the key. Some strains of ancient medical thought linked impotency and paralysis. For example, Petronius, in his *Satyricon*, describes how the main character suffered from impotency. The account compares impotency to the death of the sinews that, if left unchecked, could affect his other joints and cause full-body paralysis.[53] If, as Petronius appears to suggest, paralysis is a more extreme form of impotency, then the form of the girl's impairment may be intended to suggest an inability to participate in sexual congress altogether. Moreover, the structure of the story renders paralysis and virtue synonymous. No longer is paralysis a sign of divine judgment; it is a precursor to salvation. The *reason* it is a precursor is the manner in which it renders Peter's daughter sexually inaccessible. While the reality of this idea may be problematic (persons with disabilities are especially vulnerable to sexual assault in the modern world), it allows Peter to establish a new economy of the body, an economy in which physical infertility and undesirability are prized more highly than youth, beauty, and fertility.

VIRGINITY AND STERILITY

It might seem thus far in this chapter as if all this discussion of sexual practices in the ancient world and sexual continence in Paul is irrelevant to our study. After all, with one famous exception, no one expects virgins or monks to produce offspring. Perhaps this chapter is helpful to the voluntarily celibate, but, as Christian tradition in general *already* valued virginity and chastity, this might seem to be gilding the virginal lily. Modern readers tend to distinguish between the choice to remain chaste and thus childless and the physical condition that renders a person unable to have children. In the case of the former, the sexually inactive female is assumed to be fertile, because the natural order of the world is that women are fertile. In other words, choice is key, but so is a fundamental assumption about human biology.

This assumption becomes particularly interesting when it comes to the moral evaluation of virginity and chastity in Christian contexts. Women who remain chaste and childless by choice are assumed to be blessed, to be moral, and to be set apart. Women who are childless through biological defect are seen as broken, unnatural, and perhaps also sinful. In the history of interpretation the distinction becomes especially problematic in contexts in which fertility is linked with God's blessing and infertility with divine punishment.

This choice-driven chasm between abstinence and impotence seems natural to us. Virtue is found in the decision not to have children, a choice synonymous with remaining unmarried. This fissure, forced by Paul and his religious heirs, is less acute in the broader Greco-Roman world. While infertility was a common reason for divorce in the ancient world, there were nonetheless certain locations in which infertility was ambiguously linked to virginity.[54] In the heavenly pantheon of gods there were a number of notable virgins. Athena, the goddess of wisdom, not only remained unmarried and virginal, she was herself born "unnaturally" from the head of her father.

Artemis, the goddess of the hunt and childbirth, and proto-lesbian icon, also eschewed the company of men. In the process she garnered some interesting appellations. In his discussion of the moon and its nature, Plutarch discusses the origins of the traditional connection between the moon and Artemis. He notes "we shall say that she was thought to be Artemis on the ground that she is a virgin and childless/sterile but is helpful and beneficial to other females."[55] Plutarch refers here to the traditional understanding of the virgin goddess Artemis as the goddess of childbirth, but it is interesting that he sees sterility as a component of her identity.[56] Despite never having had the opportunity to become pregnant, he views her as sterile.[57]

The notable difference in ancient texts breaks down the moral judgments encoded in biblically derived interpretations of virginity and infertility. Plutarch sees virginity and infertility as biological and linguistic synonyms. The same interplay is evident in the work of the Greek playwright Sophocles. Toward the end of *Oedipus the King*, the famous story of the ill-fated prince who kills his father and marries his mother, the protagonist bemoans the fate that awaits his young daughters. He recognizes the shame that will follow them and says, "but who will marry you? There is no one, my children, but you are destined to perish barren (*chersous*) without husbands."[58]

The observation made by both authors is that, practically speaking, virgins are barren. They are without offspring. The ramification of virginity is childlessness. In the case of Oedipus's daughters this is a fact to be decried, but in the case of Artemis infertility was a question of choice. In broader Greco-Roman culture the distinction made by moderns between virginity and infertility breaks down.

We might wonder, then, does the hallowed status of the sexually abstinent extend to the childless in general? Certainly in old age, as the trappings of fertility fall away, some ancient commentators argued that it did. The Jewish philosopher Philo linked femininity to fertility and argued that through the shedding of this femininity—through virginity and advanced age—women were eligible to enter the ranks of the masculine philosopher and truly contemplate the divine.[59] Philo's opinion anticipates the celibacy practices of Christian late antiquity, but he also emphasizes the extent to which biological impairment caused by old age functions similarly to the more virtuous forms of elective chastity.

CONCLUSION

What these quiet voices demonstrate is that pregnancy and childbirth were not unambiguous goods for early Christians and that, for some, biological sterility could carry the privileges and advantages of celibacy. The conceptual wall that separates the morally virtuous chaste virgin from the ethically ambiguous tarnished barren women did not always exist in the ancient world. Perhaps the very problematic virtue ascribed to women whose social conditions prevented them from childbearing (widows and virgins) can be extended to women whose biological circumstances left them in the same state. In drawing out the quiet voices of the early church it is not our intention to suggest that the moral compass of the early church pointed due north. The celebration and fetishizing of virginity has had a damaging effect in the lives of many women throughout history, and we do not intend to reproduce it here. But by stressing the diversity of opinion about marriage and procreation in the ancient world and in the early church and the perennial interest in practiced celibacy, we can find alternative models of the family in the ancient world and for today.

CHAPTER 6

Barrenness and the Eschaton

As he toured ancient Palestine, Jesus was approached by a man named Jairus, one of the leaders of the local synagogue, whose daughter was extremely unwell. Jesus agreed to visit the girl and set off with Jairus and his disciples to Jairus's home. As he journeyed he was followed by the ever-present crowd. The crowd jostled and shuffled around Jesus, slowing the progress of Jairus and his guests and straining to catch a glimpse of the increasingly famous healer. A woman in the crowd, who had been unwell for twelve years with a "flow of blood," weaved her way through the mass of people toward Jesus. She had visited many doctors in the past, but she had lost all of her money and they had made her only more unwell.

The woman was convinced that, if she only touched Jesus's clothes, she would be healed. When she reached him she stretched out and clasped the hem of his garment. Power (*dunamis*) flowed out of Jesus and into the woman and she instantly felt in herself that she had been healed. Jesus was also aware of the physical transformation. He spun around in the crowd and, to the incredulity of his disciples, asked who had touched his garment. The terrified woman came forward, was absolved of her sins and commended on her faithfulness by Jesus, and was sent on her way to a priest.

This story, commonly referred to as "the woman with the hemorrhage" or "the woman with the flow of blood," was popular in antiquity, as it is to this day. It not only appears in the three Synoptic Gospels—Matthew, Mark, and Luke—but also features in ancient Christian artwork, especially on sarcophagi and on funerary art.[1] Fourth-century church historian Eusebius even refers to (and criticizes) a popular tradition that the woman with the hemorrhage had herself commissioned statues of the event.[2]

The popularity of the story is matched by its enigmatic nature. In keeping with the predisposition of post-Enlightenment scholars to diagnose and deconstruct miraculous cures according to the conventions of modern medicine, a great deal of scholarly interest in this story has lighted on the woman's condition.[3] The fact that it is a woman who has the flow of blood has led to the conclusion that the woman's ailment is gynecological. The language used to describe her condition ("flow of blood") is used by Greek writers to refer to discharge from the womb.[4] So it is not unreasonable to suppose that the same kind of condition is alluded to here in Mark, even if any kind of more specific diagnosis eludes us.

The woman is described as having had the condition for twelve years, a period of time that parallels the age of Jairus's daughter in the miracle story that immediately follows.[5] Whether symbolic or not, the mention of "twelve years" undoubtedly indicates that she has suffered for a lengthy period. The woman's condition has left her physically and financially depleted. According to Mark she has spent all she had on the care of physicians, and to no avail. The statement that she has only "grown worse" serves as an indictment of traditional medical practices.[6]

THE WOMAN'S "HEALING"

Intriguingly, this is the only healing story in the Gospels that involves a gynecological ailment. While barrenness and sterility figure prominently in the Hebrew Bible, the New Testament is surprisingly quiet on the matter. The woman—about whom we know very little—has become a blank slate upon which cultural valuations of normal women's bodies are inscribed. From the perspective of those interested in ancient medicine, the question of what happens to the woman after she has been cured is particularly important. Modern readers are often inclined to see the woman's transformation as a straightforward healing story: it is assumed that, now that the flow of blood has abated, the woman can lead a normal life—normal, in this context, meaning one in which she can marry, reproduce, and move about freely without fear of ostracization or alienation.

When read more closely, however, the nature of the woman's transformation is less clear. The process by which the woman is healed utilizes classical distinctions between hydration and dryness. The woman goes from a sodden, leaky, malleable body into a dry, hard one. The Greek the term used to describe what happens to her is *exerantho,* from the root *xeraino,* which means, literally, "dried up," "scorched," or "hardened."[7] Translations of the passage are inclined to render the term as "ceased" or "abated," but the actual valence of the cure is one of hardening and drying. The mechanics of her healing reproduce the logic of ancient medicine. According to ancient medical thought, men's bodies were naturally harder, drier, and more turgid than those of women, which were soft and malleable. The imagery of bodily hardening and drying is masculinizing. It articulates both the mechanics of her healing (the flow is dried up) and her new condition (she is hardened).

The drying of the woman's blood could have a number of meanings. It could simply mean that the abnormal bleeding has stopped and that the woman is no longer hemorrhaging.[8] She is restored, we might assume, to the "natural" state of fertility. This reading, of course, assumes that fertility *is* the natural state, something that was by no means clear in our examination of the

matriarchs. The overwhelming majority of modern biblical interpreters follow this line of interpretation.[9]

If we want to understand the healing story on its own terms,
however, we must consider the woman's condition in its ancient
context and through the lens of ancient bodily theory. The language of drying and hardening in Mark 5 could imply not merely
a return to "natural" fertility, but in fact a transition to a permanent state of hardening. Dried female bodies carried with them
overtones of barrenness. Female bodies from climates that were
naturally harder were thought to have difficulty reproducing. The
Hippocratic text *Airs, Waters, Places* states that, in places with
cold northerly winds, "the women suffer largely from barrenness
owing to the nature of the water; this is hard, permanently so,
and cold."[10] The aggressiveness of the scorching language used in
Mark might similarly denote a more permanent transformation.
She is, in effect, cauterized.

In agricultural parables employed by Mark, this withering and
scorching language is laden with heavy language of judgment
and death. It is noteworthy that on those other occasions where
xeraino is used in the Gospel of Mark it means scorched, hardened, or withered (cf. Mark 3:1; 4:6; 9:18; 11:20–21). It is used
most frequently to describe withering and wasting away. The
plants that are scorched in the parable of the sower, for example,
die. It is an unambiguously bad thing. The same trend can be de-
tected in the Septuagint, in which language of scorched plants is
set alongside human infertility as a sign of God's punishment. In
Hosea 9:16, for instance, God's judgment on Ephraim is visited in
the form of the scorching of crops and destruction of offspring:
"Ephraim is stricken, their root is dried up (*exeranthe*), they shall
bear no fruit. Even though they give birth, I will kill the cherished offspring of their womb."

The imagery of Hosea makes explicit the analogy between
human and plant fruitfulness and barrenness. And God manages

to cover his bases. He dries up the roots of the people (rendering them barren) as punishment, but if they somehow continue to have children Israel should be reassured that God will kill those children too. The same use of withering language occurs in a description of eunuchs in Isaiah 56:3. Here God instructs the people, "do not let the eunuch say, 'I am just a dry tree (*xulon xeron*).'" Once again the same language of drying is used to describe the infertile eunuch.

The association among women's fertility, plant reproduction, and scorching is a literary feature not just of biblical texts. A Greek medical papyrus recommends the following test for fertility: "The way to know it of a woman whether she will be pregnant: You should make the woman urinate on this plant, above, again, at night. When morning comes, if you find the plant scorched, she will not conceive. If you find it green, she will conceive."[11] The underlying logic is the same. Barrenness in a woman will produce the same lack of flourishing in a plant.[12] It is interesting for our reading of Mark that, in both Greek medicine and the Septuagintal passages just discussed, barrenness is expressed in terms of scorched plants. In his Gospel, Mark employs the same terminology for the scorched and destroyed plants as he does for the "healing" of the woman with the flow of blood. We might imagine that Mark, like others in the ancient world, associated female infertility with desiccated plants. In some essential sense the two were identical.[13]

Given the common use of scorching language in both Mark and in medical descriptions of barrenness in women, it is curious that modern commentators have not seen the woman as transitioning from unchecked bleeding to infertility. There are three main reasons for this. The first is the biological difference between the scorched infertility of the Septuagint and the woman with the flow of blood. In both instances we mentioned—Ephraim in Hosea 9 and the eunuch of Isaiah 53—the scorched one was male. The image, therefore, depends on the drying up of a natural biological stream. By contrast, the woman's hemorrhage is unnatural.

Flows of blood from women were—even in the most "natural" of circumstances—dangerous sources of pollution and power.[14] The abating of an unnatural flow might be construed differently than the drying up of a natural one. To put this in Hippocratic terms: if a perfect balance between sodden and desiccated was necessary for reproductive health, the woman with the flow of blood was overly saturated while the eunuch was desiccated. By drying up the woman's flow we might assume that balance is restored. We should note, however, that we do not *know* this. The language employed by Mark is the language of sterility.

The second reason for assuming that the woman's healing means the restoration of normal, fertile reproductive abilities is that the Gospel of Mark is deeply invested in healing. For the author of Mark, bodily wholeness and faith in Jesus are intimately connected. The evangelist relates numerous instances of healing of blindness, paralysis, and illness resulting from faith. From the healing of the paralytic in chapter 2 to the restoration of Bartemaeus's vision in chapter 10, faith and healing are inextricably connected. When Jesus addresses the woman he uses language of salvation. He tells her, "your faithfulness has saved you (*sesōken*); go in peace, and be healed of your affliction." English renderings of this verse will often translate salvation into healing and affliction into disease, both of which are legitimate interpretations of the Greek. The coalescing of religious salvation and bodily healing in this term encapsulates the Markan view that faithful bodies are healthy bodies.[15]

The association between health and salvation is a biblical theme, as we have already seen, and one that is firmly inscribed into the pages of Mark's Gospel. Mark constantly rehearses the interwoven discourse of salvation and healing, reproducing the two in tandem so that language and imagery of healing become synonymous with salvation. Later interpreters of the healing of the woman with the flow of blood story interpreted her healing as a prefiguration of the resurrection of the body. They argued that she was *not* restored to fertility but that in her barrenness she becomes a model of the eschatological body. The question, then, is this: what counts as healing and salvation in the Gospel of Mark and for us as readers? And, when it comes to the woman with the flow of blood, we have to ask ourselves: is being healed the same as becoming fertile? Is it possible that the idealized early Christian body is infertile?

BARRENNESS AND FERTILITY IN THE ESCHATON

One of the focal points of the Jesus movement was the looming eschaton and the Day of Judgment. The impending arrival of the apocalypse sounded like a low steady drumbeat in the background of the lives of the first Christians. Almost all scholars agree that it was the belief that the world was drawing to a close that spurred both Jesus and his followers to spread their message. With respect to early Christian views on the family, this recognition often serves an apologetic function. Interpreters of the New Testament will often remark that it was *because* the early Christians thought the end of the world was coming that they rejected marriage and procreation: the proverbial biological clock was overshadowed by a much louder, eschatological timepiece. It is noteworthy, however, that modern Christians would prefer to admit a colossal Pauline scheduling error than to confront the reality of Christian ambiguity about procreation itself, and the fact that early Christians had a theology of barrenness to accompany their asceticism.

When it comes to the specifics of the end of the world—its forms, its precise timing, and, most important, its aftermath—

early Christians were divided. Ancient Jewish views about the afterlife were diverse and amorphous. The landscape of ancient Jewish thinking about the end of the world incorporated everything from messianic hopes to a cosmic battle between the forces of light and dark to a rather more abrupt divine intervention in the inevitable decay of humanity.

Early descriptions of the resurrection utilized naturalistic imagery of flourishing, fertility, the reassuringly reliable passage of the seasons and sun, and the remarkable renewal of the phoenix. These descriptions were occasionally set in landscapes of new creation or re-creation and scheduled for a millennium of creature comforts.[16] Expectations of a period of reward, flourishing, and peace abounded and had circulated since the exile. Traditionally, it was viewed as a period in which injustice and wrongdoing would be righted. The blessed would be rewarded for their fidelity and covenantal obedience, while the wicked would be punished for their sins. Individual sufferings would be reversed—the lame would walk, the blind would see, and so on. As we already saw with ancient Jewish literature, expectations about this period of restitution, restoration, and bliss utilized imagery of earthly and human flourishing: in the eschaton, the abundance of crops would be mirrored by the healing of humanity.

Yet even as visions of the eschaton lighted on bodily transfiguration and healing, the fate of those who were biologically barren and sterile was not necessarily reversed. As intrinsic as procreation was to ancient notions of immortality, the rewards of the faithful who behaved appropriately did not include actual children. We have already encountered the passage from the Wisdom of Solomon in which the barren woman who remains celibate while alive "will have fruit when God examines souls," and the eunuch who does "no lawless deed" will be "shown special favor" for his faithfulness "and a place of delight in the temple of the Lord" (3:13–14). The promises implied in the prophecy allude to the experiences of the able-bodied procreative norm. Fruit and fruitfulness were of course common biblical metaphors for child rearing and procreation in general. More pointedly, eunuchs were not allowed to serve in the Temple as priests. Thus, this according of particular places and honors might be read as a reversal of the social constraints placed upon eunuchs. But even as these honors allude to the ordinary experiences of the fertile and "whole," they also trump and transform them. There can be no doubt that eternal eschatological "fruits" supersede the blessings of offspring in this world. Moreover, if we are to understand "the Temple of the Lord" in this passage as the eschatological or heavenly temple, it would surely outrank the earthly one. At the same time, and even as these expectations play on the reversal of earthly sufferings and disadvantages, barrenness is one arena in which bodily healing is a moot affair. While we might picture God as an eschatological adoption agency, assessing the souls of the barren, and distributing children to those who are worthy, it seems unlikely.[17] The fruits of righteousness are more likely to be eschatological gifts of personal immortality and special proximity to the divine than the temporal gift of children as numerous as the stars.

A similar interpretation of eschatological barrenness may be at work in the story of the Ethiopian Eunuch in Acts 8:26–39. In this story, the disciple Philip is traveling from Jerusalem down to Gaza when he encounters "an Ethiopian eunuch" on the way. The unnamed eunuch enjoys high social status as a "court official of Candace, queen of the Ethiopians" and as the person in charge of her entire treasury (Acts 8:27). The Ethiopian had journeyed to Jerusalem to worship and was struggling to interpret Isaiah as he journeyed home. Directed by the spirit, Philip approaches the chariot and helps the eunuch interpret the Isaianic passage as a prophecy about Jesus. As they journey the eunuch sees some water and exclaims, "What is to prevent me from being baptized?" (v. 37). The chariot stops; he is baptized by Philip; and when the eunuch comes up out of the water Philip is snatched away by the Spirit.

Traditional interpretations of the passage have focused on the way that the story of the Ethiopian eunuch's conversion fits with Luke-Acts's larger interest in the missionary expansion of the church.[18] Often these interpretations will focus on a particular aspect of the eunuch's identity: his geographical origins, ethnic categorization, political affiliation, potential cultic status in the Jerusalem temple, or gender. He is described as both a man and a eunuch.[19] There are intersecting patterns of identification at play in this character.[20]

The eunuch's status as Ethiopian courtier may intrigue modern readers, but our modern definitions of national identity should not serve as a guide for ancient constructions of identity.[21] There is something intriguing about the eunuch's presence in the temple. He has cultic interests but, technically, would not have had access to the Jerusalem temple.[22] Western-centered readings of the story have used the Ethiopian eunuch to highlight Luke's theological program, but this has come at the cost of noticing the man's race.[23] As Virginia Burrus puts it, the Ethiopian eunuch was a "black Jew, castrated man."[24] There are numerous—ideally intersecting—ways to understand the identity of the Ethiopian eunuch, but for our purposes, and following the consistent Lukan pattern of referring to him as a "eunuch" (vv. 34, 36, 38, 39), we will focus on the significance of his infertility and inability to procreate.

In a recent book on disability, Amos Yong has set the eunuch's gender in the context of modern disability.[25] Noting that the Ethiopian eunuch is not "healed" of his "condition" or otherwise transformed in Acts 8, Yong argues that the man offers evidence that disability is redeemed in the New Testament and, accordingly, that perhaps we should not expect that people will be healed of their conditions in the eschaton. While we might empathize with and approve of Yong's conclusions, Yong fails to appreciate the complex ways in which gender was constructed in the ancient world. Yong assumes that being a eunuch is a disability in the same way that being blind is a disability—the category of disability that he uses is a modern one. In order to understand the significance of the eunuch's gender and "lack" of a cure, we must explore how eunuchs were viewed in the Greco-Roman world.

Eunuchs occupied an ambiguous place in the ancient world, and the language and discourse were more complicated and stratified than our modern English term suggests. This much is evident from Matthew 19:12, where the evangelist specifies that some eunuchs were born that way, some were made eunuchs, and others made themselves eunuchs. Matthew's tripartite division mimics the taxonomy of the jurist Ulpian, who distinguishes between "eunuchs by nature, those who are made eunuchs, and any other kind of eunuchs" (*Digest* 50.16.126).[26] Self-made eunuchs (*galli*) were attached to the fertility cults of Cybele and Dea Syria, where they served as musicians.[27] The origins of the condition were socially and legally important, and this is reflected in the various technical terms used to differentiate various kinds of eunuchs.[28] Castration pre- and postpuberty had a pronounced effect on the appearance of the eunuch, but in general it should be remembered that the purpose of castration appeared to be to render the person incapable of procreation, not incapable of sexual relations.[29]

In practice, eunuchs were often slaves who were brutalized as a form of punishment, subjugation, or economic exploitation.[30] As slaves, eunuchs would already have been excluded from the idealized gender spectrum in which freeborn men participated.[31] If slavery was culturally emasculating for male slaves, the eunuch was the physical embodiment of this process.[32] Socially, eunuchs could occupy positions of great power but were distanced from traditional structures of succession and were the objects of derision.[33]

Perspectives on the social and moral status of eunuchs varied. Herodotus and Xenophon employ the language of *pistis* (trustworthiness) to describe them.[34] *Galli* were often seen as hyperreligious and filled with religious fervor. Virgil casts the eunuch as a strange, effeminate foreigner (*Aeneid* 2.693–97), an idea that may be hinted at in the association of the eunuch of Acts 8 with a foreign queen. Lucian describes them as "neither a man nor woman but something composite, hybrid and monstrous, alien to human nature" (*Eunuch* 6–11).[35] Lucian may well describe popular attitudes to eunuchs, but their inability to procreate meant that eunuchs stood outside of traditional household roles; they had access to the private worlds of women, and were particularly trusted with the care of elite women.[36] That said, eunuchs were generally not viewed as asexual.[37] According to Martial, they were skilled providers of oral sex to both men and women (Martial, *Epigrams* 3:81).

For the purposes of our interest in fertility, it is worth noting the common theme in the complex ancient taxonomies of gender: eunuchs had no biological procreative destiny. They were unable to reproduce. This biological weakness both made them the objects of derision and allowed them to rise to positions of authority because they were generally seen as more trustworthy. Despite their inability to procreate, some eunuchs were able to participate in the structures of power that transmitted inheritance from one person to another. Those who were born as eunuchs were able to adopt children and transmit property to them (but those who were made eunuchs could not).[38] Even if they were divorced from the usual social structures of the family, the channels for producing legal heirs were not necessarily closed off to them.

Given all of the complexities surrounding the eunuch in Acts 8, what can we say about the valuation of nonprocreative bodies in Luke-Acts? We can, in the first place, note that unlike others encountered by the Apostles in the course of their journeying, the Ethiopian eunuch is not physically transformed by his conversion. The extent to which the audience might have expected Philip to transform the eunuch depends on whether or not his ancient audiences saw him as defective or as of the socially ambiguous "third gender" (*tertius genus hominum*).[39] Did they know that his status was the result of an act of castration? While it is more likely that he was made a eunuch than born one, it is difficult to say.

All we can say for certain is that the Ethiopian eunuch was incapable of procreation. That Philip does not "fix" this condition suggests that the eunuch's body is already appropriately fashioned for the Kingdom of Heaven. Yong wishes to draw this out into a general statement about disability, but perhaps it is better understood in terms of the form of the eschatological body. The Ethiopian eunuch, like the woman with the flow of power, is reproductively incapacitated—and thus already perfected for the Kingdom of Heaven.

A somewhat different take on the question of fertility and infertility on the Day of Judgment emerges in Mark 13, the so-called "Markan Little Apocalypse." In this chapter, Jesus warns his apostles about the dangers and horrors of the Day of Judgment. It is a period when child will turn against parent, when time runs short and the faithful will have to flee, and when pregnancy will become a curse. The Markan Jesus says, "Woe to those who are pregnant and to those who are nursing infants in those days!"(Mark 13:17). It is certainly not the case that Mark is condemning pregnancy and child rearing; the rhetorical impact of the phrase lies in his assertion that the end of time will be a period of such horror that natural bonds will break down and causes of celebration will become a curse.

For others, the tension between fertility and eschatology was a question less of practicalities than of systems of reward. In the *Acts of Paul*, another apocryphal story of the travels and travails of the Apostles, Paul enters into a debate about the nature of the afterlife. His opponents suggest that the "rising" to which Christians can look forward is generational: in other words, we rise in our children.[40] A putative response to this idea is provided by Paul in *3 Corinthians*.[41] In *3 Corinthians* Paul objects that we rise in all of our "flesh . . . not even a hair nor an eyelash" will go astray.[42] The tension between the preservation of our bodies and the preservation of "ourselves" in our biological offspring is acutely felt here. It reflects an ancient tussle over resurrection, continued lineage, and the resurrection as reconstituted ligaments.

THE RESURRECTED BODY

Following the Day of Judgment, the new era would begin. Here too ancient authorities are divided about the nature of the afterlife. The biblical book of Daniel, for example, envisions an afterlife akin to Greco-Roman expectations of astral immortality. But discussions of life after physical death in this material world were cross-cultural. It was the subject of myth, rumor, speculation, and debate. The shape of the afterlife and discussions of its nature were the focus of intense speculation by Greek philosophers, Jewish visionaries, mystics, and priests alike. While reason and carefully cultivated personal mystical experiences played a role in these discussions, what these manifold articulations of the hereafter have in common is their uncertainty. The afterlife is essentially unknown and hypothetical. It is an experience that is predicated on assumptions about the nature of God, the good, and eternality, as well as on readings of traditional statements and texts about the nature of the soul, heaven and hell, Hades and paradise.

What this means, of course, is that discussions of what happens in heaven and what resurrected bodies will be *like* reflect contemporaneous views of ideal places, activities, bodies, and things. This is not just about good and evil; it is about aesthetics. These issues pertain to infertility insofar as most early Christians believed in the resurrection of the body. If these bodies are physical—if they can see, touch, taste, eat, breathe, and walk—then surely they can also have sex and reproduce.

One of the dominant early Christian understandings of the afterlife was that the body would be resurrected from the dead at the end of time. The resurrection of the dead was an idea rooted in the world of Hellenistic Judaism, watered by traditional and early claims about the resurrection of Jesus after his crucifixion, and cultivated in the Pauline churches. The resurrection of the dead is assumed in 1 Thessalonians 4:16–17, in which Paul promises his grieving community of followers in Thessalonica that their deceased relatives would rise first at the final trumpet, but it finds its fullest expression in 1 Corinthians 15.[43] "Fullest" is perhaps a misnomer here, because for all Paul's insistence on the resurrection of the dead, his emphasis on continuity and discontinuity and metaphors of risen bodies "glorious . . . like the stars" and sprouted like grown plants fail to put flesh on the bare bones of his theory.

Grounding his argument in the resurrection of Jesus (1 Cor 15:42), Paul is insistent that there will be a resurrected body, but its precise nature goes undescribed. Instead Paul notes merely, "So it is with the resurrection of the dead. What is sown is perishable, what is raised is imperishable. It is sown in dishonor, it is raised in glory. It is sown in weakness, it is raised in power. It is sown a physical body, it is raised a spiritual body. If there is a physical body, there is also a spiritual body" (1 Cor 15:42–44). There is in 1 Corinthians a clear relationship between the resurrected body and the earthly body. Paul describes his community as "sowing a bare seed" of the bodies that they will have in the future, but is clear that, while the bodies are related, they are not identical. It is left to future generations of Christians to parse the relationship between the two.

In the Gospel of Mark, written some thirty years after Paul's First Epistle to the Corinthians, the existence of the resurrection is something that can be assumed. In chapter 12 the Sadducees, well known for their opposition to the theory, come to Jesus to question him about his opinions on the afterlife. Their question pertains directly to levirate law:

> [The Sadducees asked him] "Teacher, Moses wrote for us that 'if a man's brother dies, leaving a wife but no child, the man shall marry the widow and raise up children for his brother.' There were seven brothers; the first married and, when he died, left no children; and the second married her and died, leaving no children; and the third likewise; none of the seven left children. Last of all the woman herself died. In the resurrection whose wife will she be? For the seven had married her." (Mark 12:19–23)

The question might sound like just the kind of technical hypothetical quandary in which we find ourselves immersed in the Mishnah, but here it is likely to be spoken in jest. It is less a genuine question about adjudicating marital relations in the afterlife than a snide commentary on the theory of bodily resurrection in general.

Adela Collins cites, by way of analogy to this passage, a question put by the "Alexandrians" to Rabbi Joshua ben Hananiah.[44] The Alexandrians enquired as to whether the resurrected dead would need to be purified on the third and seventh days to avoid ritual impurity (as those impure by contact with corpses were required to be by rabbinic law). He responded, "When they will be resurrected we shall go into the matter." The reply essentially communicates that in the resurrection all things would be revealed and the fundamental lack of knowledge that people have about the world to come.

In contrast, Jesus's confident response to the question asserts the fallacy of their belief in sexual relations in the afterlife. He states, "Is not this the reason you are wrong, that you know neither the scriptures nor the power of God? For when they rise from the dead, they neither marry nor are given in marriage, but are like angels in heaven" (12:24–25). He then proceeds to adduce biblical proof for the belief in the resurrection. But the social awkwardness of polyandry in the afterlife is moot, as the dead neither marry nor are given in marriage. Marital relations in heaven do not feature in contemporary Jewish descriptions of eschatological resurrection. Bodily resurrection is inferable from *1 Enoch* 22–27, 2 Maccabees, *4 Ezra* 7:28–44, and *2 Baruch* 29, but none of these accounts describe marriage or family.

On the basis of the famous scene of the revivification of dry bones in Ezekiel 37, at least one scholar has argued that many Jews living at the time of Jesus assumed that marital relations would continue in the resurrection.[45] This is because in this passage the bones that are brought to life go on to live normal lives and have children. At least some rabbis interpreted Ezekiel 37 as a foreshadowing of the eschatological resurrection.[46] These rabbinic sources were written sometime after the death of Jesus, so we shouldn't make sweeping statements about their relevance to first-century Palestine, but it is likely that some Jews living at the time of Jesus did believe in the continuation of marriage in the resurrection.[47]

Jesus seems to be in no doubt whatsoever about the nature of postresurrection marital life. Whereas just moments before

he had used wit to evade the questions of the Pharisees and
Herodians over tribute to Caesar (12:13–17), his response here
is straightforward and serious. The focus of his response is to
rebuff the claims of the Sadducees that they know scripture, but
in the course of rebuking them he states quite clearly that the
resurrected dead are unmarried, like the angels. Given that Jesus,
like all other ancient Jews, thought that sex should be reserved
for marriage, it seems that sex is eliminated in the afterlife. Moreover, the structural effects of marriage—of organizing society
into couples—are not present in the afterlife. For ancient Jews
and Christians the afterlife is a celebration of God, not a family
reunion. It is a vision of the afterlife that values fertility and infertility equally.

Some scholars have argued, on the basis of Jesus's statement
that we are not given in marriage in heaven, that Mark thinks that
the resurrection is spiritual, not physical, but the Markan Jesus
never says as much. All he says is that humans are like angels
with respect to marriage. While it is likely that he means humans
are transformed into angelic beings of the sort envisioned in Daniel 12 and contemporaneous texts, it is possible that Mark sees
the resurrected bodies as physical *and* barren or perhaps celibate.
Certainly this is how some Patristic authors would read him.

In the postapostolic era, proto-orthodox authors would interpret Paul as referring to the literal resurrection of physical bodies. The ambiguities about the specific valence of *soma* would be
washed away in a rhetorical contest between different Christian
authors that, in the end, tied authentic Christianity to the resurrection of the body.[48] The rhetorical contest is too protracted and
detailed for us to examine here, but it is important to note that the
nascent doctrine of the resurrection of the body played a crucial
role in defining what was and was not orthodoxy.[49] It was thus
with great care and a sense of the weightiness of the task that
Christians speculated about the nature of the resurrected body.

Over the course of the second century a gradual consensus about the eschaton and afterlife began to emerge, and the contours of the resurrected body began to be reasoned out and finely painted. Between Paul's ambiguous statement about resurrection and Augustine's methodical analysis, a number of authors jostled with one another. One key element in these discussions was the fleshing out of biblical language of eschatological healing. As we saw in our treatment of Isaiah, notions of the eschaton and life in God were frequently tied to images of bodily healing, restoration, and superabilities. This rhetoric of restoration and healing came to typify later Christians' attitudes to disability in general. Metaphors of perfection and healing could suggest the siphoning off of the objectional corruption that marred the physical body in the here and now.[50]

In his *Adversus Haereses*, Irenaeus, bishop of Lyons in the latter part of the second century, uses medical imagery to defend the corporeality of the resurrection. Throughout his treatment of the subject, Irenaeus anticipates that the second coming of Christ will bring with it widespread judgment followed by a period of eschatological cleansing: "At his coming 'the lame man shall leap as an hart, and the tongue of the dumb shall [speak] plainly, and the eyes of the blind shall be opened, and the ears of the deaf shall hear,' and that 'the hands which hang down, and the feeble knees, shall be strengthened,' and that 'the dead which are in the grave shall arise,' and that he himself 'shall take [upon him] our weaknesses, and bear our sorrows,'—[all these] proclaimed those works of healing which were accomplished by him."[51] Irenaeus structures his argument so that images of healing and resurrection parallel one another here—the "lame" walking and the dead rising are apparently synonymous acts. Death and deafness are essentially similar. The mechanics of the resurrection of the dead are described using the terminology of healing and strengthening rather than of purification or refinement. Irenaeus grounds his belief in bodily resurrection in the healing actions of Jesus during his lifetime.

For Irenaeus, the resurrection is foreshadowed in the ministry of Jesus. He poses the leading question "In what bodies did they [people Jesus healed during his earthly ministry] rise again?" and replies, "In those same, no doubt, in which they had also died." His argument mirrors Paul's statement in 1 Corinthians 15 that if there is no resurrection for followers of Jesus, there is no resurrection of Christ. But Irenaeus takes the argument further and extends it into the ministry of Jesus himself. His issue here is one of identity:

> For if it [the resurrected body] were not in the very same, then certainly those same individuals who had died did not rise again. For [the Scripture] says, "The Lord took the hand of the dead man, and said to him, Young man, I say to you, Arise. And the dead man sat up, and He commanded that something should be given him to eat; and He delivered him to his mother." . . . As, therefore, those who were healed [by Jesus] were made whole in those members [parts of the body] which had in times past been afflicted; and the dead rose in the identical bodies, their limbs and bodies receiving health, and that life which was granted by the Lord, who prefigures eternal things by temporal, and shows that it is He who is Himself able to extend both healing and life to His handiwork, that His words concerning its [future] resurrection may also be believed.[52]

Irenaeus then supplies a catena of scriptural quotations pertaining to Jesus's healings in order to demonstrate that they prefigure the resurrection. Jesus healed and raised people from the dead as proof that at the end of time God will heal and raise people from the dead in their bodies.

In offering a biblically based justification for the resurrection, Irenaeus reinforces the New Testament connection between healing and salvation, able-bodiedness and divine order. He utilizes to great effect the image of Jesus as soteriological physician come to "heal" the sinners (Mark 2:17). For Irenaeus, the continued presence of disability in the world is an indication that salvation is incomplete; the healing of the sick in the future will restore the world to its prefallen state.

At the same time, Irenaeus raises an important question about identity. He is concerned about the preservation of the individual's identity or, as Caroline Walker Bynum would call it, the individual's "me-ness" in the resurrection.[53] It is precisely for this reason that he dwells on the fate of the body and locates personal identity in the body's materiality. It must be resurrected because, without it, the person himself or herself is not truly resurrected. The sickness and impairments that currently plague the lives of some are not part of these identities; they are evidence that God's "handiwork [has been] impaired by wickedness" (5.12.6), and thus for Irenaeus they cannot find their way into the afterlife.

Irenaeus's deeply materialistic conception of the afterlife lays the groundwork for those who follow him. A pseudepigraphical treatise, *De Resurrectione* (On the Resurrection), attributed to the second-century Christian philosopher Justin Martyr, engaged skeptical philosophical opponents of bodily resurrection directly. Drawing upon Pauline notions of continuity and discontinuity and the materialistic tradition evident in Irenaeus, Pseudo-Justin argues that the body will be resurrected, only perfectly. An emblematic example for Pseudo-Justin is the role of infirmity in the resurrection. Against those who would suppose that disabled bodies rise disabled, Pseudo-Justin argues,

> Well, they say, if then the flesh rise, it must rise the same as it falls; so that if it die with one eye, it must rise one-eyed; if

lame, lame; if defective in any part of the body, in this part
the man must rise deficient. How truly blinded are they in
the eyes of their hearts! For they have not seen on the earth
blind men seeing again, and the lame walking by His word.
All things which the Saviour did, He did in the first place in
order that what was spoken concerning Him in the prophets might be fulfilled, "that the blind should receive sight,
and the deaf hear," and so on; but also to induce the belief
that in the resurrection the flesh shall rise entire. For if on
earth He healed the sicknesses of the flesh, and made the
body whole, much more will He do this in the resurrection,
so that the flesh shall rise perfect and entire. In this manner,
then, shall those dreaded difficulties of theirs be healed.[54]

Just like those of Irenaeus, Pseudo-Justin's theoretical opponents
appear to reproduce the traditional Greco-Roman idea that the
characteristics of a person's body are important for his or her
identity even after the body itself has died. If corpses are being
resuscitated, they argue, then the state of that corpse at death is
integral for determining its resurrected abilities. Pseudo-Justin's
opponents seem to be concerned with ability and identity because they have eschewed the obvious criticism of inquiring
about bodily decay and decomposed flesh. Even so there are
some clear indications that these bodily disabilities are negative.

The language of defection that Justin uses here is typical both
of the common ancient perspective that disability is deficiency
and also of the notion that these conditions form an integral and
enduring part of a person's identity. Pseudo-Justin's opponents
are not arguing for the resurrection of disabled bodies; they appear to be arguing either for astral immortality or for the immortality of the soul. Pseudo-Justin counters his philosophical opponents with biblical proof texts and salvation history. The process
of eschatological healing begun in stories of Jesus's healings in

Palestine will be completed in the eschatological transformation of the world. The author constructs a view of God's actions in history as a history of healing—a history of God acting to remove the deficient disability that mars God's otherwise perfect creation. The miraculous healings by Jesus and his followers were but an overture to the main eschatological performance.

In the frenzy of divine triage and re-creation that takes place in Pseudo-Justin's eschatological hospital there is no gynecology. Barrenness, the prototypical disability in the Hebrew Bible, is not revoked in the resurrection of the body. On the contrary, Pseudo-Justin breaks with earthly conventions and treats earthly infertility as anticipating the state of the resurrected body:

> The function of the womb is to become pregnant; and of the member of the male to impregnate. But as, though these members are destined to discharge such functions, it is not therefore necessary that they from the beginning discharge them (since we see many women who do not become pregnant, as those that are barren, even though they have wombs), so pregnancy is not the immediate and necessary consequence of having a womb; but those even who are not barren abstain from sexual intercourse, some being virgins from the first, and others from a certain time. And we see men also keeping themselves virgins, some from the first, and some from a certain time; so that by their means, marriage, made lawless through lust, is destroyed.[55]

In this passage, Pseudo-Justin turns to the function of the womb. He recognizes, in good Aristotelian form, that the "proper function" of the womb is to become pregnant, but sees barrenness as evidence against the necessity of pregnancy and the existence of procreation in heaven. In his refutation of heavenly procreation he cites the existence of barrenness and celibacy as prefigurations of the heavenly state. It is interesting that Pseudo-Justin, like other ancient authorities we examined in the previous chapter, links celibacy and sterility. Abstinence from sexual intercourse through celibacy joins the fertile to the infertile.

The effect of the passage is to reshape infertility as heavenly ideal. The barren body is reshaped as angelic. Pseudo-Justin's motivation here is to discredit the suggestion that there is procreation in heaven. But he nonetheless offers a model for evaluating the relative merits, status, and value of fertile and infertile bodies. It is the barren womb that anticipates the finality of God's plan for humanity. It is an arresting reversal of social hierarchies.

Pseudo-Justin goes on, in the following passage, to amass further evidence for infertility as divinely originating. In the tradition of Plutarch, who condemned Roman procreative behaviors through unfavorable comparison with animals, he cites examples from nature:

> And we find that some even of the lower animals, though possessed of wombs, do not bear, such as the mule; and the male mules do not beget their kind. So that both in the case of men and the irrational animals we can see sexual intercourse abolished; and this, too, before the future world. And our Lord Jesus Christ was born of a virgin, for no other reason than that He might destroy the begetting by lawless desire, and might show to the ruler that the formation of man was possible to God without human intervention. And when He had been born, and had submitted to the other conditions of the flesh—I mean food, drink, and clothing—this one condition only of discharging the sexual function He did not submit to; for, regarding the desires of the flesh, He accepted some as necessary, while others, which were unnecessary, He did not submit to. For if the flesh were deprived of food, drink, and clothing, it would be destroyed; but being deprived of lawless desire, it suffers no harm. And at the same time He foretold that, in the future world, sexual intercourse should be done away with; as He says, "The

children of this world marry, and are given in marriage; but the children of the world to come neither marry nor are given in marriage, but shall be like the angels in heaven." Let not, then, those that are unbelieving marvel, if in the world to come He do away with those acts of our fleshly members which even in this present life are abolished.[56]

The summit of Pseudo-Justin's argument is the example offered in the life of Jesus. Again appealing to similarities between virginity and sterility, he cites both the virgin birth and the celibacy of Jesus as examples of the irrelevancy of sexual acts in the divine plan. We are a far cry from both *The Da Vinci Code* and John Paul II's "Theology of the Body." For Pseudo-Justin sex is extraneous. It ranks lower in the hierarchy of bodily functions than food, drink, and clothing. Sex, and thus also childbearing and procreation, takes a tumble down the hierarchy of ancient Christian goods. If, as in Pseudo-Justin, heaven is the ideal and heavenly bodies are perfect bodies, it follows that in fullness of time barren bodies are ultimately superior. In this understanding, barrenness is not divine punishment or brokenness, it is the *telos* of human existence.

Pseudo-Justin and Irenaeus present radically materialistic visions of heaven, a materialism inherited and transmitted by Augustine, the father of Western Christianity. In his *City of God*, the resurrected body preserves the functions of the living body, even if it has no use for them. The blessed dine at heavenly banquets, even if they have no need for food. Yet the beatification of the body and the redemption of the flesh meant the obfuscation of infirmity. Even in the case of scarred martyrs, whose wounds were received as part of a divinely sanctified mission, their "blemishes" will not be visible in the world to come.[57] Augustine will not even permit us to call these marks "blemishes," so inconceivable does he find the very notion of heavenly wounds.

He is torn between his "desire to see in the kingdom of heaven the marks of the wounds which they received for Christ's name" and his belief that wounds (imperfections) do not exist in God's world.[58] In Augustine's heavenly city the body will have "no deformity, no infirmity, no heaviness, no corruption—nothing of any kind unfit for that kingdom."[59] He is insistent that anything "naturally present" in human bodies (e.g., intestines, eating) will be present at the resurrection but that "the natural" does not include "deformity" or "infirmity."[60]

While Pseudo-Justin, Irenaeus, and Augustine belong to Western orthodoxy and describe the resurrected state of the body, we know that there were other Christian groups who saw sex and reproduction as impediments to salvation in the present. In his summary of various philosophical approaches to marriage and procreation, Clement of Alexandria, a turn-of-the-second-century writer and philosopher, provides a description of an Egyptian group known as the Encratites. According to Clement, "they have received the resurrection, as they say, and for that reason they reject marriage."[61]

Other groups were less consistent. Augustine criticizes the Manicheans for avoiding procreation. In *Against Faustus* he describes this as "the unrighteous law of the Manichæans." He explains that "in order to prevent their god, whom they bewail as confined in all seeds, from suffering still closer confinement in the womb, requires married people not on any account to have children, their great desire being to liberate their god."[62] It is difficult for us to know both if this accusation accurately represents Manichean theology and whether or not the Manicheans were successful in engaging in sexual relations while avoiding pregnancy. The soft polemics against contraception embedded in Augustine's critique may foreshadow the accusations of improper use of contraceptives in religious communities today. What Clement and Augustine reveal, however, is that there were early Christians who chose to implement the principle of divine sterility in their own lives and replicate the statement of Jesus that heavenly bodies are unmarried. These groups may now be deemed heretical, but they illustrate the basic principle that, far from being anathema to divine will or a form of punishment, the refusal to have children can be an expression of heightened religiosity and a means of embodying the resurrection.

Although these groups are heretical, they represent an authentic way of living in accordance "with the Gospel" and a reading tradition in early Christianity. Among the orthodox, too, the idea of abstaining from sex in anticipation of the resurrection formed part of the conversation about virginity. In his reading of Gospel tradition, John Chrysostom remarks, "The angels do not marry nor are they given in marriage; nor does the virgin. Always are they waiting on and serving God: this too does the virgin."[63] The idea of living life with an eye on the eschaton led some Christians to eschew marriage and procreation. What they demonstrate to us is that it is not necessary to read the words of Jesus through a dominant model of fertility and prosperity.

CONCLUSION

Resurrected bodies are self-consciously idealized blanks onto which cultural and societal values are projected. In 1 Corinthians 15, Paul gave us very little with which to work. He gave us, instead, a concept: resurrected bodies are glorious bodies. And into this glorious body generations of Christian readers have read an array of physical attributes that constantly shift and yet always coalesce around notions of perfection.

In discussions of the resurrection of the body in general, the eradication of gender, race, and disability has been a source of concern to ethicists and historians. Rightly so. It is not—as Paul might say—that there is "neither Jew nor Greek, male nor female" in the Kingdom of Heaven. The result of the eradication of bodily differences is not that there is *no* race or gender in heaven, but rather that there is *only one* race and *only one* gender. Here on the celestial big screen are our projected bodily ideals. The difficulty with these homogenized cookie-cutter portraits of heavenly healing is not solely that they are projected but that they are also reflective. They inscribe and reinscribe a social hierarchy in which certain kinds of bodies are more highly prized. The idea that heavenly realities are the perfect models from which earthly realities are shoddily crafted comes crashing down when we realize that these models are crafted in our own image.[64]

The Patristic authors who argued for the resurrection of barren bodies are unlikely champions for our cause. Their motivation is much less about privileging infertility or overthrowing the dominant narrative of hyperfertility as divine blessing than it is about keeping sex out of heaven. But the prudishness of Patristic men may serve as the modern reader's tonic. In heaven, infertility is far from divine punishment. On the contrary: as we draw nearer to God, we leave behind us not only the pains of childbirth, but also the very necessity of procreation.

The understanding that the resurrected woman would be infertile was not an idiosyncratic reading of a traditional passage. On the contrary, the barrenness of the resurrected body was a fundamental tenet of proto-orthodox and Latin interpretations of the resurrected life. For all the idealization of pregnancy and childbirth during life, we would be hard-pressed to find an early Christian author who thought there would be procreation in the hereafter. While some descriptions of heaven portray all Christians as children in heaven, there is no child rearing. All receive new creation and reach maturity in God.

It is no small thing, therefore, to find that all of these perfect bodies are barren. The irony here is endless. These ancient authors are not budding identity politicians; they are corporeal idealists. And yet in the heavenly scourge that accompanies the resurrection from the dead all will find themselves eunuchs in the Kingdom of Heaven. The remarkable aspect of the elevation of infertility is not that it stands apart from other disabilities but rather that it stands as a part of a tableau of heavenly perfection. Barrenness is not the exception to the rule; it is the new rule. It is not the new normal; it is the heavenly ideal. Perhaps here the reflection of heavenly realities sheds helpful light onto earthly ones.

Conclusion

In Act IV of Shakespeare's *Macbeth*, the troubled hero visits three witches in order to learn his fate. They summon their masters—three apparitions—who predict that "none of woman born/Shall harm Macbeth." He leaves the witches with a sense of invincibility. For what man is not born of woman? It is only in the final act of the play, when he finally meets Macduff, that he learns that his rival was born via Cesarean. He was not "of woman born," but rather "from his mother's womb/untimely ripped" (V.10.15–16). In this moment Macbeth realizes that the prophecy has been fulfilled and death is close to hand.

The scene plays to all the conventions of ancient Greek Delphic prophecies. A haughty leader misunderstands a prophecy and is ultimately undone by it. In this particular case, though, what blinded Macbeth was not merely hubris, but the power of accepted notions of what is "natural" and what is unthinkable. So ingrained were the conventions of natural birth that he could conceive of no other means by which a man could enter the world. He could not imagine the exceptional birth, and thus, despite all the evidence to the contrary, he could not see Macduff coming.

Normative understandings of childbirth and fertility figuratively blind readers of the Bible as well. But in the reception of biblical prophecies it is not the closed-minded interpreter who is ultimately harmed, but rather those that the interpreter fails to see. If the Bible were to be reduced to a single concentrated message on fertility, it would be of the goodness and blessing of fertility and childbearing. There is of course nothing inherently problematic about such a position—until it entails a negative corollary, that infertility and childlessness are punishment, or curse, or simply wrong. Such an argument develops almost by necessity when, as has traditionally been the case, the Bible is indeed reduced to a single message on fertility. In the preceding chapters, we have made the case that such reductive readings of the biblical materials are misguided—that there are, in the Bible and in the cultural contexts from which it emerged, conceptions of infertility that push back strongly against the dominant paradigm.

The inability to become pregnant, or the loss of a pregnancy, is often accompanied by feelings of guilt: perhaps some activity, habit, or dietary choice is at the root of this misfortune. These feelings are greatly exacerbated when compounded with religious doctrines and norms that associate infertility with sin—be it premarital sex or some other. The infertile are encouraged, implicitly or explicitly, to look within themselves to find the root of their unhappiness, or the strength to overcome it—this especially in situations where medical testing is frowned upon.

The stories of the barren matriarchs in the Hebrew Bible directly rebut such notions. Though they do eventually give birth, it is the beginnings of their stories, not the ends, that reveal a very different attitude toward infertility. These women are as blameless as any biblical characters—and yet they suffer from childlessness. As they search for answers, they do not look within themselves for some moral flaw, but rather turn directly to God. In doing so, they replicate and reinforce a common, though often forgotten, aspect of ancient Near Eastern thought: that in order for any conception and pregnancy to take place, there has to be active intervention on the part of the deity. The default state of humanity is not fertile. God must "open the womb." And, as the stories of the matriarchs make clear, even in cases of morally perfect women, sometimes God neglects this sacred and promised duty. It is natural to want to attribute blame. But the matriarchal narratives, and the Near Eastern cultural context in which they participate, ensure that the blame does not lie with the infertile woman.

At the same time that they relieve the woman from blame, these biblical texts openly recognize that there remains a social stigma attached to infertility. In this way they speak to the present as much as to the past, for we hardly need to look far to find just such stigma attached to the childless woman—whether childless by choice or not—in our own time. By giving this stigma expression through the attitudes and voices of the narrative antagonists, however, the biblical authors send the message that such behavior is not to be condoned. It is an irony of interpretation that the attitudes expressed by Hagar and Peninnah should have become the normative stance toward infertility. But we need not be beholden to the normative stance. We can affirm instead the values embedded in and promoted by the matriarchal narratives themselves.

So much of the stigmatization of childlessness stems from the perception—and the codification of this perception in popular rhetoric—that having children is "natural," despite the fact that until the last century it was also regularly life-threatening for both mother and infant. This view of childbearing is reinforced by reference to the first biblical command, "be fruitful and multiply," which transmutes an abstract sense of the "natural" into a divinely authorized definition of what it means to be human. Cultural attitudes, and the behaviors that derive from them, are grounded in an eternally validating biblical verse.

But this is where the power of received tradition forces biblical meaning into a straitjacket. In the attempt to make the ancient words relevant in every generation, context—historical and, equally, literary—is lost. In this case what goes unobserved is that within the narrative of the Hebrew Bible, the blessing to be fruitful and multiply is not given to all humans for all time. It is bound to its contexts, be they the stories of Adam, Noah, Abraham, or Jacob. We may aspire to emulate these figures, but we are under no obligation to do so. The Bible abounds with childless, even unmarried, perfectly natural and judgment-free individuals. The raising of "be fruitful and multiply" to a universal and timeless divine imperative is an interpretive choice. It is not demanded by the text; in fact it ignores important aspects of the text's presentation of this blessing.

Most notably, universalistic interpretations of the blessing of fertility fail to notice that, after Genesis 1, it is delivered exclusively to men. Women's fertility is treated in a very different manner, with the curse of Eve in Genesis 3. The standard interpretation of this curse, as introducing pain into the labor and delivery process, is tied up with concepts of original sin, with depictions of a pain-free postpartum Mary, and, undoubtedly, with the modern notion of drug-free birth being natural and even cleansing in some spiritual sense. But as we have argued, Genesis 3 quite possibly meant something completely different: not the existence of pain in childbirth, but the existence of childbirth itself. Eve is cursed with fertility. This interpretation, which is grounded firmly in the linguistic and literary context, drastically reimagines the question of what is "natural," what is "blessed," and what is "good." And, as even some ancient biblical interpreters recognized, it shifts the responsibility for fulfilling the blessing of "be fruitful and multiply"—and any condemnation that comes with the lack of fulfillment—off the shoulders of women.

By elevating fertility to a divine mandate, traditional readings imply that barrenness diminishes the perfection of God's created order, that its existence is a blemish that must be explained (or, in modern terms, diagnosed). Yet there are passages in the Bible, specifically the curses and blessings found in Exodus, Leviticus, and Deuteronomy, that, by depicting alternative potential states of being, be they positive or negative, shine a light on the state of the world as we know it, as it was created. The world these passages depict is one in which barrenness is a given; it is not desirable, but neither is it so uncommon as to be extraordinary. In line with Mesopotamian myths depicting the origins of humanity, these biblical texts suggest that the variety of human experience is not a deficiency, but merely reality; not a bug, but a feature. This suggests a dramatic change in the way infertility, and infertile women, should be perceived and treated.

Our readings of the matriarchal narratives, the blessing and curse formulations in the Hebrew Bible, and their ancient Near Eastern contexts stand in opposition to the long-standing association of infertility with sin, punishment, and shame. It is in the book of Isaiah, however—the biblical author who uses the imagery of infertility more broadly and more deftly than any other— that we see barrenness being raised above mere acceptability. Isaiah returns to the matriarchal stories, but reimagines them, repurposes them for his own time and place, and equates the barren matriarchs with the heroine of his book, barren Mother Zion. In so doing, the prophet invests stories about the past with meaning for the future, and elevates the barren woman to something like a foreshadowing of the eschatological era to come.

From this prophetic seed bloomed a dazzling array of interpretations, discourses about the state of the infertile woman in the world to come. In one respect, the very existence of these disparate readings, and the distance between them and their biblical sources—a distance enforced by the contingencies of historical circumstance—is itself worthy of notice. Tradition is not unilinear or univocal; it need not be equated with the conventions that precipitated from it. Difference of opinion neither started nor ended with the biblical text, but has been a constant in religious discourse for all time.

More specifically, however, we may hear in the postbiblical Jewish discussions of eschatological infertility the ringing absence of any moral judgment on the barren woman. In the world to come, she will be exalted—though the nature of that exaltation, whether through restored fertility, superabundant fertility, or the absence of even the desire for fertility, is up for discussion. Because the world to come is beyond our ability to perceive, we are all guessing as to what it will be like, what will be preserved of this world, what will be valued. It says something awfully important, then, that with all this uncertainty, the secure place of the barren woman remains constant.

In turning to the New Testament and the extraordinary birth of Jesus, we found that the privileging of biological parenthood and "natural" or "normal" modes of procreation is difficult to sustain in the Gospels. The anxiety over the biological connection between God and Christ is held taut by the repulsive notion of the transcendent deity lying down with the dirt. Sinless or not, clay creatures muddy the saving waters of the incarnation. The intellectual struggle to preserve the dynasty of God while simultaneously protecting the transcendent deity from the sticky mess of reproduction found a rather elegant solution in the Gospel of Mark.

Even in a modern world supposedly oriented toward compassion, openness, and empathy, adoption and adopted children continue to receive second-class status. For every Brad Pitt and Angelina Jolie there is a low-brow chat show dedicated to scrutinizing morality and parenthood in a laboratory through DNA testing. The comparably novel ability to test paternity allows us to fixate on biological parenting and denigrate adoptive parenthood as somehow second-rate and undesirable. The common representation of adoption as charity only further smothers the ideals of parenthood with the oppressive weight of guilt and expected gratitude.

What the evidence from the Roman world shows us is that it was not always thus and does not have to be so. The adopted child was often the beloved and the process of adopting often advantageous. The same can be said of the Hebrew Bible. Whether or not legal formulas were employed, the familial group and the conception of family were more amorphous than is usually recognized. In a world before blood groups, Watson and Crick, and Maury Povich, paternity was always slightly in question. As hyperattentive as ancient peoples were to issues of parenting, begetting, and policing offspring, parenthood itself was practiced.

This interest in making rather than begetting families flourished in the writings of Paul and his interpreters. Paul's ambiguous approach to marriage and procreation, while consonant with certain elements of ancient thought, contributed to the idea that celibacy was a preferable alternative to procreation. Yet, while modern readers posit a firm moral division between childlessness by choice and childlessness by impairment, the story of Peter's daughter undermines this division. That married early Christians of the fourth and fifth centuries chose to live in celibate marriage further undermines the extent to which ancient Christians saw a stark difference between the married and those who took religious orders. Such examples deconstruct the way that we think about childlessness in society. It was one form of a life validated by God. Where we might expect to find an interest in biological offspring, early Christians placed a family of believers. It was not that imagery or metaphors of marriage and procreation were abandoned or that Christians did not procreate, but there were some blurred boundaries between the monk and the married man.

For those interested in following Paul's suggestions about procreation, their eyes were fixed firmly on heaven. It is in speculation about the afterlife that conventional understandings about infertility as divine judgment or marital failure meet their comeuppance. The barren womb is, in the opinions of Pseudo-Justin, Irenaeus, and others, a prefiguration of the eschaton. And, at the end of time, all will cease to bear children. That Irenaeus and Pseudo-Justin group barrenness with celibacy again undercuts the conventional division between the two. The most striking element of this reversal of conventional valuations of infertility is that these are authors who describe the resurrected body as eschatologically healed and biologically perfect. These are authors who restore all "defects" and "deficiencies" at the eschaton. We do not have to agree with them, but their understanding of resurrection as infertility and infertility as a prefiguration of the heavenly demonstrates its importance in the plan of God. In the end, and at the end, infertility is not deficiency, punishment, or failure; it is the God-given state.

Whatever one's approach to the Bible, as holy scripture or as ancient library, it cannot be denied that the biblical texts, and more specifically the culturally accepted perception of what those texts mean, have had enormous influence on how we in modern society view and treat infertility and those who are childless. The basic notion, explicit or implicit in virtually every religious and scholarly treatment of the Bible, that fertility is a blessing and a good permeates our literature, our pulpits, our medical establishment, and our public policy.

The strength of convention is such that often the standard interpretation comes to seem almost inevitable, inescapable: the historically dominant line of reading is assumed to be the one that was "intended" by the biblical authors. This, however, is a trick of the eye; we look backward with tunnel vision, unable to see the many possible interpretive paths that could have been taken, given different historical and cultural contingencies.

If we are to take the Bible seriously as a source of insight into the human condition, we are obligated to treat with equal seriousness those claims present in the biblical text that did not receive the blessing of orthodox tradition. As we draw back the curtain of modern "natural" assumptions about fertility we are able to hear again and rehabilitate ideas and arguments that have been buried under the accumulated centuries of interpretation. That has been the aim of this book: to pull to the surface and give new voice to ancient ideas about infertility, ideas that challenge, forcefully and quite directly, conventional views.

NOTES

NOTES TO INTRODUCTION

1. Myra Marx Ferree, "Angela Merkel. What Does It Mean to Run as a Woman?," *German Politics and Society* 24 (2006): 93–107, and idem, "The Rise and Fall of 'Mommy Politics': Feminism and German Unification," *Feminist Studies* 19 (1993): 89–115.

2. Merkel and other childless political leaders like New Zealand Prime Minister Helen Clark and "spinster" politicians such as former US Attorney General Janet Reno and former US Secretary of State Condoleezza Rice have faced sharp scrutiny about their motivations and femininity. See Donatella Campus, *Women Political Leaders and the Media* (New York: Palgrave Macmillan, 2013), 97.

3. The phenomenon of the "phantom pregnancy" (pseudocyesis) is attested in the Hippocratic corpus. That it manifests the same symptoms as pregnancy could lead to confusion about a person's procreative status. Thus, at risk of being sticklers for details, we must point out that until a woman carries a child to term it is difficult to confirm that she or her partner was actually fertile.

4. See Arthur L. Greil, "The Hidden Infertile: Infertile Women without Pregnancy Intent in the United States," *Fertility and Sterility* 93 (2010): 2080–83.

5. This concept of disability is sometimes referred to as the "cultural model" of disability. It has had a significant impact on the subfield of critical disability studies in biblical scholarship. For further discussion

of this model's use among biblical scholars and its differences from the so-called social model, see Nyasha Junior and Jeremy Schipper, "Disability Studies and the Bible," in *New Meaning for Ancient Texts: Recent Approaches to Biblical Criticisms and their Applications*, ed. Steven L. McKenzie and Jonathan Kaltner (Louisville: Westminster John Knox, 2013), 21–37; Candida R. Moss and Jeremy Schipper, "Introduction," in *Disability Studies and Biblical Literature* (New York: Palgrave Macmillan, 2011), 1–13 (here 2–8); Rebecca Raphael, *Biblical Corpora: Representations of Disability in Hebrew Biblical Literature* (LHBOTS 445; London: T&T Clark, 2008), 8–11; Jeremy Schipper, *Disability and Isaiah's Suffering Servant* (Oxford: Oxford University Press, 2011), 14–30; idem, *Disability Studies and the Hebrew Bible: Figuring Mephibosheth in the David Story* (LHBOTS 441; New York: T&T Clark, 2006), 15–24.

6. In a series of publications, sociologist Arthur L. Greil studied the socio-psychological impact of infertility on both men and women. Prior to 1997, the date of Greil's first study ("Infertilty and Psychological Distress: A Critical Review of the Literature," *Social Science and Medicine* 45 [1997]: 16–79), the majority of descriptive studies of infertility treated it as a "psychologically devastating experience, especially for women." Prior to the 1980s, when infertility treatments became accessible to the public, the majority of social-scientific research into infertility assumed that it was a condition affecting women and that it was primarily a psychological condition, in the sense both that it was rooted in psychological factors and that it caused emotional distress. With the advent of fertility treatments, the psychological theories for the cause of infertility were left by the wayside, but the notion that infertility causes psychological distress and that this stress may contribute to infertility continues to proliferate.

7. See Arthur L. Greil and Julia McQuillan, "Help-Seeking Patterns among Subfecund Women," *Journal of Reproductive and Infant Psychology* 22 (2004): 305–19.

8. Access to care greatly affects the experience of infertility in both developing and developed countries. Ethnic minorities in the United States, the United Kingdom, and the Netherlands have less access to care than do non-Hispanic whites; see L. J. Beckman and S. M. Harvey, "Current Reproductive Technologies: Increased Access and Choice?," *Journal of Social Issues* 61 (2005): 1–20; M. Bitler and L. Schmidt, "Health Disparities and Infertility: Impacts of State Level Mandates," *Fertility and Steril-*

ity 85 (2006): 858–64; L. Culley and N. Hudson, "Disrupted Reproduction and Deviant Bodies: Pronatalism and British South Asian Communities," *International Journal of Diversity in Organisations, Communities and Nations* 5 (2006): 117–26, and idem, "Public Understandings of Science: British South Asian Man's Conceptions of Third Party Assisted Conception," *International Journal of Interdisciplinary Social Sciences* 2 (2007): 79–86; M. B. Henne and K. Bundorf, "Insurance Mandates and Trends in Infertility Treatments," *Fertility and Sterility* 89 (2008): 66–73; M. C. Inhorn and M. H. Fakih, "Arab Americans, African Americans, and Infertility: Barriers to Reproduction and Medical Care," *Fertility and Sterility* 85 (2005): 844–52; and L. White, J. McQuillan, and A. L. Greil, "Explaining Disparities in Treatment Seeking: The Case of Infertility," *Fertility and Sterility* 85 (2005): 853–57. While these studies rarely adjust for religious beliefs, it should be noted that in Massachusetts less educated and poor women are underrepresented; see T. Jain, "Socioeconomic and Racial Disparities among Infertility Patients Seeking Care," *Fertility and Sterility* 85 (2005): 876–81.

9. See E. C. Feinberg et al., "Economics May Not Explain Hispanics' Underutilization of Assisted Reproductive Technology and Services," *Fertility and Sterility* 88 (2007): 1439–41. There may be a correlation between the underrepresentation of Hispanic women at military fertility clinics and the high proportion of Hispanics who self-identify as practicing Roman Catholics.

10. John Chrysostom, *De sacerdotio* 3.16.318.

11. Lynn Clark Callister, "The Pain and the Promise of Unfilled Dreams: Infertile Couples," in *Handbook of Families and Health: Interdisciplinary Perspectives*, ed. D. Russell Crane and Elaine S. Marshall (Thousand Oaks, CA: Sage, 2006), 96–112 (here 98).

12. For the distinction, see Erving Goffman, *Stigma: Notes on the Management of Spoiled Identity* (Englewood Cliffs, NJ: Prentice Hall, 1963), 4.

13. Nancy J. Herman and Charlene E. Miall, "Positive Consequence of Stigma: Two Case Studies in Mental and Physical Disability," *Qualitative Sociology* 13 (1990): 251–69 (here 253).

14. http://www.catholicnews.com/data/stories/cns/1402247.htm.

15. http://time.com/2911630/japan-politician-sorry-for-heckling-female-colleague/.

16. Ruth Sunderland, "Childless Is Not a Synonym for Weird," *Guardian*, May 23, 2009, http://www.guardian.co.uk/commentisfree/2009/may/24/women-feminism-childless-ruth-sunderland.

17. Callister, "Pain and the Promise," 98.

18. Quoted in Laura Clark, "Childless Women 'Vilified by Bosses': Why Not Having a Family Could Ruin Your Career," *Daily Mail*, May 18, 2009, http://www.dailymail.co.uk/femail/article-1183895/Childless-women-vilified-bosses-Why-NOT-having-family-ruin-career.html.

19. James G. Evans, "Barrenness: Its Cause, Curse, and Cure," *Physical Culture* 9 (1903): 428–29.

20. http://www.cch.com/press/news/2010/20100308t.asp.

21. This does not mean that women who elect to have large families feel comfortable in society as a whole. Just as childless women are cast as cold and unfeminine, women with large families report feeling stigmatized as fundamentalists who unduly and selfishly contribute to overpopulation and the depletion of the world's resources.

22. The issue of how to treat this passage was a live one even in the ancient world (see John Chrysostom, "Homily XIV," "Homily IX"; Augustine, *De Trinitate* XII.7.11; Jerome, *Letter LXXIX. To Salvina* 7). For an overview of the question, see Stanley E. Porter, "What Does It Mean to Be 'Saved by Childbirth' (1Timothy 2.15)?," *JSNT* 49 (1993): 87. More apologetic arguments include that of George Montague, who argues that Paul "could hardly mean that women needed to be childbearers in order to be saved, since he commends virginity in 1 Cor 7:25–35. Rather, he is pointing to the more usual state of life of women" (George T. Montague, et al., *First and Second Timothy, Titus*, Catholic Commentary on Sacred Scripture [Grand Rapids, MI: Baker, 2008], 69). Others, like Benjamin Fiore, see the author as maintaining social order and promoting conventional Jewish social ethics (Benjamin Fiore, *The Pastoral Epistles: First Timothy, Second Timothy, Titus*, Sacra Pagina Series, ed. Daniel J. Harrington [Collegeville, MN: Liturgical Press, 2007], 69) or as having written this passage as part of anti-Gnostic propaganda (see Sebastian Fuhrmann, "Saved by Childbirth: Struggling Ideologies, the Female Body and a Placing of 1 Tim 2:15a," *Neotestamentica* 44 [2010]: 34).

23. Jessie Fischbein, *Infertility in the Bible: How the Matriarchs Changed Their Fate and How You Can Too* (Jerusalem: Devora, 2005), 132.

24. See, e.g., R. Matthews and A. M. Matthews, "Infertility and Involuntary Childlessness: The Transition to Nonparenthood," *Journal of Marriage and the Family* 48 (1986): 641–49.

25. On the persistently "abled" bias in religious tradition and in scholarship, see particularly Amos Yong, *The Bible, Disability, and the Church: A New Vision of the People of God* (Grand Rapids, MI: Eerdmans, 2011).

26. Charis M. Thompson, "Fertile Ground: Feminists Theorize Infertility," in *Infertility Around the Globe: New Thinking on Childlessness, Gender and Reproductive Technologies*, ed. Marcia C. Inhorn and Frank van Balen (Berkeley: University of California Press, 2002), 53–57.

27. D. C. Parry, "Work, Leisure, and Support Groups: An Examination of the Ways Women with Infertility Respond to Pronatalist Ideology," *Sex Roles* 53 (2005): 337–46; T.-J. Su and Y.-C. Chen, "Transforming Hope: The Lived Experience of the Infertile Woman Who Terminated Treatment after In Vitro Fertilization Failure," *Journal of Nursing Research* 14 (2006): 46–53; M. Ulrich and A. Weatherall, "Motherhood and Infertility: Viewing Motherhood through the Lens of Infertility," *Feminism & Psychology* 10 (2000): 323–26.

CHAPTER 1: THE MATRIARCHS AS MODELS

1. On this meaning of the ever-difficult phrase *mana 'aḥat 'appayim* in 1 Sam 1:5, see S. R. Driver, *Notes on the Hebrew Text and the Topography of the Books of Samuel* (Oxford: Clarendon, 1960), 7–8.

2. All translations from the Hebrew Bible are those of the NJPS, and all those of the Apocrypha and New Testament are from the NRSV, unless otherwise noted.

3. In addition to the reference to the aphrodisiacal properties of the mandrake in Song 7:14, see Theophrastus, *Enquiry into Plants* 9.9.1 and perhaps also Aristotle, *De somno et vigilia* 456b, where mandrakes are clearly marked as a narcotic. See the discussion in R. K. Harrison, "The Mandrake and the Ancient World," *EvQ* 28 (1956): 87–92.

4. See the characterization of these stories by Athalya Brenner, *The Israelite Woman: Social Role and Literary Type in Biblical Narrative* (Sheffield: JSOT, 1985), 93: "Their chief aim in life is to become biological mothers."

5. Esther Fuchs points out that while there are men in the Bible who seem to avoid reproduction—Onan in Genesis 38 most notably—there are no such women, as if to suggest that "woman is not even shown to be capable of *not* desiring sons" ("The Literary Characterization of Mothers and Sexual Politics in the Hebrew Bible," *Semeia* 46 [1989]: 151–66 [here 162]). To this point we may add the presence in Ugaritic myth of a childless female deity, 'Anat, who is portrayed as being desperate to bear a son (see Hennie J. Marsmann, *Women in Ugarit and Israel: Their Social and Religious Position in the Context of the Ancient Near East* [OTS 49; Leiden: Brill, 2003], 209–11).

6. For a brief overview of this so-called Dark Age, see Amihai Mazar, *Archaeology of the Land of the Bible*, vol. 1 (ABRL; New York: Doubleday, 1992), 287–91.

7. Carol Meyers, *Discovering Eve: Ancient Israelite Women in Context* (New York: Oxford University Press, 1988), 71.

8. Ibid., 165–66.

9. The major exceptions would be the state administration, which was typically very small, and the temple-based economies at the sanctuaries scattered throughout the land.

10. Carol Meyers, "The Family in Early Israel," in *Families in Ancient Israel* (The Family, Religion, and Culture; Louisville: Westminster John Knox, 1997), 1–47 (here 27).

11. Meyers, *Discovering Eve*, 61.

12. See Daniel I. Block, "Marriage and Family in Ancient Israel," in *Marriage and Family in the Biblical World*, ed. Ken M. Campbell; Downers Grove, IL: InterVarsity, 2003), 33–102 (here 94).

13. Meyers, "Family," 32–33.

14. KTU 1.17 i 26–32.

15. In the Bible, we find the clearest references to it in prohibitions, particularly in Leviticus. Of course, these very prohibitions attest to the presence and prevalence of just such a cult in Israelite society at large. On the cult of the dead in ancient Israel, see the seminal work of Elizabeth Bloch-Smith, *Judahite Burial Practices and Beliefs about the Dead* (JSOTS 123; Sheffield: Sheffield Academic, 1992), 109–51.

16. Karel van der Toorn, *Family Religion in Babylonia, Syria, and Israel* (SHCANE 7; Leiden: Brill, 1996), 62; Gay Robins, *Women in Ancient Egypt* (London: British Museum, 1993), 76–77.

17. The rabbis turned having a son from a desideratum into a near requirement: "The Holy One, blessed be he, is filled with anger against any one who does not leave a son to be his heir" (*b. B. Bat.* 116a).

18. Candida R. Moss, *The Myth of Persecution: How Early Christians Invented a Story of Martyrdom* (New York: HarperOne, 2013), 32; Elizabeth A. Castelli, *Martyrdom and Memory: Early Christian Culture Making* (New York: Columbia University Press, 2004).

19. See, from a Mesopotamian prayer for fertility, "Give me a name and a descendant!" (Karel van der Toorn, *From Her Cradle to Her Grave: The Role of Religion in the Life of the Israelite and the Babylonian Woman* [BibSem 23; Sheffield: JSOT, 1994], 80). So too a Mesopotamian medical text: "That woman will become [pregnant] and she will acquire a name" (Marten Stol, *Birth in Babylonia and the Bible: Its Mediterranean Setting* [Groningen: Styx, 2000], 53).

20. Carol Meyers, *Rediscovering Eve: Ancient Israelite Women in Context* (New York: Oxford University Press, 2013), 98–99.

21. By the rabbinic period, the centrality of childbirth had become even more entrenched: "For what was the world created except for being fruitful and multiplying?" (*m. Eduy.* 1.13). This phrase, "be fruitful and multiply," is translated here and throughout according to the more traditional NRSV, rather than the NJPS, which has "be fertile and increase."

22. http://www.medicalnewstoday.com/articles/259262.php.

23. Richard Whitekettle, "Human Reproduction in the Textual Record of Mesopotamia and Syria-Palestine during the First and Second Millennia B.C." (Ph.D. diss., Yale University, 1995), 38. See similarly the marriage contract quoted in Raymond Westbrook, "The Female Slave," in *Gender and Law in the Hebrew Bible and the Ancient Near East*, ed. Victor H. Matthews, Bernard M. Levinson, and Tikva Frymer-Kensky (Sheffield: Sheffield Academic, 1998), 216. In the biblical text it is pointedly the women who have the idea and make the offer, while in the Mesopotamian marriage contracts it appears to be the man who is the active party.

24. Note the ancient Sumerian proverb: "Marrying several wives is human; getting many children is divine" (Karel van der Toorn, *Sin and Sanction in Israel and Mesopotamia: A Comparative Study* [Assen: Van Gorcum, 1985], 85). The rabbis surmised that Elkanah married Peninnah at Hannah's urging, just as Sarah had urged Abraham to take Hagar as a concubine (*Pes. Rab.* 43.6).

25. Whitekettle, "Human Reproduction," 41.

26. Martha Roth, "Marriage and Matrimonial Property in the First Millennium B.C.," in *Women's Earliest Records from Ancient Egypt and Western Asia*, ed. B. S. Lesko (BJS 166; Atlanta: Scholars, 1989), 245–60 (here 251).

27. *m. Yeb.* 6.6. See further Judith R. Baskin, *Midrashic Women: Formations of the Feminine in Rabbinic Literature* (Brandeis Series on Jewish Women; Hanover, NH: Brandeis University Press, 2002), 126–28. In some modern Muslim societies, men are encouraged to take a second wife if the first proves to be infertile. See A. Merve Demircioğlu, "The Rhetoric of Belief and Identity Making in the Experience of Infertility," *Culture and Religion* 11 (2010): 51–67 (here 59); Callister, "Pain and the Promise," 98.

28. Marsmann, *Women*, 176.

29. Miriam Lichtheim, *Ancient Egyptian Literature: Volume III: The Late Period* (Berkeley: University of California, 2006), 79.

30. *t. Yeb.* 8.4. See also Philo, *Special Laws* 3.6.34–36.

31. On the generalized meaning of the phrase "something obnoxious," *'erwat dabar*, see Jeffrey Tigay, *The JPS Torah Commentary: Deuteronomy* (Philadelphia: Jewish Publication Society, 1996), 221.

32. Virtually the same options—divorce or taking a second wife—remain the standard protocols in modern Nigeria. See M. O. Araoye, "Epidemiology of Infertility: Social Problems of the Infertile Couples," *Western African Journal of Medicine* 22 (2003): 190–96.

33. Although there is no clear evidence of the participation of women in the Israelite ancestral cult, this may be due simply to the limited scope and genre of our sources. It is noteworthy that in Mesopotamia there is no question of the inclusion of female ancestors in the cult of the dead; we have an Old Babylonian prayer for the ancestor cult in which the names and relationships of the deceased are to be recited, including grandmother, mother, and sister (van der Toorn, *Family Religion*, 52–54).

34. On celibacy in the ancient world, see Dale Launderville, *Celibacy in the Ancient World: Its Ideal and Practice in Pre-Hellenistic Israel, Mesopotamia, and Greece* (Collegeville, MN: Liturgical Press, 2010).

35. John Van Seters, "The Problem of Childlessness in Near Eastern Law and the Patriarchs of Israel," *JBL* 87 (1968): 401–8 (here 403–4).

36. Ibid., 403; A. K. Grayson and John Van Seters, "The Childless Wife in Assyria and the Stories of Genesis," *Orientalia* 44 (1975): 485–86.

37. Brenner, *Israelite Woman*, 94. Though she means this as ironic commentary on the way that women are depicted by the male authors of the Bible, Brenner's characterization of the social phenomenon may well be accurate, if overstated for rhetorical reasons.

38. *Gen. Rab.* 71.5. On the rabbinic appreciation of the untenable social situation of a barren woman, see Baskin, *Midrashic Women*, 130–31.

39. A midrash describes Sarah reprimanding Abraham for this very reason: "Had you said 'We are childless,' then as he gave you a child, so would he have given me; since, however, you said 'I go childless' (Gen 15:2), he gave you a child but not me. . . . Had you said 'to us you have given no offspring,' then as he gave you so would he have given me; since, however, you said 'to me you have given no offspring' (Gen 15:3), he gave to you but not to me" (*Gen. Rab.* 45.5).

40. Fuchs, "Literary Characterization," 162.

41. See Gay Becker, "Metaphors in Disrupted Lives: Infertility and Cultural Constructions of Continuity," *Medical Anthropology Quarterly* 8 (1994): 383–410 (here 384).

42. Stol, *Birth*, 36.

43. Whitekettle, "Human Reproduction," 86–88.

44. *Gen. Rab.* 71.6; *b. Avod. Zar.* 5a. See also "One who has no child is as if dead and demolished" (*Gen. Rab.* 45.2).

45. *Tanḥ. B.* Wayyetse 19.

46. The rabbis accurately assessed the situation by equating infertile women with prisoners: trapped with no means of escape, surviving by the will of others alone; at the same time, unwilling or unworthy to show one's face in public for the shame (*Gen. Rab.* 71.1).

47. See Fuchs, "Literary Characterization," 157–58.

48. See Stol, *Birth*, 35.

49. Whitekettle, "Human Reproduction," 37. For the Egyptian reference to the seed/field metaphor, see Miriam Lichtheim, *Ancient Egyptian Literature: Volume I: The Old and Middle Kingdoms* (Berkeley: University of California Press, 1973), 69: "She is a fertile field for her lord." In rabbinic literature, a similar metaphor is used in which rain is described as "the husband of the earth" (*b. Ta'an* 6b), with reference to Isa 55:10—"For as the rain and the snow come down from heaven, and do not return there until they have watered the earth, making it bring forth and sprout"—in

which the word "bring forth" is the same Hebrew term as that used for bearing a child. The fertilized field is feminine, whether the masculine partner is seed or rain.

50. A Mesopotamian curse has been taken as evidence of male infertility: "May your semen dry up like that of a barren eunuch" (JoAnn Scurlock and Burton R. Andersen, *Diagnoses in Assyrian and Babylonian Medicine: Ancient Sources, Translations, and Modern Medical Analyses* [Urbana-Champaign: University of Illinois Press, 2005], 113). The image employed in this curse, however, is not of a male with normal sexual function who is unable to produce offspring, but of a male with abnormal sexual function: with "dried up" semen. This image suggests at least the inability to ejaculate, if not also the inability to achieve an erection, and thus falls more accurately under the category of male impotency rather than male infertility. Similarly, the Ugaritic epic of Aqhat depicts a king, Dan'il, who prays desperately for a son, the absence of which might suggest that he suffers from male infertility (on the assumption that, as king, he had his pick of sexual partners). Yet the emphasis of his plea is on the specific maleness of the desired offspring: he wants an heir to the throne—this is the thrust of his meaning when he mentions that his brothers all have sons, as they would then stand in the line of royal accession—and a child that will care for him in his old age. Daughters, who were not fit to rule and who left the paternal home for that of their eventual spouse, served neither purpose. Infertility per se is not at issue here.

51. Robert D. Biggs, *Šaziga: Ancient Mesopotamian Potency Incantations* (Locust Valley, NY: J. J. Augustin, 1967), 17, 26–27.

52. Though it should be noted that whereas there may be some question as to the origin and divine intent behind female infertility, at least in Mesopotamian texts there was no such uncertainty when it came to male impotency. The choices were evidently either divine punishment or sorcery (for the texts, see ibid., 3, 46). For a nuanced take on the issues of power and responsibility implied in the divine/sorcery binary, see I. Tzvi Abusch, "Witchcraft, Impotence, and Indigestion," in *Disease in Babylonia*, ed. I. L. Finkel and M. J. Geller (Cuneiform Monographs 36; Leiden: Brill, 2007), 146–59.

53. Note the sexual identity laid out in an Egyptian letter from the late second millennium BCE: "You are not a man since you can't make your wives pregnant" (Robins, *Women*, 77).

54. Gary M. Beckman, *Hittite Birth Rituals*, 2nd ed. (Studien zu den Boğazköy-Texten 29; Wiesbaden: Harrassowitz, 1983), 2–3.

55. There is also a rabbinic parallel, in a midrash on the story of Samson's mother. "There was a quarrel between Manoah and his wife, he saying to her, 'you are barren and this is the reason why you do not bear,' while she said to him, 'you are barren and this is the reason why I have not borne.' But in fact Manoah was not barren"—because the divine messenger appears to Samson's mother, and tells her explicitly, "You are barren"—"in order to make peace between her and her husband" (*Num. Rab.* 10.5). This midrash admits the existence of male infertility, which is an innovation over the biblical text. But the "peace" won by the arrival of the divine messenger was surely of little comfort to Samson's mother.

56. Ruth's husband is named Maḥlon, which translates roughly as "Sicky"— perhaps in subtle recognition of the fact not only that he would die young, but that he suffered some reproductive impairment as well. Cf. Kirsten Nielsen, *Ruth* (OTL; Louisville: Westminster John Knox, 1997), 42.

57. On levirate marriage, see Dvora Weisberg, *Levirate Marriage and the Family in Ancient Judaism* (Waltham, MA: Brandeis University Press, 2009); Eryl W. Davies, "Inheritance Rights and the Hebrew Levirate Marriage," *VT* 31 (1981): 138–44, 257–68; note that Davies, like many others, routinely conflates the categories of "sonlessness" and "childlessness." See also Block, "Marriage," 93, who misdefines the levirate marriage along these lines: "union between *yebama*, a widow whose husband has died without having fathered any offspring, and the *yabam*, the brother of the deceased." The legal narrative in Num 27:1–11 of the daughters of Zelophehad depicts precisely the situation of "sonlessness": a father who dies, leaving only five daughters and no male offspring to inherit. The law that emerges from this situation is that daughters should inherit, but as the continuation of this tradition makes clear in Num 36, they are then to marry within the clan so that the familial inheritance does not pass to another tribe. This alternative levirate tradition may envision that the remarriage of the widow to her brother-in-law should take place only when there are no offspring whatsoever, and thus tacitly suggests the possibility of male infertility. On the other hand, it is a reasonable assumption that Zelophehad's wife was also dead, as she was a member of the condemned generation of the wilderness (Baruch A. Levine, *Numbers 21–36* [AB 4A; New York: Doubleday 2000], 358; Jacob Milgrom, *The JPS Torah Commentary: Numbers* [Philadelphia: Jewish

Publication Society, 1990], 231), and thus the law in Numbers refers only to a situation in which levirate marriage proper was impossible. As Levine points out (*Numbers 21–36*, 358), this is also what is depicted in the book of Ruth: Naomi cannot undergo levirate marriage because she is past the age of child-bearing (Ruth 1:11–12).

58. In rabbinic literature, however, the biblical whispers are sounded aloud. Although, as noted earlier, a man is required to take a second wife if his first one fails to bear children within ten years, the wife is also permitted to ask for a divorce and remarry, upon which she and her second husband are granted their own ten-year period (*m. Yeb.* 6.6). The talmudic commentary on this mishna makes it explicit that the lack of offspring could well be the husband's fault, which is why he is required to give her a divorce if she asks for it (*b. Yeb.* 64a). The Talmud then goes on to state, without compunction, that Isaac himself was barren (ibid.). Even in the medieval period, however, Jewish scholars still maintained that women are "responsible for miscarriage and infertility more than men" (Naḥmanides on Exod 23:26).

59. http://www.sciencedaily.com/releases/2005/06/050622134550.htm.

60. Schipper, *Disability and Isaiah's Suffering Servant*, 21.

61. An Egyptian medical text regarding a woman who is unable to conceive describes her as unwilling to get out of her bed (Pnina Galpaz-Feller, "Pregnancy and Birth in the Bible and Ancient Egypt (Comparative Study)," *BN* 102 [2000]: 42–53 [here 45]).

62. As Avalos says, "Hannah seems depressed by her condition, and she is treated as an inferior by the rival wife" (*Illness and Health Care in the Ancient Near East: The Role of the Temple in Greece, Mesopotamia, and Israel* [Harvard Semitic Museum Monographs 54; Atlanta: Scholars, 1995], 332); we might change the word "and" to "because," at least in large part.

63. In Zeph 3:18–19 the word is associated other physical disabilities. See Saul M. Olyan, *Disability in the Hebrew Bible: Interpreting Mental and Physical Differences* (New York: Cambridge University Press, 2008), 37.

64. The ancient rabbis, in a midrash on this passage, naturally filled in this narrative gap, and in what is, for our purposes, a remarkable manner: they say that when visitors would come, "Hagar would tell them, 'My mistress Sarah is not inwardly what she is outwardly; she appears to be a righteous woman, but she is not. For had she been a righteous woman,

see how many years have passed without her conceiving, whereas I conceived in one night!'" (*Gen. Rab.* 45.4). Hagar, in short, ascribes to Sarah
the sin she assumes must be at the root of her mistress's infertility. See
also a similar story with regard to Rachel, *MHG* Gen 30:23. Even Peninnah's taunt is filled out in cruel form, *Pes. Rab.* 43:8.

65. Here we deviate slightly from the NJPS translation, reading "because"
instead of "that" for the word *ki.*

66. This situation was inscribed into ancient Mesopotamian law in the Code
of Hammurabi (LH 146–47).

67. See Victor H. Matthews, "Honor and Shame in Gender-Related Legal
Situations in the Hebrew Bible," in *Gender and Law in the Hebrew Bible
and the Ancient Near East,* ed. Victor H. Matthews, Bernard M. Levinson,
and Tikva Frymer-Kensky (JSOTS 262; Sheffield: Sheffield Academic,
1998), esp. 98–100.

68. On shame in the Bible and ancient Israel, see Lyn M. Bechtel, "Shame
as a Sanction of Social Control in Biblical Israel: Judicial, Political, and
Social Shaming," *JSOT* 49 (1991): 47–76; idem, "The Perception of Shame
within the Divine-Human Relationship in Biblical Israel," in *Uncovering Ancient Stones,* ed. Lewis M. Hopfe (Winona Lake, IN: Eisenbrauns,
1994), 79–92.

69. See Bechtel, "Shame"; idem, "Perception."

70. van der Toorn, *Sin,* 86.

71. *1 Enoch* 98:5. Translation from E. Isaac, "1 (Ethiopic Apocalypse of)
Enoch," in *The Old Testament Pseudepigrapha,* vol. 1, ed. James H. Charlesworth (ABRL; New York: Doubleday, 1983), 5–89 (at 78). I am including
here the additional text found in one Greek manuscript because it was
simply too apropos to ignore.

72. *Song Rab.* II.14,8; similarly *Gen. Rab.* 45.4.

73. *Tanḥ. B.* Wayyera' 32. See also *b. Roš. Haš.* 16b, in which Sarah is said to
be punished for calling on God to judge between Abraham and herself
(Gen 16:5).

74. *Gen. Rab.* 60.13; *Song Rab.* II.14,8.

75. *Gen. Rab.* 71.7. Conversely, Rachel recognized that Leah must be righteous since she had borne children (*Gen. Rab.* 71.6).

76. *Pes. Rab.* 43.4.

77. *Gen. Rab.* 45.4; *Song Rab.* II.14,8.

78. *Pes. Rab.* 43.5. Baskin, *Midrashic Women*, 133, puts a fine point on these interpretations: "All of these inadequate explanations, however, are trivial responses to childlessness, which was most often a source of anguish and affliction. They constitute a powerful declaration of the futility of all human efforts in explaining the mysteries of suffering."

79. Demircioğlu, "Rhetoric," 57.

80. Harald M. Wahl, "Ester, das adoptierte Waisenkind. Zur Adoption im Alten Testament," *Biblica* 80 (1999): 78–99 (here 92; see also 97).

81. Ludwig Köhler, *Hebrew Man* (London: SCM, 1956), 42.

82. Leo G. Perdue, "The Israelite and Early Jewish Family," in *Families in Ancient Israel* (The Family, Religion, and Culture; Louisville: Westminster John Knox, 1997), 163–222 (here 189).

83. van der Toorn, *Sin*, 86.

84. Galpaz-Feller, "Pregnancy," 46.

85. van der Toorn, *Cradle*, 79.

86. See Joel S. Baden and Candida R. Moss, "The Origin and Interpretation of *ṣāra'at* in Leviticus 13–14," *JBL* 130 (2011): 643–62.

87. See van der Toorn, *Sin*, 79: "The recognition of a supernatural involvement in a disease had to be supplemented by further explanations; it certainly did not coincide with an indictment of sin."

88. Hector Avalos has read this prophetic intercession as evidence for "wider social implications for the health care system . . . that this system sometimes requires the consultation of the prophet-as-intermediary regardless of the existence of the patient's ability to contact Yahweh directly through prayer" (*Illness*, 262). Yet we cannot overlook the fact that the patriarchs and matriarchs, who—Abraham in this episode alone excluded—are not depicted as prophets, are able to both contact Yahweh directly through prayer and plead for their own fertility. There are two salient differences between Abimelech and the patriarchs and matriarchs: Abimelech is not an Israelite, and, perhaps more important, Abimelech alone is said to have been explicitly punished.

89. Some scholars have attempted to identify other biblical passages that seem to link infertility with a defined sin: the ordeal of the adulterous woman in Num 5, the sexual laws of Lev 20, and the story of Michal in 2 Sam 6 (see, e.g., van der Toorn, *Sin*, 86). None of these cases are either clear or convincing. The law of Num 5 seems most likely to deal not with

infertility, but with miscarriage: the jealous husband believes his wife is carrying a child that is not his, and if the curse-waters she drinks cause miscarriage, his suspicions are confirmed (cf. Baruch A. Levine, *Numbers 1–20* [AB 4; New York: Doubleday 1994], 202). In support of this reading are the rabbinic statements that women incapable of conceiving, including the barren, are exempt from undergoing this ordeal (*m. Soṭ* 4.3). In Lev 20:20–21, the key word of punishment is *'aririm*, which appears only twice elsewhere in the Hebrew Bible and, though it was translated as "childless" even from ancient times, its precise meaning remains unclear; it seems just as likely to mean "prohibited from having heirs" in a more legal sense (see G. R. Driver, "Linguistic and Textual Problems: Jeremiah," *JQR* 28 [1937]: 97–129 [here 115]). In this reading the punishment for sexual relations with a paternal uncle's wife or a brother's wife would be far closer to that determined for marrying one's sister, which is excommunication (*karet*; Lev 20:17), the proximity of the punishments echoing the similarity of the crimes. Finally, the case of David's wife Michal at best only alludes to infertility as divine punishment. The text does not say that she is barren, only that after having an altercation with David she did not have any children until she died. Most commentators claim that the situation depicted here is one not of divine disfavor but of marital disfavor: she and David never shared a bed again (see, e.g., P. Kyle McCarter, *II Samuel* [AB 9; New York: Doubleday, 1984], 187). The rabbis read the phrase "until the day of her death" (2 Sam 6:23) as meaning that Michal actually died in childbirth (*b. Sanh.* 21a), an indication at least that those keen readers did not consider her to have been barren. For further discussion of Michal's status, see Jeremy Schipper, "Disabling Israelite Leadership: 2 Samuel 6:23 and Other Images of Disability in the Deuteronomistic History," in *This Abled Body: Rethinking Disabilities in Biblical Studies*, ed. Hector Avalos, Sarah M. Melcher, and Jeremy Schipper (Atlanta: Society of Biblical Literature, 2007), 103–13.

90. van der Toorn, *Cradle*, 79.

91. A midrash describes God and the divine court debating Sarah's merits, and finding her worthy of offspring (*Tanḥ. B.* Wayyera' 34).

92. On the contrast between the positive depiction of Samson's mother and her hapless husband, see Fuchs, "Literary Characterization," 155–56.

93. Mary Callaway suggests that the story of Hannah picks up on themes found in psalms of individual lament, and that the author is alluding to

"the tradition of the righteous man who is in distress and harassed by his adversaries" (*Sing, O Barren One: A Study in Comparative Midrash* [SBLDS 91; Atlanta: Scholars, 1986], 47).

94. A rabbinic midrash transmutes Hannah's feelings almost into vindictiveness toward God, as she attempts to turn God's own laws to her benefit: knowing that in Numbers 5 it is said that a woman accused and acquitted of adultery "will conceive" (Num 5:28), Hannah threatens to seclude herself with another man so that she will be accused, and so that upon being found innocent of wrongdoing she will become pregnant (*Pes. Rab.* 43.3). The response to this midrash denies such a possibility, for the very reason that "if this was so, then all barren women would go and seclude themselves (with other men)" (*b. Ber.* 31b).

95. van der Toorn, *Cradle*, 79–80.

96. "While Deuteronomy stressed that obedience brings blessings and disobedience brings curses, one cannot go on to assume (as many since Deuteronomy did assume—see the book of Job) that suffering indicates one is not elect while riches or ease on earth indicates that one is elect." James A. Sanders, "The Ethic of Election in Luke's Great Banquet Parable," in *Essays in Old Testament Ethics*, ed. James L. Crenshaw and John T. Willis (New York: Ktav, 1974), 245–71 (here 258), quoted in Callaway, *Sing*, 92. This misunderstanding of deuteronomic theology persists in scholarship: see, e.g., Wahl, "Ester," 95: "According to deuteronomistic theology, God punishes the disobedient with infertility, the loss of children, and existential threat to children."

97. *Tanḥ. B.* Wayyera' 34.

98. Naturally enough, the rabbis of the Talmud were unwilling to leave such a gap in the text; again, the way that they fill it is noteworthy. They depict Hezekiah asking Isaiah what he has done to deserve his sickness, to which Isaiah responds, "because you did not engage in being fruitful and multiplying" (*b. Ber.* 10a). That is, the rabbis ascribe Hezekiah's illness to divine punishment for not even attempting to have children—a nearly perfect confluence of the various issues taken up in this chapter.

99. Moss and Schipper, "Introduction," 3.

100. This is somewhat in line with the language of Avalos, *Illness*, 332, who employs the concept of Yahweh as "sender/controller," a term that permits a range of potential levels of involvement.

101. In one midrash, it is argued that Sarah and Rebekah were barren because they were each lacking an ovary, a situation that is remedied miraculously by God (*Gen Rab.* 47.2; 53.5; 63:5). An alternative reading has Sarah lacking a womb altogether (*Pes. Rab.* 42.4).

102. van der Toorn, *Cradle,* 78.

103. KTU 1.17 ii 24–47. See Marsmann, *Women,* 214–16.

104. Cited in Stol, *Birth,* 35.

105. Cited in ibid., 35. See also P. Kah. 30.

106. For archaeological details of the geographical and chronological distribution of these Israelite figurines, see Raz Kletter, *The Judean Pillar-Figurines and the Archaeology of Asherah* (BAR International Series 636; Oxford: Tempus Reparatum, 1996), 40–48.

107. Whitekettle, "Human Reproduction," 58.

108. Pierpont Morgan Library M662B 22 includes an appeal by a man that his wife might conceive (translated in Marvin Meyer and Richard Smith, eds., *Ancient Christian Magic: Coptic Texts of Ritual Power* [Princeton: Princeton University Press, 1999], 176). For further examples of oracular and documentary texts pertaining to pregnancy, childbirth, and the importance of procuring male progeny, see Jane Rowlandson, *Women and Society in Greek and Roman Egypt* (Cambridge: Cambridge University Press, 1998), 280–98.

109. London Oriental Manuscript 5525 asks for protection for a pregnant woman possibly afflicted by demons (translated in Meyer and Smith, *Ancient Christian Magic,* 120).

110. Rylands 100 (translated in Meyer and Smith, *Ancient Christian Magic,* 125).

111. The Schmidt papyrus describes an instance in which a woman, Esrmpe, went to a local cemetery in Hermopolis Egypt where she read an invocation to the local spirit from a papyrus before leaving the papyrus at the shrine. Her complaint was that her husband was avoiding her sexually and, thus, denying her a son. David Frankfurter hypothesizes that the papyrus was tied to a figurine representing herself as pregnant: "A Plea to a Local God for a Husband's Attentions," in *Religions of Late Antiquity in Practice,* ed. Richard Valantasis (Princeton: Princeton University Press, 2000), 230–31. We are grateful to David for sharing with

us his unpublished paper: "'It Is Esrmpe Who Appeals!' Place, Object, and Performance in the Quest for Pregnancy in Roman Egypt."

112. While it focuses more on the modern period, Marcia C. Inhorn's *Quest for Conception: Gender, Infertility and Egyptian Medical Tradition* (Philadelphia: University of Pennsylvania Press, 1994) offers an outstanding introduction to this issue.

113. See Block, "Marriage," 80: "Children were viewed primarily as the product of divine action."

114. For other biblical metaphors for this process, see Claudia D. Bergmann, *Childbirth as a Metaphor for Crisis: Evidence from the Ancient Near East, the Hebrew Bible, and 1QH XI, 1–18* (BZAW 382; Berlin: de Gruyter, 2008), 61–62: "All of these images have in common a description of the child's life during the embryonic stage as a *divinely initiated* turning of nature into culture" (at 62; italics added).

115. In this light we should also understand Ezek 24:27; 33:22, which, though they use the language of dumbness, are clearly meant metaphorically, as Ezekiel has spoken already (beginning in Ezek 4:14).

116. Outside of body parts, we might also consider Deut 28:12 in this regard: "The Lord will open for you his bounteous store, the heavens, to provide rain for your land." This is not describing the natural rains to which Israel is accustomed, but to extraordinary weather; the context is that of the blessings that will accrue to Israel if they obey the deuteronomic covenant. See similarly Mal 3:10: "I will surely open the floodgates of the sky for you and pour down blessings on you."

117. Robert K. Ritner, "A Uterine Amulet in the Oriental Institute Collection," *JNES* 43 (1984): 209–21.

118. *Gen. Rab.* 73.4. See similarly *Deut. Rab.* 7.6; *Tanḥ. B.* Wayyera' 35; *Pes. Rab.* 42.7; *b. Taʿan* 2a.

119. On the persistent use of metaphor in the attempt to describe the experience of infertility, see Becker, "Metaphors."

120. Leah is often listed among the barren women of the Bible, almost certainly precisely because the Bible says that Yahweh "opened her womb," a phrase otherwise associated only with infertility. Yet there is no indication in the text that this is the case: she is not called barren as Sarah, Rebekah, Rachel, and Samson's mother are; it is never said that God has closed her womb, as it is of Hannah; when Leah names her

children, she does so always in light of Jacob's preference for Rachel, and never with reference to any inability to conceive. Though there are some rabbinic statements that suggest that Leah was barren (e.g., *PRK* 20:1), it seems that this notion was a relatively late midrashic development (see Louis Ginzberg, *Legends of the Jews*, vol. 1 [Philadelphia: Jewish Publication Society, 2003], 288n171).

121. This observation gives increased meaning to the rabbinic dictum "No one is ever healed unless he has been previously smitten" (*Pes. Rab.* 42.3).

122. An almost identical locution is found in the description of Sarah: "She was barren; she had no child" (Gen 11:30). There are two differences. The first is that here the second clause describes a state rather than an action (or lack of action): not that Sarah bore no children, but that she had none. Perhaps this can be read to exclude the possibility of Sarah having any children through adoption or surrogacy; perhaps not. The second difference is that the two clauses of the verse are coordinated asyndetically, that is, they could be read as the same statement expressed twice rather than as two distinct statements. The difference in the Hebrew is but a single vertical stroke, the letter *waw*.

123. This is not to take away from the artistic literary parallelism of "You are barren and have borne no children / but you will become pregnant and will bear a son," as observed by J. Cheryl Exum, "Promise and Fulfillment: Narrative Art in Judges 13," *JBL* 99 (1980): 43–59 (here 47).

124. A midrash describes Moses's mother, Jochebed, being divorced from her husband Amram, and therefore being "barren," in the period between the births of Aaron and Miriam and the birth of Moses (*Pes. Rab.* 43.4). In this story infertility is seen as identical with not only an inability to conceive but even a lack of opportunity. Note the conventional perspective expressed by Rachel Havrelock, "The Myth of Birthing the Hero: Heroic Barrenness in the Hebrew Bible," *BibInt* 16 (2008): 154–78: "No one can call a woman with four children barren" (161).

125. The rabbis, in discussing how long it takes before a woman's infertility is firmly established, settle initially on a period of twenty years (*b. Yeb.* 64b); yet they immediately allow for the possibility that, in fact, she could bear her first child after thirty or more years of trying (*b. Yeb.* 65a). Elsewhere, however, they tell a story of a woman who loses the ability to bear children after only twelve years (*b. Ket.* 62b).

126. Rabbinic law prohibits a woman incapable of bearing children from participating in the process of levirate marriage (*m. Yeb.* 8:5). Here, however, the word for this woman is not the usual one for barren, *ʿkārâ*, but rather *ʾaylônît*—a woman who does not achieve puberty (*b. Yeb.* 80b). The distinction made in the rabbinic literature between these two types of women is an important one—yet it should also be noted that it is possible even for the *ʾaylônît* to become pregnant (*m. Gitt.* 4.8).

127. Cited in Stol, *Birth*, 34.

128. P. Carlsberg VI; E. Iverson, "Papyrus Carlsberg No. VIII: With Some Remarks on the Egyptian Origin of Some Popular Birth Prognoses," *Historisk-filologiske Meddelelser udgivet af det Kgl. Danske Videnskabernes Selskab* 26 (1939): 1–31 (here 25).

129. Stol, *Birth*, 37; Erica Reiner, "Babylonian Birth Prognoses," *ZA* 72 (1982): 124–38 (here 133).

130. P. Kah. 27.

131. Reiner, "Babylonian Birth Prognoses," 134–37.

132. P. Carlsberg IV/P. Kahun 28. On the dependence of later medical texts on these Egyptian documents, see particularly Iverson, "Papyrus Carlsberg." It may be noted that the category of tests involving "fumigation" was a rather popular one; we also find, for one particularly egregious example, P. Carlsberg V: "Another [test] to distinguish between a woman who shall give birth and one who shall not. You shall fumigate her with excrements of hippopotamus through her vulva. If she vomits with her mouth at once, she will not give birth; if she gets flatus from her posterior at once then she will give birth" (Iverson, "Papyrus Carlsberg," 23).

133. Stephanie Dalley, "Etana," in *The Context of Scripture*, vol. 1, ed. William W. Hallo (Leiden: Brill, 1997), 453–57.

134. Stol, *Birth*, 52–54.

135. Cited in ibid., 53.

136. P. Berlin 192.

137. On the use in Islam of ostensibly "natural" or "man-made" means to become pregnant while still maintaining divine control over fertility, see Demircioğlu, "Rhetoric," 58. For a comparable, though not quite parallel, argument in Judaism, see Judith N. Lasker and Harriet L. Par-

met, "Rabbinic and Feminist Responses to Reproductive Technology," *Journal of Feminist Studies in Religion* 6 (1990): 117–30 (here 121).

138. Though see the careful treatment of this topic in Stol, *Birth*, 56–58. Havrelock suggests that the mandrakes were a means of drawing God's attention to Rachel's plight ("Myth," 173).

139. The rabbis make this case explicitly in *Gen. Rab.* 45.2, where Sarah discounts the idea that charms will be effective when she says "The Lord has kept me from bearing." On the other hand, we find in the Talmud the statement that in the world to come there will be a tree with leaves that cure infertility (*b. Sanh.* 100a).

140. This knowledge may have been lost to a degree: Augustine claims that old women can conceive only with young men, and vice versa (*Civ.* 16.28).

141. Stol, *Birth*, 58–59.

142. This age is defined by the rabbis, amusingly, as "When she is called 'Mother So-and-So' and does not mind" (*Gen. Rab.* 47.3).

143. Stol, *Birth*, 58–59.

144. Similar is the narrative of the Shunammite woman in 2 Kgs 4:14–17. Though this narrative is sometimes invoked as another story of infertility (e.g., Callaway, *Sing*, 17; Fuchs, "Literary Characterization," 158–59), it need not be read as such. The woman is never called barren, nor even said to be childless; she is said specifically to have no son (a detail that is lacking in all of the true infertility passages). Here there is no question of the lack of a son being her fault; the text emphasizes that it is her husband who has grown too old to produce offspring (2 Kgs 4:14). This is a story in which it is the lack of an heir that is at stake—it is not unimportant that the woman is said to be wealthy (2 Kgs 4:8) or that the focus is on the lack of a son. It is not the woman who is healed in any way in this story; if anyone, it is her elderly husband—perhaps yet another whisper of male infertility? See, at least for the claim that the woman's fertility is not at issue here, if not for the conclusion that Elisha is the child's true father, Fokkelien van Dijk-Hemmes, "The Great Woman of Shunem and the Man of God: A Dual Interpretation of 2 Kings 4.8–37," in *The Feminist Companion to Samuel and Kings*, ed. Athalya Brenner (Sheffield: Sheffield Academic Press, 1994), 218–30.

145. On the following, see Michael V. Fox, "The Sign of the Covenant: Circumcision in the Light of the Priestly *'ot* Etiologies," *RB* 81 (1974):

557–96; Howard Eilberg-Schwartz, *The Savage in Judaism: An Anthropology of Israelite Religion and Ancient Judaism* (Bloomington: Indiana University Press, 1990), 141–76.

146. Eilberg-Schwartz, *Savage*, 141–76.

CHAPTER 2: THE BLESSING AND THE CURSE

1. *m. Yeb.* 6.6. The force of this law is evident from a midrash that explains why Noah had no sons until he was five hundred years old. In this story, Noah knew that his generation would be evil, and so did not want to contribute to it, but after five hundred years he acceded to the divine will: "The Holy One has commanded Adam about fruitfulness and multiplying . . . yet I am dying without children" (*Tanḥ. B.* Bereishit 39). Similarly we may point to some more legalistic texts that appeal to the requirement to procreate: the ruling that during a time of famine, when there is not enough food for the mouths that already exist, it is prohibited to engage in conjugal relations—unless one does not already have children, in which case it is permitted in order to fulfill the obligation to be fruitful and multiply (*b. Ta'an.* 11a); or the prohibition on selling a Torah scroll, with the single exception being to finance a wedding, again for the purpose of promoting the fulfillment of the divine imperative to procreate (*b. Meg.* 27a).

2. See Jeremy Cohen, *"Be Fertile and Increase, Fill the Earth and Master It": The Ancient and Medieval Career of a Biblical Text* (Ithaca: Cornell University Press, 1989), 79–80, 124–33, 158–65.

3. *Paedagogus* 2.10.83.

4. See Demircioğlu, "Rhetoric," 54.

5. Alexander Carlebach and Judith Baskin, "Barrenness and Fertility," in *Encyclopedia Judaica*, 2nd ed., ed. Michael Berenbaum and Fred Skolnik (Detroit: Macmillan, 2007), 174–75 (here 174).

6. Dorothy Jean Weaver, "Barrenness & Fertility," in *The IVP Women's Bible Commentary*, ed. Catherine Clark Kroeger and Mary J. Evans (Downers Grove, IL: InterVarsity, 2002), 156–58.

7. Act 1, scene IV, line 27.

8. Leah appears only in genealogies (Gen 35:23, 26; 46:15, 18), in the list of family members buried in the cave of Machpelah (Gen 49:31; though her death and burial are nowhere narrated), and in the blessing given to

Ruth (Ruth 4:11). Bilhah and Zilpah, similarly, appear only in references to their offspring (Gen 35:22, 25, 26; 37:2; 46:18, 25; 1 Chr 7:13).

9. Many commentators, sensing this problem, attempt to relocate this divine speech before Jacob has had any of his children; see, e.g., Hermann Gunkel, *Genesis* (Macon, GA: Mercer University Press, 1997), 373; Gerhard von Rad, *Genesis* (OTL; Philadelphia: Westminster, 1972), 339. Such a solution only serves to indicate the predominance of the traditional understanding of "be fruitful and multiply."

10. In traditional Jewish exegesis, the words of Gen 1:28 are considered a blessing, while those of Gen 9:1 are—despite the fact that here too it says "God blessed Noah and his sons"—considered a command. See Rashi and Ramban on Gen 9:1; see more recently Nahum Sarna, *The JPS Torah Commentary: Genesis* (Philadelphia: Jewish Publication Society, 1989), 13.

11. It is for this reason that the great medieval Jewish commentator ibn Ezra (on Gen 1:28) states plainly that God's first words to humanity are a blessing.

12. See, perhaps most eloquently, the booklet of David Daube: *The Duty of Procreation* (Eugene: Wipf & Stock, 1977).

13. See Block, "Marriage," 81, who roughly translates all of the individual blessings of fertility, including "be fruitful and multiply," as "May the Lord bless you, and may you have many children."

14. Technically, according to the priestly author who wrote the words "be fruitful and multiply" in Gen 1:28, the first man and woman had only a single child, Seth (Gen 5:3).

15. See note 10 above.

16. Cf. Cohen, *"Be Fertile and Increase,"* 235: "Rather than a commitment to the entire human species, 'be fertile and increase' signified the election of Israel."

17. The connection between these two mentions of "filling the earth" was made by Umberto Cassuto, *A Commentary on Genesis*, vol. 2 (Jerusalem: Magnes, 1992), 51–52.

18. See Norbert Lohfink, "'Subdue the Earth?' Genesis 1:28," in *Theology of the Pentateuch* (Minneapolis: Fortress, 1994), 1–17 (here 8).

19. The only possible exception is Ruth 4:11, where the people of Bethlehem express their wish that God make Ruth "like Rachel and Leah, both of whom built up the House of Israel." On this as a blessing of fertility, see Nielsen, *Ruth*, 89–90.

20. The church fathers, in an attempt to uphold the virtues of celibacy and virginity, came to the same conclusion, although on supercessionist grounds: that the command to "be fruitful and multiply" was only a temporary one. See Cohen, *"Be Fertile and Increase,"* 243–44.

21. See the perceptive statements of Lohfink, " 'Subdue the Earth?,' " 8: "The 'blessing of creation' is by no means a blessing that applies to all future generations. The priestly document supposes that some day the blessing of fruitfulness will have achieved its purpose, that humanity will have reached the necessary numbers and that it will then no longer need to increase any further."

22. For a general overview of property inheritance in the Hebrew Bible, see Richard H. Hiers, "Transfer of Property by Inheritance and Bequest in Biblical Law and Tradition," *Journal of Law and Religion* 10 (1993–94): 121–55. See also Naomi Steinberg, *Kinship and Marriage in Genesis: A Household Economics Perspective* (Minneapolis: Fortress, 1993), 5–34.

23. See the rabbinic statement: "The fruit of a woman's body is blessed only from the fruit of a man's body" (*b. Ber.* 51b).

24. As has long been noted, in the biblical world wives are considered property, and just as this passage does not list the animals or other movable goods that Jacob's family brought to Egypt, neither does it list the wives. The only women who are mentioned in this list are unwed daughters: Dinah (Gen 46:15) and Serah, the daughter of Asher (Gen 46:17). On the status of women as property, see J. Harold Ellens, *Sex in the Bible: A New Consideration* (Westport, CT: Praeger, 2006), 67–82.

25. The standard work on genealogies in the Hebrew Bible is Robert R. Wilson, *Genealogy and History in the Biblical World* (New Haven: Yale University Press, 1977). On the roles of women in the genealogies, see Ingeborg Löwisch, "Gender and Ambiguity in the Genesis Genealogies: Tracing Absence and Subversion through the Lens of Derrida's *Archive Fever*," in *Embroidered Garments: Priests and Gender in Biblical Israel*, ed. Deborah W. Rooke (Hebrew Bible Monographs 25; Sheffield: Sheffield Phoenix, 2009), 60–73. Fuchs points out that even the narratives of the barren matriarchs, examined in the previous chapter, can be construed as dramatizing "the idea that woman's reproductive potential should be and can be controlled only by men" ("Literary Characterization," 161).

26. *m. Yeb.* 6.6. See also *Gen. Rab.* 8.12; *Tanḥ. B.* Noah 18; *PRK* 22.2. For discussion, see Cohen, *"Be Fertile and Increase,"* 140–44.

27. A rabbinic story from the Talmud depicts a woman who, upon learning that she is not obligated in the command of procreation, immediately drinks a sterility potion (*b. Yeb.* 65b).

28. Baskin, *Midrashic Women*, 119–26, shows how, in fact, understanding women as religiously or legally required to procreate would cause havoc for the male-dominated social system of the rabbis, potentially encouraging sexual licentiousness and certainly supporting female sexual independence.

29. See, e.g., Sarna, *Genesis*, 27; C. F. Keil and F. Delitzsch, *Commentary on the Old Testament*, vol. 1 (Peabody, MA: Hendrickson, 1996), 64, who state quite plainly that their traditional rendering of Gen 3:16 is absolutely dependent on the statement of 1:28.

30. This reading of the Eden narrative is common among the church fathers; though they read this chapter correctly in our view, they do so only by virtue of forcing an allegorical interpretation onto "be fruitful and multiply" in Gen 1:28, as an attempt to link sexuality with original sin. For an overview, see Cohen, *"Be Fertile and Increase,"* 237–38.

31. Meyers, *Rediscovering Eve*, 88–93.

32. See *b. Eruv.* 100b, where the rabbis elaborate the curse of Eve as covering every aspect of the reproductive process: menstruation, loss of virginity, pregnancy, childbirth, and even raising children. The same statement appears in *Gen. Rab.* 20.6, with the additional curse of miscarriage.

33. One early Jewish tradition denies the possibility that God could curse those whom he had just blessed (*2 Enoch* 31:7). Another, however, reads the text more along the lines suggested here: "Three were cursed, and their curses were beyond any limit, namely, the serpent, the woman, and the slave. But Adam is not included among the cursed ones" (Ginzberg, *Legends*, 79).

34. This is true even of the story in Gen 2–3; though the man is created first, once woman has entered the world there is no differentiation of status between them. In fact, one of the notable aspects of Eden is that there are effectively no lines along which gendered status could be differentiated: there is no labor, there are no children, there is no cult. The text recognizes in Gen 3:16b that the gender-status link comes into effect only after Eden.

35. The text famously mentions six hundred thousand men above the age of twenty; most approximations that include women and children expand

this number to two million (see, e.g., S. R. Driver, *The Book of Exodus* [CBC; Cambridge: Cambridge University Press, 1918], 101).

36. Cf., e.g., Richard D. Nelson, *Deuteronomy* (OTL; Louisville: Westminster John Knox, 2002), 350; Ronald Clements, "Deuteronomy," in *The New Interpreter's Bible*, vol. 2 (Nashville: Abingdon, 1998), 514; Patrick D. Miller, *Deuteronomy* (Interpretation; Louisville: Westminster John Knox, 1990), 213.

37. It is often overlooked or forgotten that these wild beasts were no mere fantasy, as they are today: there were lions in Israel in biblical times.

38. Note the rest of the verse, with its blessings on "the offspring of your cattle, the calves of your herd, and the lambs of your flock"—not that the animals will be fertile, but that they will have healthy offspring. See similarly Deut 7:13.

39. The medieval Jewish commentators took it in precisely the way we are rejecting here: they read "make you fruitful" as a promise that there would be no infertility, and "multiply you" as a promise of many descendants (ibn Ezra and Naḥmanides on Lev 26:9). Yet it is impossible to read the same words this way in their earlier appearances, where, as we have noted, those who received this blessing did not have many children (Jacob excepted).

40. The association of rain and fertility is drawn explicitly in the Talmud (*b. Ta'an* 8a–b), where it is noted that many of the same verbs are used for both rain and women: "withhold," "bear," and "remember."

41. So, for example, in discussing the deuteronomic blessing and curses, Perdue claims that "the greatest curse was sterility and the cutting off of progeny" ("Household, Theology, and Contemporary Hermeneutics," in *Families in Ancient Israel* [The Family, Religion, and Culture; Louisville: Westminster John Knox, 1997], 223–57 [here 227]). Block states that "whether due to barrenness or misfortune, childlessness was viewed as a curse," with references to the passages from Leviticus and Deuteronomy discussed here ("Marriage," 80).

42. Biggs, *Saziga*, 3.

43. Book of Overthrowing Apep, 28.1. See, from the same corpus, "His egg shall not flourish and his seed shall not be established, and his seed shall not be established and his egg shall not flourish" (27.13).

44. Whitekettle, "Human Reproduction," 57.

45. Beckman, *Hittite Birth Rituals*, 3.

46. See Moshe Weinfeld, *Deuteronomy and the Deuteronomic School* (Winona Lake, IN: Eisenbrauns, 1992), 59–157.

47. *ANET* 206.

48. Beckman, *Hittite Birth Rituals*, 3–4.

49. *ANET* 538. On the relationship of Esarhaddon's Treaty to Deuteronomy, see recently Bernard M. Levinson, "Esarhaddon's Succession Treaty as the Source for the Canon Formula in Deuteronomy 13:1," *JAOS* 130 (2010): 337–47, and the bibliography cited there.

50. W. G. Lambert and A. R. Millard, *Atra-Hasis: The Babylonian Story of the Flood* (Oxford: Oxford University Press, 1969), 103.

51. Tikva Frymer-Kensky, "What the Babylonian Flood Stories Can and Cannot Teach Us about the Genesis Flood," *BAR* 4 (1978): 32–41.

52. Jacob Klein, "Enki and Ninmah," in *The Context of Scripture*, vol. 1, ed. William W. Hallo (Leiden: Brill, 1997), 516–18. For further discussion, see Schipper, *Disability Studies and the Hebrew Bible*, 63–64; Neal H. Walls, "The Origins of the Disabled Body: Disability in Ancient Mesopotamia," in Avalos, Melcher, and Schipper, *This Abled Body*, 13–30 (here 16–19).

CHAPTER 3: MOTHER ZION AND THE ESCHATON

1. There is abundant scholarly discussion regarding the possibility that Isa 40–66 should itself be divided into two parts, chapters 40–55 and 56–66, the latter part being attributed to yet a third hand, often designated "Trito-Isaiah." While it is clear that the last chapters of Isaiah were written later than 40–55, there is much evidence to suggest that they are, in fact, by the same prophet. See the survey of scholarship on this, and further arguments in this direction, by William L. Holladay, "Was Trito-Isaiah Deutero-Isaiah after All?," in *Writing and Reading the Scroll of Isaiah: Studies of an Interpretive Tradition*, vol. 1, ed. C. C. Broyles and C. A. Evans (VTSup 70; Leiden: Brill, 1997), 193–217. For the purposes of this book, which deals more with the received biblical text than with its compositional history, such concerns may be secondary in any case.

2. On this variety of female imagery for Zion in Isaiah and elsewhere, see Tikva Frymer-Kensky, *In the Wake of the Goddesses: Women, Culture, and the Biblical Transformation of Pagan Myth* (New York: Free Press, 1992), 168–78.

3. Callaway, *Sing*, 67. The only other place the phrase appears is in the description of Samson's mother (Judg 13:2). For the fullest alignment of Isaiah's prophecies with the matriarchs, see W. A. M. Beuken, "Isaiah liv: The Multiple Identity of the Person Addressed," *OTS* 19 (1974): 29–70 (esp. 37–43).

4. Claus Westermann, *Isaiah 40–66* (OTL; Philadelphia: Westminster, 1969), 272.

5. The miraculous reversal of infertility is used elsewhere as a symbol of God's power: not only in the matriarchal narratives, but also in Ps 113:9: "He sets the barren woman among her household as a happy mother of children."

6. On the need to read the metaphor as it relates to the real-world experience of women in ancient Israel, see John F. A. Sawyer, "Daughter of Zion and Servant of the Lord in Isaiah: A Comparison," *JSOT* 44 (1989): 89–107; Katheryn Pfisterer Darr, *Isaiah's Vision and the Family of God* (Literary Currents in Biblical Interpretation; Louisville: Westminster John Knox, 1994), 178.

7. On intertextuality and allusion, see Candida R. Moss, "Nailing Down and Tying Up: Lessons in Intertextual Impossibility from the Martyrdom of Polycarp," *Vigiliae Christianae* 67 (2013): 117–36.

8. It should be noted that it is not necessary to assume that Isaiah had before him the actual text of Genesis. The patriarchal (and matriarchal) stories were part of the larger body of Israelite traditions, and reference could be made to them without explicit citation of earlier written documents. Again, however, we are interested here in how the prophet reconfigures the matriarchal stories for the present-day reader, for whom both Isaiah and Genesis are part of the continuous text of the Hebrew Bible. On the potential biblical allusions in Isaiah, see Patricia Tull Willey, *Remember the Former Things: The Recollection of Previous Texts in Second Isaiah* (SBLDS 161; Atlanta: Scholars, 1997); in a different manner, Benjamin D. Sommer, *A Prophet Reads Scripture: Allusion in Isaiah 40–66* (Stanford: Stanford University Press, 1998).

9. See, e.g., Joseph Blenkinsopp, *Isaiah 40–55* (AB 19A; New York: Doubleday, 2002), 312. Sawyer, "Daughter of Zion," 102, states that "the application of this language to the exiles has momentarily disturbed the consistency of the imagery," though to his credit he does not see this as problematic.

10. This language thematically recalls Isa 26:18: "We were with child, we writhed; it is as though we had given birth to wind."

11. See J. Gerald Janzen, "Rivers in the Desert of Abraham and Sarah and Zion (Isaiah 51:1–3)," *HAR* 10 (1986), 139–51 (here 141).

12. In light of the archaeological evidence that Israel was not as thoroughly uninhabited during the Exile as the biblical authors and conventional readings claim (for a thorough treatment, see Oded Lipschits, *The Fall and Rise of Jerusalem: Judah under Babylonian Rule* [Winona Lake, IN: Eisenbrauns, 2005]), the prophetic emphasis on this notion of emptiness ties together even more closely these two types of barrenness, geopolitical and maternal. It is as if the prophet discursively empties the land beyond the historical reality precisely in order to align it with the metaphor of the barren mother.

13. On the use of orchard imagery to symbolize fertility, see Eilberg-Schwartz, *Savage*, 156–62. There is, admittedly, some internal conflict in the imagery of Eden used here: Eden, though an undeniable paradise, was also a barren place. It is only in the canonical context, alongside "be fruitful and multiply" from Gen 1, that Eden becomes a site of human, rather than arborial, fruitfulness. It is not entirely obvious, from the narrative context of Gen 2–3 alone, how the swift delivery of Zion's children could "remind people of the paradisiacal situation of Eden" (Christl Maier, *Daughter Zion, Mother Zion: Gender, Space, and the Sacred in Ancient Israel* [Minneapolis: Fortress, 2008], 202): birth was not painless before the curse of Gen 3:16, it was nonexistent.

14. Cf. Westermann, *Isaiah 40–66*, 236.

15. See the convincing exposition of this imagery by Janzen, "Rivers." On the possibility that Eden was imagined as Jerusalem by the author of Gen 2, see Lawrence E. Stager, "Jerusalem as Eden," *BAR* 26 (2000): 36–47; idem, "Jerusalem and the Garden of Eden," *ErIsr* 26 (1999): 183*–94*.

16. Maier's claim ("Zion's Body as a Site of God's Motherhood in Isaiah 66:7–14," in *Daughter Zion: Her Portrait, Her Response*, ed. Mark J. Boda, Carol J. Dempsey, and LeAnn Snow Flesher [SBLAIL 13; Atlanta: Society of Biblical Literature, 2012], 225–43) that this is the only text in Isaiah in which Zion bears new children would seem to ignore entirely the explicit reference to barrenness in Isa 54:1.

17. In the narrative, of course, Sarah suckles only one child, Isaac. Yet Isaiah astutely recognizes, as we argued in the previous chapter, that the

promise of progeny given to Abraham and fulfilled through Sarah is not describing the birth of a single child in a single generation, but entails the creation of an entire nation. Thus he refers to Sarah as the one "who brought you"—plural—"forth" (Isa 51:2; see Callaway, *Sing*, 60). Isaiah credits Sarah in a way that the narratives of Genesis suggest, but never explicitly state.

18. The words "exiled and disdained" in this verse have been taken by some to be a later explanatory gloss (see, e.g., Westermann, *Isaiah 40–66*, 221; Blenkinsopp, *Isaiah 40–55*, 309). Yet this hardly seems necessary, as the context in vv. 14–19 has already made the equation clear.

19. On the history of Jerusalem's feminine personification, see Mark E. Biddle, "The Figure of Lady Jerusalem: Identification, Deification and Personification of Cities in the Ancient Near East," in *The Biblical Canon in Comparative Perspective*, ed. K. Lawson Younger Jr., William W. Hallo, and Bernard F. Batto (Scripture in Context 4; Ancient Near Eastern Texts and Studies 11; Lewiston: Edwin Mellen, 1991), 173–94.

20. On the potential social anxieties regarding women, see the incisive statement of Ben Sira 42:9–10.

21. On the unity of these verses, and the chapter as a whole, see Beuken, "Isaiah liv," 43 and passim.

22. See Westermann on this passage: "It is not anything she does, such as behaving immorally, that involves her in shame, but childlessness as such" (*Isaiah 40–66*, 273).

23. Scholarship commonly elides shame and vulnerability, as though they are identical phenomena; see, e.g., Darr, *Isaiah's Vision*, 180: "The disgrace of widowhood foregrounds the vulnerability of being without a protector or provider."

24. The closest parallel is Lam 1:1: "She that was great among nations has become a widow." Even here, however, the mention of shame is delayed considerably, until Lam 1:8, where it is tied to her "uncleanness" (Lam 1:9), and the references to widowhood do not recur. Deutero-Isaiah is famously dependent on Lamentations, so it is possible that this verse stands, in part, behind the language of Isa 54:4.

25. Thus we may avoid simply labeling this as a mixed metaphor, or as a metaphor that encloses a variety of potentially conflicting images, as in, e.g., Maier, *Daughter Zion*, 172, 174.

26. See ibid., 174: "While the 'husband' has not died but abandoned his wife, she may still feel like a widow."

27. In a fascinating reading, S. Borocin-Knol ("Zion as an 'Agunah? An Interpretation of Isaiah 49:14; 50:1 and 54:6–8," in *"Enlarge the Site of Your Tent": The City as Unifying Theme in Isaiah*, ed. Archibald L. H. M. van Wieringen and Annemarieke van der Woude [OTS 58; Leiden: Brill, 2011], 191–206) has proposed that Zion in Isaiah may be understood as having the (later) rabbinic status of an *'agunah*: a woman "chained to a marriage that no longer exists" (191). There are two possible ways that one achieves this status: a couple may be estranged, but the husband refuses to provide his wife with a formal religious divorce (which, given Yahweh's eventual return, is an interesting parallel); or "the husband has gone missing and his death cannot be proven" (191). In this latter case, intriguingly, the woman is described by the term "living widow" (a term taken from 2 Sam 20:3). Zion, in Isaiah, may also be something of a "living widow"—her husband, Yahweh, having left, she not knowing whether or when he may return, and none of it through any fault of her own.

28. See Knud Jeppesen, "Mother Zion, Father Servant," in *Of Prophets' Visions and the Wisdom of Sages*, ed. Heather A. McKay and David J. A. Clines (JSOTS 162; Sheffield: JSOT, 1993), 109–25 (here 124–25); Lena-Sofia Tiemeyer, "Isaiah 40–55: A Judahite Reading Drama," in *Daughter Zion: Her Portrait, Her Response*, ed. Mark J. Boda, Carol J. Dempsey, and Le-Ann Snow Flesher (SBLAIL 13; Atlanta: Society of Biblical Literature, 2012), 55–75 (here 71–74). The language of Isa 49:14—"The Lord has forsaken me"—strongly recalls the individual laments found in the Psalms, perhaps most famously that of Ps 22:1: "My God, my God, why have you forsaken me?" A common feature of these psalms of lament is that there is no admission of guilt on the part of the speaker: what is being expressed is the anguish over unprovoked divine abandonment. Or perhaps even more: "Zion's lament . . . articulates an accusation of YHWH" (Maier, *Daughter Zion*, 164).

29. See Walter Brueggemann, *Isaiah 40–66* (Westminster Bible Companion; Louisville: Westminster John Knox, 1998), 153: "Yahweh 'bailed out' of the marriage, perhaps because Yahweh could not tolerate the humiliation of a barren wife." Such a reading is obliquely suggested by Sawyer, "Daughter of Zion," 94: "A husband promises never again to lose his

temper, never again to walk out on his wife, leaving her childless and humiliated." Julian Morgenstern ("Isaiah 49–55," *HUCA* 36 [1965]: 1–35 [here 24]) and Mark J. Boda ("The Daughter's Joy," in Boda, Dempsey, and Flesher, *Daughter Zion*, 321–42 [here 330]) treat this as a case of the divine husband leaving his wife, Zion, while she was still young, before she had given birth; yet this reading does not take into account either the explicit language of barrenness or the mention of widowhood.

30. See Darr, *Isaiah's Vision*, 46–84.

31. See Jeppesen, "Mother Zion," 124–25.

32. This may be, as Sawyer ("Daughter of Zion," 98), Darr (*Isaiah's Vision*, 222), Maier (*Daughter Zion*, 202), and others suggest, an allusion to the imagined female state before God cursed Eve in Gen 3:16 (taking the conventional reading of that verse, rather than that of Meyers advocated for in the previous chapter); if so, this text too connects the barren matriarch to the traditions of creation.

33. This connection to the patriarchs was noted by Westermann, *Isaiah 40–66*, 272–73; Blenkinsopp, *Isaiah 40–55*, 362.

34. See Blenkinsopp, *Isaiah 40–55*, 362; John L. McKenzie, *Second Isaiah* (AB 20; Garden City, NY: Doubleday, 1968), 139.

35. Isaiah takes up the language of the utopian pentateuchal blessings in 65:20: "No more shall there be an infant or gray-beard who does not live out his days" (Isa 65:20); see Exod 23:26, "I will let you enjoy the full count of your days."

36. The connection to Sarah here is seen by Blenkinsopp, *Isaiah 56–66* (AB 19B; New York: Doubleday, 2003), 305.

37. See Westermann, *Isaiah 40–66*, 419–20.

38. For an overview of the hermeneutical development of the barren matriarch tradition in these texts, see Callaway, *Sing*, 115–39.

39. *PRK* 20.1.

40. Cf. Callaway, *Sing*, 123: "While her barrenness is seen in the present, her fruitfulness is yet to come."

41. This same commentary is applied elsewhere to Isa 54:11; see *PRK* 18.3.

42. *PRK* 20.3.

43. For an overview of these various positions and their historical development within rabbinic circles, see Efraim Urbach, *The Sages: Their Concepts and Beliefs*, 2 vols. (Jerusalem: Magnes, 1975), 2:666–92.

44. See Norman W. Porteous, "Jerusalem-Zion: The Growth of a Symbol," in *Verbannung und Heimkehr: Beiträge zur Geschichte und Theologie Israels im 6. und 5. Jahrhundert v. Chr*, ed. Arnulf Kuschke (Tübingen: J. C. B. Mohr, 1961), 235–52.

45. For an overview of the New Jerusalem passages from the Second Temple period, see Lorenzo diTommaso, *The Dead Sea New Jerusalem Text: Contents and Contexts* (TSAJ 110; Tübingen: Mohr Siebeck, 2005), 112–50.

46. See, however, the talmudic ruling that a man whose children have died has failed to fulfill the command of "be fruitful and multiply," a ruling that is applied also to men who have no offspring at all (*b. Yeb.* 62a–b).

47. This primordial Jerusalem is alluded to also by the rabbis when they enumerate those things that existed before the creation of the world, a list that typically includes the Temple (*Gen. Rab.* 1.4; *b. Pes.* 54a).

48. *Gen. Rab.* 77.1.

49. On this tradition, and the complications inherent in it, see Frederick E. Greenspahn, "Why Prophecy Ceased," *JBL* 108 (1989): 37–49. The self-aggrandizement on the part of the rabbis in this tradition—which may well have been intended as a rebuke to Christian claims—comes through clearly in the statement that "a wise man" (i.e., the rabbis) "is superior to a prophet" (*b. B. Bat.* 12a). The rabbis are now those who possess the authority once held in Israel by the prophets. For our purposes, a particularly fine example of this is the rabbinic story of a barren woman and her husband who came to R. Simeon b. Yoḥai to be divorced, according to the rabbinic law. The man tells his wife that she may take any precious object from his house when she returns to her father's house after the divorce. The wife gets the husband drunk and takes him to her father's house, declaring him to be the object most precious to her. R. Simeon hears of this, prays on their behalf, and the woman becomes pregnant. The moral of the story is that "even as the Holy One remembers barren women"—the very words of the midrash quoted above—"righteous men also have the power to remember barren women" (*PRK* 22.2). This text thus quite intentionally reverses that of *Gen. Rab.* 77.1, and puts the rabbi in the position of the prophet.

50. This is an answer given in modern Muslim societies as well: that earthly infertility will be rewarded with a child in heaven. See Demircioğlu, "Rhetoric," 57.

51. *Pes. Rab.* 42.4; *PRK* 22.1.

52. *b. Sanh.* 100a; *b. Shek.* 17a.

53. *b. Kallah Rabbati* 52a. This notion parallels other rabbinic texts that describe superabundant fruitfulness for plants and trees in the eschatological era: e.g., "Each and every month [a tree] will bear fruit" (*b. Shek.* 17a).

54. Hence the rabbinic recognition that there can be no procreation for the immortal; see, e.g., *Gen. Rab.* 12.7.

55. *b. Ber.* 17a.

56. *Ag. Ber.* 106–7. On this text, see Callaway, *Sing,* 117–20.

57. *Pes. Rab.* 43.4.

58. Cf. Mark 9:43–48, and the brief treatment of this text in Moss and Schipper, "Introduction," 1–2; *m. Nid.* 2.1. Also part of this broader discourse is Ben Sira 16:3: "To die childless is better than to have ungodly children"; here the sin is in the next generation, but the preferral, and acceptance, of impairment remains.

59. On Philo's discussions of infertility, see Callaway, *Sing,* 94–100.

60. *De Congressu Eruditionis gratia* 3.

61. *De Vita Contemplativa* 68.

62. *De Praemiis et Poenis* 158–59.

63. Callaway, *Sing,* 99.

CHAPTER 4: THE SON OF GOD AND THE CONCEPTION OF THE NEW AGE

1. For overviews of the biblical intertexts, see Leander Keck, "The Spirit and the Dove," *NTS* 17 (1970): 41–67, and Stephen Gero, "The Spirit as a Dove at the Baptism of Jesus," *NovT* 18 (1976): 17–35.

2. Jon D. Levenson, *The Death and Resurrection of the Beloved Son* (New Haven: Yale University Press, 1995), 30, 228.

3. In the Hebrew Bible, the spirit of God can confer a variety of gifts including special strength (Judg 14:6, 19) and leadership skills (Judg 3:10; 1 Sam 16:13). The spirit is closely associated with the ecstatic gifts of prophecy (Num 11:25; 1 Sam 10:6, 10) and can even transfer a person, noncorporeally, to another location (Ezek 3:12; 8:3; 11:1).

4. "Son of God" is absent from Codex Sinaiticus and several other important textual witnesses. It seems highly unlikely that a scribe would omit

the potent title, and we cannot argue that scribes were tired in the very first sentence of the text. Thus it is all but certain to be secondary. On the textual evidence for the title "Son of God" in Mark 1:1, see Bart D. Ehrman, "The Text of Mark in the Hands of the Orthodox," *LQ* 5 (1991): 143–56 (esp. 149–52).

5. LXX Isa 61:1–2.

6. Edward P. Dixon, "Descending Spirit and Descending Gods: An Interpretation of the Spirit's 'Descent as a Dove' in Mark 1:10," *JBL* 128 (2009): 759–80.

7. So Adela Yarbro Collins, *Mark: A Commentary* (Hermeneia; Minneapolis: Fortress, 2007), 149–50.

8. For a survey of various views on messianic uses, see Adela Yarbro Collins and John J. Collins, *King and Messiah as Son of God: Divine, Human, and Angelic Messianic Figures in Biblical and Related Literature* (Grand Rapids, MI: Eerdmans, 2008).

9. As Michael Peppard observes, "Roman adoption . . . was not enacted to stabilize the life of a child, but to stabilize the future of a father." Michael L. Peppard, *The Son of God in the Roman World: Divine Sonship in Its Social and Political Context* (New York: Oxford University Press, 2012), 60.

10. So Mason Hammond, *The Augustan Principate in Theory and Practice during the Julio-Claudian Period* (Cambridge, MA: Harvard University Press, 1933); idem, *The Antonine Monarchy* (Rome: American Academy in Rome, 1959); idem, "The Transmission of Powers of the Roman Emperor from the Death of Nero in A.D. 68 to that of Alexander Severus in A.D. 235," *Memoirs of the American Academy in Rome* 24 (1956): 63–133; Herbert Nesselhauf, "Die Adoption des römischen Kaisers," *Hermes* 83 (1955): 477–95.

11. Clifford Ando, *Imperial Ideology and Provincial Loyalty in the Roman Empire* (Berkeley: University of California Press, 2000), 24, cited in Peppard, *Son of God*, 27. It should be noted that Ando's original statement pertains to the figure of the emperor in general as a rallying point and "common reference point" (23) for those groups under their control.

12. Hammond, "Transmission," 63. He concludes that—prior to the reign of Severus, at least—the emperor's selection of his successor as indicated by adoption was "the determining factor in securing the support of the army and the confirmation of the senate" (67).

13. Cassius Dio, *Roman History* 69.20.

14. Adoption had its own risks. The Roman historian Tacitus describes Claudius's adoption of Nero as "ruinous" (Ann. 12.25.2) and has Otho describe Piso's "ill-starred adoption" ("infaustam adoptionem"; Hist. 1.38).

15. Clifford Ando and, following Ando, Michael Peppard have seen adoption, and Augustinian adoption in particular, as a means to harness charismatic authority (Ando, *Imperial Ideology*, 32–34; Peppard, *Son of God*, 68–69). Embedded within adoption were two forms of authority: charismatic and legal authority. Peppard: "Through the mechanism of adoption, Augustus successfully solved what Weber identified as the primary problem with charismatic authority—its transmission to another individual" (Peppard, *Son of God*, 69–70).

16. Brian K. Harvey, "Two Bases of Marcus Aurelius Caesar and the Roman Imperial Succession," *Historia: Zeitschrift für Alte Geschichte* 53 (2004): 46–60.

17. Christiane Kunst, *Römische Adoption: Zur Strategie einer Familienorganisation* (Hennef: Marthe Clauss, 2005), 15. Cf. Diodorus Siculus's reports of "barbarians" reenacting the process of biological birthing as part of their adoption ceremony.

18. First published in Alan H. Gardiner, "Adoption Extraordinary," *JEA* 26 (1941): 23–29. On the wealth of secondary literature on the Adoption Paprus, see, especially, C. J. Eyre, "The Adoption Papyrus in Social Context," *JEA* 78 (1992): 207–21. Translations here follow Eugene Cruz-Uribe, "A New Look at the Adoption Papyrus," *JEA* 74 (1988): 220–23 with corrections from S. Allam, "A New Look at the Adoption Papyrus (Reconsidered)," *JEA* 76 (1990): 189–91.

19. So Gardiner, "Adoption Extraordinary," 25–26.

20. So Eyre, "Adoption Papyrus," 210–11.

21. Peppard, *Son of God*, nn115, 116.

22. Donald Senior, "With Swords and Clubs: The Setting of Mark's Community and His Critique of Abusive Power," *BTB* 17 (1987): 10–20, and John R. Donahue, "Windows and Mirrors: The Setting of Mark's Gospel," *CBQ* 57 (1995): 1–26.

23. We are inferring this on the basis of *1 Enoch*. Of course, as was pointed out to us by Prof. James VanderKam in correspondence, if we possessed copies of the writings of Enoch's rivals, the situation might be quite different!

24. Paul does not know Mary's name, much less the concept of a virgin birth (so Joseph A. Fitzmyer, "The Birth of Jesus in the Pauline Writings," in *Mary in the New Testament,* ed. Raymond E. Brown (Philadelphia: Fortress, 1978), 33–49. The antiquity of the concept of the virgin birth has been much debated. It lies outside the scope of this book to review the data, as our focus is on the canonical portraits of infertility, child bearing, and parenting. For a review of this question, see Geza Vermes, *Jesus the Jew: A Historian's Reading of the Gospels* (Philadelphia: Fortress, 1973), 213–22; John P. Meier, *The Vision of Matthew: Christ, Church, and Morality in the First Gospel* (New York: Paulist, 1991), 220–30; and Raymond E. Brown, *The Birth of the Messiah: A Commentary on the Infancy Gospels* (ABRL; New York: Doubleday, 1993), 517–42, the latter two of whom argue that some hint of a premature pregnancy must have been a part of the earliest tradition, or else it would have been omitted. Or, for that matter, in the hypothetical source document Q, which many scholars believe was a literary source for Matthew and Luke.

25. This problem is studiously avoided by many commentators who assume that Jesus simply could have been both. See D. R. A. Hare, *Matthew* (Interpretation; Louisville: Westminster John Knox, 1993), 8; M. L. Strauss, *The Davidic Messiah in Luke-Acts: The Promise and Its Fulfillment in Lukan Christology* (JSNTS 110; Sheffield: Sheffield Academic Press, 1995), 126–29; D. Flusser, *Jesus,* 2nd ed. (Jerusalem: Magnes, 1998), 25; E. D. Freed, *The Stories of Jesus' Birth: A Critical Introduction* (St. Louis: Chalice, 2001), 21. There's a perverse yet intelligible logic to this assumption: in the context of a virgin birth surely dual parentage is not the most surprising detail. Others attempt to make theological lemonade from biological lemons. See, for example, the statement of H. Milton that this "paradox . . . denies any attempt to reduce Jesus Christ to a mere inspired prophet, or to a pagan demigod, or to a phantom" ("The Structure of the Prologue to St Matthew's Gospel," *JBL* 81 [1962]: 175–81 [here 177–78]).

26. See Matt 1:1, 9:27; 12:3, 23; 15:22; 20:30–31; 21:9; 21:15. With respect to Matt 1:20, the second occasion upon which Joseph is addressed as Son of David, some scholars have argued that this is a redactional insertion on the basis that elsewhere the title is reserved for Jesus alone. See W. D. Davies and Dale C. Allison Jr., *A Critical and Exegetical Commentary on the Gospel According to Saint Matthew,* vol. 1 (Edinburgh: T&T Clark, 1988), 207–8.

27. See the survey in Yigal Levin, "Jesus, 'Son of God' and 'Son of David': The 'Adoption' of Jesus into the Davidic Line," *JSNT* 28 (2006): 415–42 (here 422n18).

28. An interesting feature of this argument is its sheer lack of specificity. As noted by Levin, "when pressed for either precedence or proof of such adoption the vast majority of commentators refer to 'Jewish custom' or 'Jewish Law'" ("Jesus," 422). Some scholars cite Mishnah—"If a man says 'This is my son, he may be believed'" (*m. B. Bat* 8.6)—or the levirate marriage laws of Deut 25:5–6 as a precedent for adoption. But, as we have seen, levirate marriage was not legal adoption; on the contrary, the first son born was legally the heir of the deceased husband. Legally speaking there was no structure by which Jewish men adopted sons. Practically speaking, and taking the broad view of adoption envisioned in Matthew, there are plenty of examples of nonpaternal/filial transference of property and of adoption by women. See Levin, "Jesus," 422.

29. Charles Brian Rose, *Dynastic Commemoration and Imperial Portraiture in the Julio-Claudian Period* (Cambridge: Cambridge University Press, 1997), 14.

30. Epidaurian Miracle Inscription 1.2 in Emma J. Edelstein and Ludwig J. Edelstein, *Asclepius: A Collection and Interpretation of the Testimonies* (Baltimore: Johns Hopkins University Press, 1945).

31. Edelstein and Edelstein, *Asclepius*, 237.

32. See, for example, the case of French noblewoman Madeleine d'Auvermont, who in 1637 gave birth to a healthy child. The birth was scandalous as her husband had been abroad for years. When tried for adultery, Madame d'Auvermont claimed that she had thought intensely of her spouse and had dreamed about him at night. The child, she claimed, had been conceived by the power of her imagination. Medical and theological experts concurred that such a feat was possible, and the Parliament of Grenoble declared that the child was the legitimate son and heir to M. Hieronyme Auguste de Montleon. The mother, somewhat audaciously, named her child Emanuel. See Thomas Bartholin, *Historiarum anatomicarum variorum centuria V et VI* (Hafniae, 1661), 296.

33. This argument does suffer somewhat from the fact that, at least so far as the Hebrew Bible and rabbinic interpretation are concerned, Tamar and Bathsheba are both perfectly Israelite.

34. Celsus, quoted in Origen, *Contra Celsum* 1.28.

35. Matthew even amplifies the prostitute quotient in his genealogy by introducing Rahab into the Davidic lineage, an innovation that is entirely his own. With, in theory, virtually any female available—or, of course, the opportunity to mention no female at this juncture at all—Matthew has chosen the most prominent prostitute in the entire Hebrew Bible.

36. For the evidence of this with respect to the census, see Francois Bovon, *Luke 1: A Commentary on the Gospel of Luke 1:1–9:50* (Hermeneia; Philadelphia: Fortress, 2002), 82–85.

37. Ibid., 85.

38. For a discussion of this, see Joan E. Cook, *Hannah's Desire, God's Design: Early Interpretations of the Story of Hannah* (JSOTS 282; Sheffield: Sheffield University Press, 1999), 91–118.

39. K. H. Rengstorf, "Doulos," *TDNT* 2 (1962): 266–69, 273–79.

40. For an overview of slavery in the ancient world, see J. Albert Harill, *Slaves in the New Testament: Literary, Social and Moral Dimensions* (Minneapolis: Fortress, 2006).

41. Sandra R. Joshel, "Nurturing the Master's Child: Slavery and the Roman Child-Nurse," *Signs* 2 (1986): 3–22. Slave wet nurses did elicit anxiety on the part of some ancient commentators. Plutarch's *The Education of Children* expresses concern about foreign wet nurses contaminating children (3E 4A).

42. Jennifer A. Glancy, *Corporeal Knowledge: Early Christian Bodies* (New York: Oxford University Press, 2010), 83. The problem is not merely one of uncovering or dwelling on genitalia. The genitalia of Jesus are often on display in Christian art. It is theological equivocation, not prudishness, that obscures them.

43. *Jewish Antiquities* II.218.

44. *Exod. Rab.* 1.20, *b. Sot.* 12a. Some have argued that, in the rabbinic period, there was a shift from interest in general communal punishment to a focus on individual pain and suffering. The correlation of individual righteousness and freedom from pain that we see here may be part of this larger trend. See Martha Himmelfarb, *Tours of Hell: An Apocalyptic Form in Jewish and Christian Literature* (Philadelphia: University of Pennsylvania Press, 1983).

45. In a chapter on Mary, Jennifer Glancy briefly sketches the impact of theories of pain and childbirth in Western tradition. See Glancy, *Corporeal Knowledge*, 81–136.

46. Elaine Zwelling, "The History of Lamaze Continues: An Interview with Elisabeth Bing," *Journal of Perinatal Education* 9 (2000): 15–21, cited in Glancy, *Corporeal Knowledge*, 89.

47. For an overview, see Harold W. Attridge, "The Relentless Quest for the Beloved Disciple," in *Early Christian Voices: In Texts, Traditions and Symbols*, ed. David H. Warren, Ann Graham Brock, and David W. Pao (BIS 66; Leiden: Brill, 2003), 71–80.

48. Origen, *Contra Celsum* 1.69.

49. *T. Chullin* 2.22–24.

50. Pauline Christology does not focus on divine sonship. While there are seven references to Jesus as "Son" in Romans and four in Galatians, there are over two hundred references to Jesus as "Lord." It is noteworthy that when Paul talks about sonship, he does so in the context of discussing inheritance and access to the covenantal promises made to Abraham. The only juncture at which Paul discusses *how* Christ comes to be in a narrative form is the Christological hymn found in Phil 2:6–11. Once again, however, Paul demurs on the issue of sonship. It is on the lordship of Jesus that the Apostle to the Gentiles focuses.

CHAPTER 5: CHASTITY, MARRIAGE, AND GENDER IN THE CHRISTIAN FAMILY

1. For overviews of Paul's treatment of marriage in 1 Cor. 7, see J.-M. Cambier, "Doctrine paulinienne du marriage chrétien: Étude critique de 1 Co 7 et d'Ep 5,21–33 et essai de leur traduction actuelle," *ÉgT* 10 (1979): 13–59; C. C. Caragounis, "'Fornication' and 'Concession'? Interpreting 1 Cor 7,1–7," in *The Corinthian Correspondence*, ed. R. Bieringer (BETL 125; Leuven: Leuven University Press, 1996), 543–59; Will Deming, *Paul on Marriage and Celibacy: The Hellenistic Background of 1 Corinthians 7* (SNTSMS 83; Cambridge: Cambridge University Press, 1995), 1–46.

2. A number of scholars have observed that the tension created by Paul's vacillation between denouncement of marriage and his provision of exceptions to this rule is both the cause of exegetical strife and characteristic of 1 Corinthians. See Judith M. Gundry-Volf, "1 Cor 7:5b in the Light of a Hellenistic-Jewish Tradition on Abstinence to 'Devote Leisure.' Sufficiency in Paul and Philo," in *Paulus-Werk und Wirkung. Festschrift*

für Andreas Lindemann zum 70. Geburtstag, ed. Paul-Gerhard Klumbies and David S. du Toit (Tübingen: Mohr Siebeck, 2013), 21–44 (22–23).

3. For an analysis of Paul's treatment of marriage as a concession, see Hans Lietzmann, *An die Korinther I, II* (HNT 9; Tübingen: Mohr, 1969), 30; Hans Conzelmann, *1 Corinthians: A Commentary on the First Epistle to the Corinthians* (Hermeneia; Philadelphia: Fortress, 1975), 118; Helmut Merklein, *Der erste Brief an die Korinther*, vol. 2 (ÖTK 7; Gütersloh: Gütersloher Verlagshaus Gerd Mohn, 2000), 110–11; Archibald Robertson and Alfred Plummer, *A Critical and Exegetical Commentary on the First Epistle of St. Paul to the Corinthians*, 2nd ed. (ICC; Edinburgh: T&T Clark, 1971), 135. Against these, see Joseph A. Fitzmyer, *First Corinthians* (AB 32; New Haven: Yale University Press, 2008), 282, who argues that Paul's use of imperatives in 1 Cor 7:2–3 is closer to a command than a concession.

4. So Dale B. Martin, "Paul without Passion: On Paul's Rejection of Desire in Sex and Marriage," in *Constructing Early Christian Families: Family as Social Reality and Metaphor*, ed. Halvor Moxnes (London: Routledge, 1997), 201–15.

5. One of the complications here is that Paul has a tendency to introduce an opinion or proscription on a measure only to supply exceptions to the rule. A variety of explanations of this phenomenon have been offered. Henry Chadwick sees it as apologetic, arguing that Paul "manages to combine an ability to retreat so far as to seem to surrender almost everything in principle to the opposition with an ability to make practical recommendations not easily reconciled with the theory he virtually accepts" (Henry Chadwick, "'All Things to All Men' (1 Cor. IX.22)," *NTS* 1 [1954/55]: 261–75 [264]). A. C. Wire agrees and, like Chadwick, is convinced that Paul states his agreement with the ascetic stance but in fact takes a more promarriage position. See *The Corinthian Women Prophets: A Reconstruction through Paul's Rhetoric* (Minneapolis: Fortress, 1990), 72–97. Margaret Mitchell sees the oscillations as part and parcel of Paul's rhetorical strategy and his desire to draw various divided groups together (Margaret M. Mitchell, *Paul and the Rhetoric of Reconciliation: An Exegetical Investigation of the Language and Composition of 1 Corinthians* [HUTh 28; Tübingen: Mohr Siebeck, 1991], 235–37). Others have tried to historicize the situation and see Paul as charting the difficult terrain between various Jewish understandings of marriage: e.g., P. J.

Tomson, *Paul and the Jewish Law: Halakha in the Letters of the Apostle to the Gentiles* (Compendia Rerum Iudaicarum ad Novum Testamentum. Section III: Jewish Traditions in Early Christian Literature 1; Assen: Van Corcum, 1990), 105–8. While there were certainly tensions surrounding the merits of celibacy and marriage in ancient Judaism, it might be an oversimplification to locate the various positions concretely—as Tomson does—in the Essenes and the "mainstream."

6. For an overview of self-restraint in general, see Judith M. Gundry-Volf, "Controlling the Bodies: A Theological Profile of the Corinthian Sexual Ascetics (1 Cor 7)," in *The Corinthian Correspondence*, ed. R. Bieringer (BETL 125; Leuven: Leuven University Press, 1996), 519–41. Some have grounded Paul's argument in Second Temple Jewish parallels (Eccl 3:5; Joel 2:16; Zech 12:12–24; *m. Ned* 5.6; *t. Ned* 5.6; and *T. Naph* 8.8: "there is a season [for a man] to have sexual intercourse with his wife, and a season to abstain therefrom for his prayer"). Gundry convincingly argues for Philonic analogues to Pauline thought. On Philo as an ascetic, see Hermann Strathmann, *Geschichte der früchristlichen Askese bis zur Entstehung des Mönchtums, vol. 1: Die Askese in der Umgebung des wedenden Christentums* (Leipzig: Deichert, 1914), 125–47, 148–57 and Kathy L. Gaca, "Philo's Principles of Sexual Conduct and Their Influence on Christian Platonist Sexual Principles," *Studia Philonica Annual* 8 (1996): 21–39.

7. For the argument that by "concession" Paul means something approximate to "compassionate understanding," see Gundry-Volf, "1 Cor. 7:5b," 28.

8. Scholarly discussions of the language of divine gifts of *charisms* in 1 Corinthians operate in light of unvoiced commitments to marriage as good. For a rather strained effort to turn marriage into a charism, see Fitzmyer, *First Corinthians*, 282. Conversely, we should note that Paul does list *enkrateia* among the fruits of the spirit in Gal 5:23.

9. So Jennifer Wright Knust, *Abandoned to Lust: Sexual Slander and Ancient Christianity* (Gender, Theory, and Religion; New York: Columbia University Press, 2005), 80–84.

10. See, e.g., Fitzmyer, *First Corinthians*, 317.

11. Pregnant women and nursing mothers occasionally feature in biblical oracles about judgment. *4 Ezra* 16.44–46 specifically warns against having children in a period of eschatological unrest.

12. So Joel Marcus, *Mark 8–16* (Yale Anchor Commentary 27; New Haven: Yale University Press, 2002), 895–96. War was a great hardship on new mothers. Josephus relays a potentially apocryphal story of a young mother cannibalizing her own child (*Jewish War* 6.201–19 cited in Marcus, *Mark 8–16*, 892).

13. Equally untenable is the psychoanalytical perspective that Paul himself suffers from a form of psychological disorder that leads him to these regulations. See A. R. Eickhoff, "A Psychoanalytic Study of St. Paul's Theology of Sex," *Pastoral Psychology* 18, no. 173 (1967): 35–72, and criticisms in Fitzmyer, *First Corinthians*, 274.

14. See Halvor Moxnes, "What Is a Family? Problems in Constructing Early Christian Families," in *Constructing Early Christian Families: Family as Social Reality and Metaphor*, ed. Halvor Moxnes (London: Routledge, 1997), 13.

15. On how religious perspectives have shaped the interpretation of Paul's views of good sex, see Martin, "Paul without Passion," 204.

16. Soranus, *Gynecology* I.33.

17. On the "disease of virgins," see Helen King, "Green Sickness: Hippocrates, Galen and the Origins of the 'Disease of Virgins,'" *International Journal of the Classical Tradition* 2 (1996): 372–87.

18. For an excellent overview of ancient Roman attitudes to sex, see Kyle Harper, *From Shame to Sin: The Christian Transformation of Sexual Morality in Late Antiquity* (Revealing Antiquity 20; Cambridge, MA: Harvard University Press, 2013), 79–86.

19. Galen, *On the Preservation of Health* 1.5. See the discussion in Vivian Nutton, *Ancient Medicine*, 2nd ed. (Abingdon: Routledge, 2013), 47–48, and Dale B. Martin, *The Corinthian Body* (New Haven: Yale University Press, 1995), 146–53, 216–17.

20. Galen, *On the Preservation of Health* 1.1, 2.2.

21. On food, see Galen, *On the Affected Parts* 6.5; on wine, see Dionysius, *Ach. Tat.* 2.3.3; Galen, *On the Preservation of Health* 1.11, 5.5; and Plutarch, *Morals* 701F. See the discussion on food and sex in Teresa Shaw, *The Burden of the Flesh: Fasting and Sexuality in Early Christianity* (Minneapolis: Fortress, 1998), 99.

22. See Athenaeus, *Deipnosophists* 10.444d. See also Ps-Aristotle's statement that "wine makes men inclined to love (*aphrodisiastikous*)" (*Problems* 30.1).

23. The best study of Roman marriage remains Susan Treggiari, *Roman Marriage: Iusti Coniuges from the Time of Cicero to the Time of Ulpian* (Oxford: Clarendon, 1991).

24. Soranus, *Gynecology* I.42.

25. Ibid., I.42.

26. Keith Hopkins, "Contraception in the Roman Empire," *Comparative Studies in Society and History* 8 (1965): 124–51.

27. See Suetonius, *Life of Augustus* 34. It is worth noting that citizenship was restricted in the first century CE.

28. In Mary R. Lefkowitz and Maureen B. Fant, *Women's Life in Greece and Rome: A Source Book in Translation*, 3rd ed. (Baltimore: Johns Hopkins University Press, 2005), 103.

29. Cassius Dio, *Roman History* 54.16.1.

30. Propertius, *Elegy* 2.7.

31. Tom Stoppard, *The Invention of Love* (Boston: Faber and Faber, 1997). For a history of love and the evolution of modern theories of love, see Simon May, *Love: A History* (New Haven: Yale University Press, 2011).

32. Plutarch, *On Affection for Offspring* 493 E–F.

33. Ibid., 493 F.

34. The *kinaidos* or "girlie man" is often assumed to be an exclusive attraction to passive homosexual relations. But the *kinaidos* could also experience passionate attraction to women. It was "his addiction to pleasure that led him to lose his manly sense of propriety and allow himself to be penetrated" (Harper, *From Shame to Sin*, 56). On softness and pleasure, see Holt N. Parker, "Love's Body Anatomized: The Ancient Erotic Handbooks and the Rhetoric of Sexuality," in *Pornography and Representation in Greece and Rome*, ed. Amy Richlin (Princeton: Princeton University Press, 1992), 90–110.

35. Dio. Or. 3.34.

36. Polybius, *Histories* 10.19.6, LCL emended translation.

37. Achilles Tatius, *Leucippe and Clitophon* 5.20.5. For a discussion of the concept of male virginity in general, see Christian Laes, "Male Virgins in Latin Inscriptions from Rome," in *Religion and Socialization in Antiquity and the Middle Ages*, ed. K. Mustakallio, S. Katajala-Peltomaa, and V. Vuolanto (Rome: Acta Instituti Finlandiae, 2013), 105–19.

38. For the view that the early Stoics did not denounce *eros* as a passion, see Kathy L. Gaca, "Early Stoic Eros: Sexual Ethics of Zeno and Chrysippus and Their Evaluation of the Greek Erotic Tradition," *Apeiron* 33 (2000): 207–38.

39. Musonius Rufus, *On Sex* frag. 12. Translation from Cora E. Lutz, "Musonius Rufus: 'The Roman Socrates,'" *Yale Classical Studies* 10 (1947): 85–87.

40. *Gen. Am.* 675.

41. Philo, *Joseph* 43.

42. Philo, *Spec. Laws* 3:36.

43. Michael Satlow, *Tasting the Dish: The Rabbinic Rhetorics of Sexuality* (BJS 303; Atlanta: Scholars, 1995), 225.

44. Juvenal, *Satiries* 6.366–78. Galen in *On the Usefulness of the Parts of the Body* 4.190.16 describes how eunuchs who were castrated as children retained sexuality and were thus able to have sex without issue.

45. For Stoic sexual ethics, see Martin, "Paul without Passion," 201–15. For precedents in Jewish asceticism, see Stephen C. Barton, "The Relativization of Family Ties in the Jewish and Graeco-Roman Traditions," in Moxnes, *Constructing Early Christian Families*, 81–102.

46. Justin Martyr, *2 Apology* 1–2, describes a Christian woman suing her pagan husband for divorce on grounds of immorality.

47. Dale B. Martin, *Sex and the Single Savior* (Philadelphia: Westminster John Knox, 2006), 115.

48. For this dating, see Jan N. Bremmer, "Aspects of the Acts of Peter: Women, Magic, Place and Date," in *The Apocryphal Acts of Peter: Magic, Miracles, and Gnosticism*, ed. Jan N. Bremmer (SAAA 3; Leuven: Peeters, 1998), 1–20 (here 18).

49. Constantin von Tischendorf, Max Bonnet, and Richard Adelbert Lipsius, *Acta Apostolorum Apocrypha*, vol. 1 (Darmstadt: Wissenschaftliche Buchgesellschaft, 1959). For English translations, see "The Acts of Peter," in *The Apocryphal New Testament*, ed. John K. Elliott (Oxford: Clarendon, 1993), 397–427; Wilhelm Schneemelcher, "The Acts of Peter," in *New Testament Apocrypha*, ed. Wilhelm Schneemelcher and R. McL. Wilson (Cambridge: James Clark, 1991), 285–317.

50. On this, see Raphael, *Biblical Corpora*, 13. In an unpublished paper, Anna Rebecca Solevag notes that the *Acts of Peter* replaces "deaf" with "dumb"

(Anna Rebecca Solevag, "Disability and Sexuality in the *Acts of Peter*" (paper, Society of Biblical Literature, Chicago, November 18, 2012) .

51. Anathea Portier-Young, " 'Eyes to the Blind': A Dialogue between Tobit and Job," in *Intertextual Studies in Ben Sira and Tobi*, ed. J. Corley and V. Skemp (Washington, DC: Catholic Biblical Association, 2005), 14–27 (esp. 17–21), and Micah Kiel, "Tobit's Theological Blindness," *CBQ* 72 (2011): 281–98. Both make the good point that blindness symbolizes death, but both assume that Tobit's physical blindness is a cipher for a deeper spiritual blindness. While that seems to be the case in the *Acts of Peter*, the argument is less compelling for Tobit. For an analysis of the connection between blinding and almsgiving in Tobit, see Gary Anderson, *Charity: The Place of the Poor in the Biblical Tradition* (New Haven: Yale University Press, 2013), 71–78.

52. For this view, see Wilhelm Schneemelcher, "The Acts of Peter: Introduction," in *New Testament Apocrypha*, ed. Wilhelm Schneemelcher and R. McL. Wilson (Cambridge: James Clark, 1991), 271–85 (at 279); Christine M. Thomas, *The Acts of Peter, Gospel Literature, and the Ancient Novel: Rewriting the Past* (Oxford: Oxford University Press, 2003), 17–20, 68. The story of Peter's daughter is preserved in the Coptic Berlin papyrus, while the story about the gardener's daughter is from the apocryphal Epistle of Titus.

53. Petronius, *Satyricon* 131 (Heseline, LCL).

54. On infertility and divorce, see Carolyn A. Osiek and David L. Balch, *Families in the New Testament World: Households and House Churches in Context* (Louisville: Westminster John Knox Press, 1997), 133, which cites the legendary divorce case of Spurius Carvilius (231 BCE), who claimed that his wife was barren.

55. Plutarch's *Moralia*, *The Face of the Moon* 938 F LCL.

56. Plato, *Theaetetus* 149 B and *Cornutus* 34.

57. Scholarly analysis on the virginity of Artemis has argued, quite vociferously, that she represents not cold sterility but, rather, fertility. The connection is evocative of the tension that makes martyrs the healers of infirmity, and polar opposites the cures of illness. At the same time, the intricate binding of fertility and sterility pushes back against modern notions. They are not bifurcated: like attracts opposite.

58. Sophocles, *Oedipus Tyrannus* 1502.

59. So Ross S. Kraemer, "Monastic Jewish Women in Greco-Roman Egypt: Philo Judaeus on the Therapeutrides," *Signs* 14 (1989): 342–70.

CHAPTER 6: BARRENNESS AND THE ESCHATON

1. See, for example, the fourth-century Sarcophagi of the Spouses, sometimes called the Trinity Sarcophagus, currently housed in the Museum of Ancient Arles.
2. Eusebius, *Church History* 7.18.
3. For a discussion of this, see Candida R. Moss, "The Man with the Flow of Power: Porous Bodies in Mark 5:25–34," *JBL* 129, no. 3 (2010): 507–19 (508–11).
4. E.g., Aristotle, *Historia Animalium* 3.19 and discussion in Lesley Dean-Jones, *Women's Bodies in Classical Greek Science* (Oxford: Clarendon, 1994), 129; Rebecca Flemming, *Medicine and the Making of Roman Women: Gender, Nature, and Authority from Celsus to Galen* (New York: Oxford University Press, 2000).
5. Technically it also precedes the story, making this a prime example of the "Markan literary sandwich." For a discussion of the literary function of this device, see James R. Edwards, "Markan Sandwiches: The Significance of Interpolations in Markan Narratives," *NovT* 31 (1989): 193–216.
6. Mark is not alone here. Many in the ancient world criticized the competency of doctors. For a discussion of the xenophobia and suspicion that surrounded doctors and was perpetuated by some of them, see Nutton, *Ancient Medicine*, 14–16.
7. *"Xeraino" LSJ* 1190.
8. Mary Rose D'Angelo, "Gender and Power in the Gospel of Mark: The Daughter of Jairus and the Woman with the Flow of Blood," in *Miracles in Jewish and Christian Antiquity: Imagining Truth*, ed. John C. Cavadini (Notre Dame Studies in Theology 3; Notre Dame: University of Notre Dame Press, 1999), 83–109 (here 98).
9. See summaries in Collins, *Mark*, 280–84, and Joel S. Marcus, *Mark 1–8* (AB 27; New York: Doubleday, 2000), 356–61.
10. Hippocrates, *Airs, Waters, Places* 4 (all references are Penguin Edition, ed. G.E.R. Lloyd [1978] unless otherwise indicated).

11. *PDM* xiv. 956–60. Translated in Hans D. Betz, ed., *The Greek Magical Papyri in Translation: Including the Demotic Spells*, vol. 1 (Chicago: University of Chicago Press, 1986).

12. There is an implicit link between human and plant biology here. The same link is implied in the use of our modern term of "barren" to refer to both fields and women.

13. There is a kind of interesting irony here. Menstrual blood itself was associated with death and drying up. See Pliny the Elder: "Contact with [menstrual blood] turns new wine sour, crops touched by it become barren, grafts die, seed in gardens are dried up, the fruit of trees fall off, the edge of steel and the gleam of ivory are dulled, hives of bees die, even bronze and iron are at once seized by rust, and a horrible smell fills the air; to taste it drives dogs mad and infects their bites with an incurable poison." *Natural History* 7.64 (Rackham, LCL).

14. The definitive work on menstrual blood and pollution is Mary Douglas, *Purity and Danger: An Analysis of Concepts of Pollution and Taboo* (Abingdon: Routledge, 2002), esp. 171–82.

15. In Mark *sozein* is used both to denote the rescuing of a person from death or physical ailment (3:4; 5:28, 34; 6:56; 10:52; 13:20; 15:30, 31) and the acquisition of eternal life (8:35; 10:26; 13:13). For a discussion, see Collins, *Mark*, 279, 749.

16. On materialism in the Apostolic Fathers, see Angelo P. O'Hagan, *Material Re-creation in the Apostolic Fathers* (TUGAL 100; Berlin: Akademie-Verlag, 1968).

17. It is interesting that in his description of the ideal state Plato does envision such a system of redistribution. He discusses the use of reward-based population control to either inhibit or encourage fertility and adoption in order to maintain a stable and constant number of households (*Laws* 5.740b-d).

18. See, for example, Scott Shauf, "Locating the Eunuch. Characterization and Narrative Context in Acts 8:26–40," *CBQ* 71 (2009): 762–75.

19. A very marginal position downplays the interest in gender altogether and argues that "eunuch" was just a synonym for a court official or minister. See the sociological reflections of L. A. Coser, *Greedy Institutions: Patterns of Undivided Commitment* (New York: Free Press, 1974).

20. Marianne B. Kartzow and Halvor Moxnes, "Complex Identities: Ethnicity, Gender and Religion in the Story of the Ethiopian Eunuch (Acts

8:26–40)," *Religion and Theology* 17 (2010): 184–204; Martin Leutzsch, "Eunuch und Intersektionalität: ein multiperspektivischer Versuch zu Apg 8, 26–40," in *Doing Gender—Doing Religion: Fallstudien zur Intersektionalität im frühen Judentum, Christentum und Islam*, ed. Ute E. Eisen, Christine Gerber, and Angela Standhartinger (WUNT 302; Tübingen: Mohr Siebeck, 2013), 405–30.

21. N. A. Dahl, "Nations in the New Testament," in *New Testament Christianity for Africa and the World*, ed. M. Glasswell and E. W. Fasholé-Luke (London: SPCK, 1974), 54–68.

22. Ibid., 62.

23. D. K. Williams, "Acts," in *True to Our Native Land: An African-American Commentary on the New Testament*, ed. B. K. Blount (Minneapolis: Fortress, 2007), 225–28 (227).

24. Virginia Burrus, "The Gospel of Luke and the Acts of the Apostles," in *A Postcolonial Commentary on the New Testament Writings*, ed. F. F. Segovia and R. S. Sugirtharajah (London: T & T Clark, 2007), 133–55 (149–50).

25. Yong, *Bible, Disability, and the Church.*

26. For a further discussion of this system, see Mathew Kuefler, *The Manly Eunuch. Masculinity, Gender Ambiguity, and Christian Ideology in Late Antiquity* (Chicago: University of Chicago Press, 2011).

27. Lucian, *De Syria dea* 51; Catullus, *carmina* 63; Ovid, *Fasti* 4.183–86; 4.351–366.

28. Ulpian's neat distinction is undone by the overlap between terms like *spado* and *castratus*. While many commentators argue that a *castratus* is one who is *caste natus* (i.e., born without testicles) and a *spado* is one who had them removed, this may be grounded in faulty etymology. The *thlibidae* or *thlasie*, whose testicles had been damaged but not removed, were sometimes categorized as *spado*.

29. Sean D. Burke, *Queering the Ethiopian Eunuch: Strategies of Ambiguity in Acts* (Minneapolis: Fortress, 2013), 97.

30. F. S. Spencer, *The Portrait of Philip in Acts: A Study of Roles and Relations* (JSNTSup67; Sheffield: Sheffield Academic Press, 1992), 138.

31. Kartzow and Moxnes, "Complex Identities," 197.

32. Maud Gleason, *Making Men: Sophists and Self-Presentation in Ancient Rome* (Princeton: Princeton University Press, 1995).

33. Bruce J. Malina, *The New Testament World: Insights from Cultural Anthropology* (Atlanta: John Knox, 1981), 175, and Halvor Moxnes, *Putting Jesus in His Place. A Radical Vision of Household and Kingdom* (Louisville: Westminster John Knox, 2003), 78–80.

34. Herodotus describes how foreigners valued eunuchs more highly as slaves precisely because of their trustworthiness (*Histories* 8.105), and Xenophon elaborates that Cyrus believed that—without wives or children—eunuchs would exhibit greater fidelity toward their patron than anyone else (*Cyropaedia* 7). For the body of the eunuch as a faithful body, see C. Grottanelli, "Faithful Bodies: Ancient Greek Sources on Oriental Eunuchs," in *Self, Soul and Body in Religious Experience*, ed. Albert I. Baumgarten with Jan Assmann and Guy G. Stroumsa (Leiden: Brill, 1998), 404–16.

35. Mikeal C. Parsons, *Body and Character in Luke and Acts. The Subversion of Physiognomy in Early Christianity* (Grand Rapids, MI: Baker, 2006), 134–35.

36. K. M. Ringrose, *Eunuchs and the Social Construction of Gender in Byzantium* (Chicago: University of Chicago Press, 2003), 206. Examples of eunuchs serving in this role can be found in Greek literature in Polybius, *Historiae* 22.22; Plutarch, *Artaxerxes* 16.1; *Callirhoe* 5.9.

37. L. E. Roller, "The Ideology of the Eunuch Priest," in *Gender and the Body in the Ancient Mediterranean*, ed. M. Wyke (Oxford: Blackwell, 1998), 118–35 (127).

38. Gaius 1.103: "Both forms of adoption agree in this point, that persons incapable of procreation by natural impotence (*spadones*) are permitted to adopt."

39. Historia Augusta, *Severus Alexander* 23.7.

40. Acts of Paul, Coptic MS version, paras. 14, 39, in M. R. James, ed., *The Apocryphal New Testament* (Oxford: Oxford University Press, 1924), 275, 280.

41. For histories of *3 Corinthians*, see Vahan Hovhanessian, *Third Corinthians: Reclaiming Paul for Christian Orthodoxy* (Studies in Biblical Literature 18; New York: Peter Lang, 2000), 1–79; Steve Johnston, "La correspondance apocryphe entre Paul et les Corinthiens: Un pseudépigraphe Paulinien au service de la polémique anti-gnostique de la fin du IIe siècle" (master's diss., L'Université Laval, 2004), 1–77. The heretics envisioned in *3 Corinthians* have been variously identified as Marcion-

ites, Valentinians, Ophites, Saturnilus, Simon Magus, and the "gnostics." For a discussion of the way that *3 Corinthians* fits into the landscape of ancient contestations of orthodoxy, see Benjamin L. White, "Reclaiming Paul? Reconfiguration as Reclamation in *3 Corinthians*," *JECS* 17 (2009): 497–523.

42. "Third Corinthians," in James, *Apocryphal New Testament*, 288–92.

43. On the possible Jewish background of Paul's vision of resurrection in 1 Thess 4:16–17, see Candida R. Moss and Joel S. Baden, "1 Thess 4.13–18 in Rabbinic Perspective," *NTS* 58 (2012): 199–212.

44. *b. Nid.* 69b, 70b.

45. H. L. Strack and Paul Billerbeck, *Kommentar zum Neuen Testament aus Talmud und Midrasch*, 6 vols. (Munich: Beck, 1924–56), 1:593.

46. Ibid., 1.895 and Collins, *Mark*, 561n120.

47. Pace Collins, who argues that Ezek. 37 is about corpse resuscitation not resurrection (*Mark*, 560–61). While Collins is no doubt correct with respect to the original context in which Ezekiel was written, authorial intent is irrelevant when it comes to first-century interpretations. If there is a problem with Billerbeck's argument it is that it lacks first-century support, not that it assumes that first-century readers were bad historical critics. First-century readers weren't conversant in post-Enlightenment interpretive methodologies.

48. For the view that resurrection of the body is a hallmark of orthodoxy, see Origen, *On First Principles* 2.10.3; Justin Martyr, *Dialogue with Trypho* 80; Athenagoras, *On the Resurrection* 1.

49. For the role that the resurrection of the body played in both articulating resistance to dominant political structures and defining in-group identity, see Claudia Setzer, *Resurrection of the Body in Early Judaism and Early Christianity* (Leiden: Brill, 2004).

50. See Candida R. Moss, "Heavenly Healing: Eschatological Cleansing and the Resurrection of the Dead in the Early Church," *Journal of the American Academy of Religion* 79, no. 3 (2011): 1–27.

51. Irenaeus, *Adversus Haereses* 4.33.11 (ANF 2.14).

52. Ibid., 5.13.1 (ANF 1.539).

53. Caroline Walker Bynum, *The Resurrection of the Body in Western Christianity, 200–1336* (New York: Columbia University Press, 1995). 25.

54. Pseudo-Justin, *On the Resurrection* 4.

55. Ibid., 3.
56. Ibid., 3.
57. Augustine, *City of God* 22.19.1149–1150.
58. Ibid., 22.19.1149. We sympathize with the sentiment but disagree with Beth Felker Jones's reading of this passage in which she suggests that Augustine thinks blemishes will be beautiful in the body of Christ (*Marks of His Wounds: Gender Politics and Bodily Resurrection* [Oxford: Oxford University Press, 2007], 29). Her suggestion that blemish is redefined as glorious is wonderful but, to us at least, seems to misrepresent Augustine's view. We take her point, however, that it is in his description of the martyrs that Augustine comes closest to allowing disability into his divine city.
59. Augustine, *City of God* 22.20.1152.
60. Ibid., 22.20.1152. Augustine writes that there will be two sexes at the eschaton because a woman's sex is not a defect. God created two sexes, so God will restore them both (22.17.1145).
61. Clement, *Stromateis* 3.48.1.
62. Augustine, *Against Faustus* 22.30. And see also *Manichean Ways of Life* 15.37; 16.49; 18.65–66; 19.73.
63. John Chrysostom, *On Virginity* 125.126.
64. On the construction of heavenly bodies and the question of "abledness," see particularly Amos Yong, *Theology and Down Syndrome: Reimagining Disability in Late Modernity* (Waco, TX: Baylor University Press, 2007), 259–92 and Moss, "Heavenly Healing," 27.

BIBLIOGRAPHY

Abusch, I. Tzvi. "Witchcraft, Impotence, and Indigestion." Pages 146–59 in *Disease in Babylonia*. Edited by I. L. Finkel and M. J. Geller. Cuneiform Monographs 36. Leiden: Brill, 2007.

Allam, S. "A New Look at the Adoption Papyrus (Reconsidered)." *Journal of Egyptian Archaeology* 76 (1990): 189–91.

Anderson, Gary. *Charity: The Place of the Poor in the Biblical Tradition*. New Haven: Yale University Press, 2013.

Ando, Clifford. *Imperial Ideology and Provincial Loyalty in the Roman Empire*. Berkeley: University of California Press, 2000.

Araoye, M. O. "Epidemiology of Infertility: Social Problems of the Infertile Couples." *Western African Journal of Medicine* 22 (2003): 190–96.

Attridge, Harold W. "The Relentless Quest for the Beloved Disciple." Pages 71–80 in *Early Christian Voices: In Texts, Traditions and Symbols*. Edited by David H. Warren, Ann Graham Brock, and David W. Pao. Biblical Interpretation Series 66. Leiden: Brill, 2003.

Avalos, Hector. *Illness and Health Care in the Ancient Near East: The Role of the Temple in Greece, Mesopotamia, and Israel*. Harvard Semitic Museum Monographs 54. Atlanta: Scholars, 1995.

Baden, Joel S. and Candida R. Moss. "The Origin and Interpretation of ṣāraʿat in Leviticus 13–14." *Journal of Biblical Literature* 130 (2011): 643–62.

Bartholin, Thomas. *Historiarum anatomicarum variorum centuria V et VI*. Hafniae, 1661.

Barton, Stephen C. "The Relativization of Family Ties in the Jewish and Graeco-Roman Traditions." Pages 81–102 in *Constructing Early Christian Families: Family as Social Reality and Metaphor*. Edited by Halvor Moxnes. London: Routledge, 1997.

Baskin, Judith R. *Midrashic Women: Formations of the Feminine in Rabbinic Literature*. Brandeis Series on Jewish Women. Hanover, NH: Brandeis University Press, 2002.

Bechtel, Lyn M. "The Perception of Shame within the Divine-Human Relationship in Biblical Israel." Pages 79–92 in *Uncovering Ancient Stones*. Edited by Lewis M. Hopfe. Winona Lake, IN: Eisenbrauns, 1994.

———. "Shame as a Sanction of Social Control in Biblical Israel: Judicial, Political, and Social Shaming." *Journal for the Study of the Old Testament* 49 (1991): 47–76.

Becker, Gay. "Metaphors in Disrupted Lives: Infertility and Cultural Constructions of Continuity." *Medical Anthropology Quarterly* 8 (1994): 383–410.

Beckman, Gary M. *Hittite Birth Rituals*. 2nd ed. Studien zu den Boğazköy-Texten 29. Wiesbaden: Harrassowitz, 1983.

Beckman, L. J. and S. M. Harvey. "Current Reproductive Technologies: Increased Access and Choice?" *Journal of Social Issues* 61 (2005): 1–20.

Bergmann, Claudia D. *Childbirth as a Metaphor for Crisis: Evidence from the Ancient Near East, the Hebrew Bible, and 1QH XI, 1–18*. Beihefte zur Zeitschrift für die alttestamentliche Wissenschaft 382. Berlin: de Gruyter, 2008.

Betz, Hans D., ed. *The Greek Magical Papyri in Translation: Including the Demotic Spells*. Vol. 1. Chicago: University of Chicago Press, 1986.

Beuken, W. A. M. "Isaiah liv: The Multiple Identity of the Person Addressed." *Oudtestamentische Studiën* 19 (1974): 29–70.

Biddle, Mark E. "The Figure of Lady Jerusalem: Identification, Deification and Personification of Cities in the Ancient Near East." Pages 173–94 in *The Biblical Canon in Comparative Perspective*. Edited by K. Lawson Younger Jr., William W. Hallo, and Bernard F. Batto. Scripture in Context 4. Ancient Near Eastern Texts and Studies 11. Lewiston: Edwin Mellen, 1991.

Biggs, Robert D. *Saziga: Ancient Mesopotamian Potency Incantations*. Locust Valley, NY: J. J. Augustin, 1967.

Bitler, M. and L. Schmidt. "Health Disparities and Infertility: Impacts of State Level Mandates." *Fertility and Sterility* 85 (2006): 858–64.

Blenkinsopp, Joseph. *Isaiah 40–55*. Anchor Bible 19A. New York: Doubleday, 2002.

———. *Isaiah 56–66*. Anchor Bible 19B. New York: Doubleday, 2003.

Bloch-Smith, Elizabeth. *Judahite Burial Practices and Beliefs about the Dead.* Journal for the Study of the Old Testament Supplement Series 123. Sheffield: Sheffield Academic Press, 1992.

Block, Daniel I. "Marriage and Family in Ancient Israel." Pages 33–102 in *Marriage and Family in the Biblical World.* Edited by Ken M. Campbell. Downers Grove, IL: InterVarsity, 2003.

Boda, Mark J. "The Daughter's Joy." Pages 321–42 in *Daughter Zion: Her Portrait, Her Response.* Edited by Mark J. Boda, Carol J. Dempsey, and LeAnn Snow Flesher. Society of Biblical Literature Ancient Israel and Its Literature 13. Atlanta: Society of Biblical Literature, 2012.

Borocin-Knol, S. "Zion as an 'Agunah? An Interpretation of Isaiah 49:14; 50:1 and 54:6–8." Pages 191–206 in *"Enlarge the Site of Your Tent": The City as Unifying Theme in Isaiah.* Edited by Archibald L. H. M. van Wieringen and Annemarieke van der Woude. Oudtestamentische Studiën 58. Leiden: Brill, 2011.

Bovon, Francois. *Luke 1: A Commentary on the Gospel of Luke 1:1–9:50.* Hermeneia. Philadelphia: Fortress, 2002.

Bremmer, Jan N. "Aspects of the Acts of Peter: Women, Magic, Place and Date." Pages 1–20 in *The Apocryphal Acts of Peter: Magic, Miracles, and Gnosticism.* Edited by Jan N. Bremmer. Studies on the Apocryphal Acts of the Apostles 3. Leuven: Peeters, 1998.

Brenner, Athalya. *The Israelite Woman: Social Role and Literary Type in Biblical Narrative.* Sheffield: JSOT, 1985.

Brown, Raymond E. *The Birth of the Messiah: A Commentary on the Infancy Gospels.* Anchor Bible Reference Library. New York: Doubleday, 1993.

Brueggemann, Walter. *Isaiah 40–66.* Westminster Bible Companion. Louisville: Westminster John Knox, 1998.

Burke, Sean D. *Queering the Ethiopian Eunuch: Strategies of Ambiguity in Acts.* Minneapolis: Fortress, 2013.

Burrus, Virginia. "The Gospel of Luke and the Acts of the Apostles." Pages 133–55 in *A Postcolonial Commentary on the New Testament Writings.* Edited by F. F. Segovia and R. S. Sugirtharajah. London: T & T Clark, 2007.

Bynum, Caroline Walker. *The Resurrection of the Body in Western Christianity, 200–1336.* New York: Columbia University Press, 1995.

Callaway, Mary. *Sing, O Barren One: A Study in Comparative Midrash.* Society of Biblical Literature Dissertation Series 91. Atlanta: Scholars, 1986.

Callister, Lynn Clark. "The Pain and the Promise of Unfulfilled Dreams: Infertile Couples." Pages 96–112 in *Handbook of Families and Health: Interdisciplinary Perspectives.* Edited by D. Russell Crane and Elaine S. Marshall. Thousand Oaks, CA: Sage, 2006.

Cambier, J.-M. "Doctrine paulinienne du marriage chrétien: Étude critique de 1 Co 7 et d'Ep 5,21–33 et essai de leur traduction actuelle." *Église et théologie* 10 (1979): 13–59.

Campus, Donatella. *Women Political Leaders and the Media.* New York: Palgrave Macmillan, 2013.

Caragounis, C. C. " 'Fornication' and 'Concession'? Interpreting 1 Cor 7,1–7." Pages 543–59 in *The Corinthian Correspondence.* Edited by R. Bieringer. Bibliotheca ephemeridum theologicarum Lovaniensium 125. Leuven: Leuven University Press, 1996.

Carlebach, Alexander and Judith Baskin. "Barrenness and Fertility." Pages 174–75 in *Encyclopedia Judaica.* 2nd ed. Edited by Michael Berenbaum and Fred Skolnik. Detroit: Macmillan, 2007.

Cassuto, Umberto. *A Commentary on Genesis.* Vol. 2. Jerusalem: Magnes, 1992.

Castelli, Elizabeth A. *Martyrdom and Memory: Early Christian Culture Making.* New York: Columbia University Press, 2004.

Chadwick, Henry. " 'All Things to All Men' (1 Cor. IX.22)." *New Testament Studies* 1 (1954/55): 261–75.

Clark, Laura. "Childless Women 'Vilified by Bosses': Why Not Having a Family Could Ruin Your Career." *Daily Mail,* May 18, 2009. http://www.dailymail.co.uk/femail/article-1183895/Childless-women-vilified-bosses-Why-NOT-having-family-ruin-career.html.

Clements, Ronald. "Deuteronomy." Page 514 in *The New Interpreter's Bible,* vol. 2. Nashville: Abingdon, 1998.

Cohen, Jeremy. *"Be Fertile and Increase, Fill the Earth and Master It": The Ancient and Medieval Career of a Biblical Text.* Ithaca: Cornell University Press, 1989.

Collins, Adela Yarbro. *Mark: A Commentary.* Hermeneia. Minneapolis: Fortress, 2007.

Collins, Adela Yarbro and John J. Collins. *King and Messiah as Son of God: Divine, Human, and Angelic Messianic Figures in Biblical and Related Literature.* Grand Rapids, MI: Eerdmans, 2008.

Conzelmann, Hans. *1 Corinthians: A Commentary on the First Epistle to the Corinthians.* Hermeneia. Philadelphia: Fortress, 1975.

Cook, Joan E. *Hannah's Desire, God's Design: Early Interpretations of the Story of Hannah.* Journal for the Study of the Old Testament Supplement Series 282. Sheffield: Sheffield University Press, 1999.

Coser, L. A. *Greedy Institutions: Patterns of Undivided Commitment.* New York: Free Press, 1974.

Cruz-Uribe, Eugene. "A New Look at the Adoption Papyrus." *Journal of Egyptian Archaeology* 74 (1988): 220–23.

Culley, L. and N. Hudson. "Disrupted Reproduction and Deviant Bodies: Pronatalism and British South Asian Communities." *International Journal of Diversity in Organisations, Communities and Nations* 5 (2006): 117–26.

——. "Public Understandings of Science: British South Asian Man's Conceptions of Third Party Assisted Conception." *International Journal of Interdisciplinary Social Sciences* 2 (2007): 79–86.

Dahl, N. A. "Nations in the New Testament." Pages 54–68 in *New Testament Christianity for Africa and the World.* Edited by M. Glasswell and E. W. Fasholé-Luke. London: SPCK, 1974.

Dalley, Stephanie. "Etana." Pages 453–47 in *The Context of Scripture,* vol. 1. Edited by William W. Hallo. Leiden: Brill, 1997.

D'Angelo, Mary Rose. "Gender and Power in the Gospel of Mark: The Daughter of Jairus and the Woman with the Flow of Blood." Pages 83–109 in *Miracles in Jewish and Christian Antiquity: Imagining Truth.* Edited by John C. Cavadini. Notre Dame Studies in Theology 3. Notre Dame: University of Notre Dame Press, 1999.

Darr, Katheryn Pfisterer. *Isaiah's Vision and the Family of God.* Literary Currents in Biblical Interpretation. Louisville: Westminster John Knox, 1994.

Daube, David. *The Duty of Procreation.* Eugene: Wipf & Stock, 1977.

Davies, Eryl W. "Inheritance Rights and the Hebrew Levirate Marriage." *Vetus Testamentum* 31 (1981): 138–44, 257–68.

Davies, W. D. and Dale C. Allison, Jr. *A Critical and Exegetical Commentary on the Gospel According to Saint Matthew.* Vol. 1. Edinburgh: T&T Clark, 1988.

Dean-Jones, Lesley. *Women's Bodies in Classical Greek Science.* Oxford: Clarendon, 1994.

Deming, Will. *Paul on Marriage and Celibacy: The Hellenistic Background of 1 Corinthians 7.* Society for New Testament Studies Monograph Series 83. Cambridge: Cambridge University Press, 1995.

Demircioğlu, A. Merve. "The Rhetoric of Belief and Identity Making in the Experience of Infertility." *Culture and Religion* 11 (2010): 51–67.

diTommaso, Lorenzo. *The Dead Sea New Jerusalem Text: Contents and Contexts*. Texte und Studien zum antiken Judentum 110. Tübingen: Mohr Siebeck, 2005.

Dixon, Edward P. "Descending Spirit and Descending Gods: An Interpretation of the Spirit's 'Descent as a Dove' in Mark 1:10." *Journal of Biblical Literature* 128 (2009): 759–80.

Donahue, John R. "Windows and Mirrors: The Setting of Mark's Gospel." *Catholic Biblical Quarterly* 57 (1995): 1–26.

Douglas, Mary. *Purity and Danger: An Analysis of Concepts of Pollution and Taboo*. Abingdon: Routledge, 2002.

Driver, G. R. "Linguistic and Textual Problems: Jeremiah." *Jewish Quarterly Review* 28 (1937): 97–129.

Driver, S. R. *The Book of Exodus*. Cambridge Bible Commentary. Cambridge: Cambridge University Press, 1918.

——. *Notes on the Hebrew Text and the Topography of the Books of Samuel*. Oxford: Clarendon, 1960.

Edelstein, Emma J. and Ludwig J. Edelstein. *Asclepius: A Collection and Interpretation of the Testimonies*. Baltimore: Johns Hopkins University Press, 1945.

Edwards, James R. "Markan Sandwiches: The Significance of Interpolations in Markan Narratives." *Novum Testamentum* 31 (1989): 193–216.

Ehrman, Bart D. "The Text of Mark in the Hands of the Orthodox." *Lutheran Quarterly* 5 (1991): 143–56.

Eickhoff, A. R. "A Psychoanalytic Study of St. Paul's Theology of Sex." *Pastoral Psychology* 18, no. 173 (1967): 35–72.

Eilberg-Schwartz, Howard. *The Savage in Judaism: An Anthropology of Israelite Religion and Ancient Judaism*. Bloomington: Indiana University Press, 1990.

Ellens, J. Harold. *Sex in the Bible: A New Consideration*. Westport, CT: Praeger, 2006.

Elliott, John K, ed. *The Apocryphal New Testament*. Oxford: Clarendon, 1993.

Evans, James G. "Barrenness: Its Cause, Curse, and Cure." *Physical Culture* 9 (1903): 428–29.

Exum, J. Cheryl. "Promise and Fulfillment: Narrative Art in Judges 13." *Journal of Biblical Literature* 99 (1980): 43–59.

Eyre, C. J. "The Adoption Papyrus in Social Context." *Journal of Egyptian Archaeology* 78 (1992): 207–21.

Feinberg, E. C., F. W. Larsen, R. M. Wah, R. J. Alvero, and A. Y. Armstrong. "Economics May Not Explain Hispanics' Underutilization of Assisted

Reproductive Technology and Services." *Fertility and Sterility* 88 (2007): 1439–41.

Ferree, Myra Marx. "Angela Merkel. What Does It Mean to Run as a Woman?" *German Politics and Society* 24 (2006): 93–107.

———. "The Rise and Fall of 'Mommy Politics': Feminism and German Unification." *Feminist Studies* 19 (1993): 89–115.

Fiore, Benjamin. *The Pastoral Epistles: First Timothy, Second Timothy, Titus.* Sacra Pagina Series. Edited by Daniel J. Harrington. Collegeville, MN: Liturgical Press, 2007.

Fischbein, Jessie. *Infertility in the Bible: How the Matriarchs Changed Their Fate and How You Can Too.* Jerusalem: Devora, 2005.

Fitzmyer, Joseph A. "The Birth of Jesus in the Pauline Writings." Pages 33–49 in *Mary in the New Testament.* Edited by Raymond E. Brown. Philadelphia: Fortress, 1978.

———. *First Corinthians.* Anchor Bible 32. New Haven: Yale University Press, 2008.

Flemming, Rebecca. *Medicine and the Making of Roman Women: Gender, Nature, and Authority from Celsus to Galen.* New York: Oxford University Press, 2000.

Flusser, D. *Jesus.* 2nd ed. Jerusalem: Magnes, 1998.

Fox, Michael V. "The Sign of the Covenant: Circumcision in the Light of the Priestly *'ot* Etiologies." *Revue biblique* 81 (1974): 557–96.

Frankfurter, David. "A Plea to a Local God for a Husband's Attentions." Pages 230–31 in *Religions of Late Antiquity in Practice.* Edited by Richard Valantasis. Princeton: Princeton University Press, 2000.

Freed, E. D. *The Stories of Jesus' Birth: A Critical Introduction.* St. Louis: Chalice, 2001.

Frymer-Kensky, Tikva. *In the Wake of the Goddesses: Women, Culture, and the Biblical Transformation of Pagan Myth.* New York: Free Press, 1992.

———. "What the Babylonian Flood Stories Can and Cannot Teach Us about the Genesis Flood." *Biblical Archaeology Review* 4 (1978): 32–41.

Fuchs, Esther. "The Literary Characterization of Mothers and Sexual Politics in the Hebrew Bible." *Semeia* 46 (1989): 151–66.

Fuhrmann, Sebastian. "Saved by Childbirth: Struggling Ideologies, the Female Body and a Placing of 1 Tim 2:15a." *Neotestamentica* 44 (2010): 34.

Gaca, Kathy L. "Early Stoic Eros: Sexual Ethics of Zeno and Chrysippus and Their Evaluation of the Greek Erotic Tradition." *Apeiron* 33 (2000): 207–38.

——. "Philo's Principles of Sexual Conduct and Their Influence on Christian Platonist Sexual Principles." *Studia Philonica Annual* 8 (1996): 21–39.

Galpaz-Feller, Pnina. "Pregnancy and Birth in the Bible and Ancient Egypt (Comparative Study)." *Biblische Notizen* 102 (2000): 42–53.

Gardiner, Alan H. "Adoption Extraordinary." *Journal of Egyptian Archaeology* 26 (1941): 23–29.

Gero, Stephen. "The Spirit as a Dove at the Baptism of Jesus." *Novum Testamentum* 18 (1976): 17–35.

Ginzberg, Louis. *Legends of the Jews.* Vol. 1. Philadelphia: Jewish Publication Society, 2003.

Glancy, Jennifer A. *Corporeal Knowledge: Early Christian Bodies.* New York: Oxford University Press, 2010.

Gleason, Maud. *Making Men: Sophists and Self-Presentation in Ancient Rome.* Princeton: Princeton University Press, 1995.

Goffman, Erving. *Stigma: Notes on the Management of Spoiled Identity.* Englewood Cliffs, NJ: Prentice Hall, 1963.

Grayson, A. K. and John Van Seters, "The Childless Wife in Assyria and the Stories of Genesis." *Orientalia* 44 (1975): 485–86.

Greenspahn, Frederick E. "Why Prophecy Ceased." *Journal of Biblical Literature* 108 (1989): 37–49.

Greil, Arthur L. "The Hidden Infertile: Infertile Women without Pregnancy Intent in the United States." *Fertility and Sterility* 93 (2010): 2080–83.

——. "Infertility and Psychological Distress: A Critical Review of the Literature." *Social Science and Medicine* 45 (1997): 16–79.

Greil, Arthur L. and Julia McQuillan. "Help-Seeking Patterns among Subfecund Women." *Journal of Reproductive and Infant Psychology* 22 (2004): 305–19.

Grottanelli, C. "Faithful Bodies: Ancient Greek Sources on Oriental Eunuchs." Pages 404–16 in *Self, Soul and Body in Religious Experience.* Edited by Albert I. Baumgarten with Jan Assmann and Guy G. Stroumsa. Leiden: Brill, 1998.

Gundry-Volf, Judith M. "Controlling the Bodies: A Theological Profile of the Corinthian Sexual Ascetics (1 Cor 7)." Pages 519–41 in *The Corinthian Correspondence.* Edited by R. Bieringer. Bibliotheca ephemeridum theologicarum Lovaniensium 125. Leuven: Leuven University Press, 1996.

——. "1 Cor 7:5b in the Light of a Hellenistic-Jewish Tradition on Abstinence to 'Devote Leisure.' Sufficiency in Paul and Philo." Pages 21–44 in *Paulus-Werk und Wirkung. Festschrift für Andreas Lindemann zum 70.*

Edited by Paul-Gerhard Klumbies and David S. du Toit. Tübingen: Mohr Siebeck, 2013.

Gunkel, Hermann. *Genesis.* Macon, GA: Mercer University Press, 1997.

Hammond, Mason. *The Antonine Monarchy.* Rome: American Academy in Rome, 1959.

——. *The Augustan Principate in Theory and Practice during the Julio-Claudian Period.* Cambridge, MA: Harvard University Press, 1933.

——. "The Transmission of Powers of the Roman Emperor from the Death of Nero in A.D. 68 to That of Alexander Severus in A.D. 235." *Memoirs of the American Academy in Rome* 24 (1956): 63–133.

Hare, D. R. A. *Matthew.* Interpretation. Louisville: Westminster John Knox, 1993.

Harill, J. Albert. *Slaves in the New Testament: Literary, Social and Moral Dimensions.* Minneapolis: Fortress, 2006.

Harper, Kyle. *From Shame to Sin: The Christian Transformation of Sexual Morality in Late Antiquity.* Revealing Antiquity 20. Cambridge, MA: Harvard University Press, 2013.

Harrison, R. K. "The Mandrake and the Ancient World." *Evangelical Quarterly* 28 (1956): 87–92.

Harvey, Brian K. "Two Bases of Marcus Aurelius Caesar and the Roman Imperial Succession." *Historia: Zeitschrift für Alte Geschichte* 53 (2004): 46–60.

Havrelock, Rachel. "The Myth of Birthing the Hero: Heroic Barrenness in the Hebrew Bible." *Biblical Interpretation* 16 (2008): 154–78.

Henne, M. B. and K. Bundorf. "Insurance Mandates and Trends in Infertility Treatments." *Fertility and Sterility* 89 (2008): 66–73.

Herman, Nancy J. and Charlene E. Miall. "Positive Consequence of Stigma: Two Case Studies in Mental and Physical Disability." *Quantitative Sociology* 13 (1990): 251–69.

Hiers, Richard H. "Transfer of Property by Inheritance and Bequest in Biblical Law and Tradition." *Journal of Law and Religion* 10 (1993–94): 121–55.

Himmelfarb, Martha. *Tours of Hell: An Apocalyptic Form in Jewish and Christian Literature.* Philadelphia: University of Pennsylvania Press, 1983.

Holladay, William L. "Was Trito-Isaiah Deutero-Isaiah after All?" Pages 193–217 in *Writing and Reading the Scroll of Isaiah: Studies of an Interpretive Tradition,* vol. 1. Edited by C. C. Broyles and C. A. Evans. Supplements to Vetus Testamentum 70. Leiden: Brill, 1997.

Hopkins, Keith. "Contraception in the Roman Empire." *Comparative Studies in Society and History* 8 (1965): 124–51.

Hovhanessian, Vahan. *Third Corinthians: Reclaiming Paul for Christian Orthodoxy*. Studies in Biblical Literature 18. New York: Peter Lang, 2000.

Inhorn, Marcia C. *Quest for Conception: Gender, Infertility and Egyptian Medical Tradition*. Philadelphia: University of Pennsylvania Press, 1994.

Inhorn, M. C. and M. H. Fakih. "Arab Americans, African Americans, and Infertility: Barriers to Reproduction and Medical Care." *Fertility and Sterility* 85 (2005): 844–52.

Isaac, E. "1 (Ethiopic Apocalypse of) Enoch." Pages 5–89 in *The Old Testament Pseudepigrapha*, vol. 1. Edited by James H. Charlesworth. Anchor Bible Reference Library. New York: Doubleday, 1983.

Iverson, E. "Papyrus Carlsberg No. VIII: With Some Remarks on the Egyptian Origin of Some Popular Birth Prognoses." *Historisk-filologiske Meddelelser udgivet af det Kgl. Danske Videnskabernes Selskab* 26 (1939): 1–31.

Jain, T. "Socioeconomic and Racial Disparities among Infertility Patients Seeking Care." *Fertility and Sterility* 85 (2005): 876–81.

James, M. R., ed. *The Apocryphal New Testament*. Oxford: Oxford University Press, 1924.

Janzen, J. Gerald. "Rivers in the Desert of Abraham and Sarah and Zion (Isaiah 51:1–3)." *Hebrew Annual Review* 10 (1986): 139–51.

Jeppesen, Knud. "Mother Zion, Father Servant." Pages 109–25 in *Of Prophets' Visions and the Wisdom of Sages*. Edited by Heather A. McKay and David J. A. Clines. Journal for the Study of the Old Testament Supplement Series 162. Sheffield: JSOT, 1993.

Johnston, Steve. "La correspondance apocryphe entre Paul et les Corinthiens: Un pseudépigraphe Paulinien au service de la polémique antignostique de la fin du IIe siècle." Master's dissertation, L'Université Laval, 2004.

Jones, Beth Felker. *Marks of His Wounds: Gender Politics and Bodily Resurrection*. Oxford: Oxford University Press, 2007.

Joshel, Sandra R. "Nurturing the Master's Child: Slavery and the Roman Child-Nurse." *Signs* 2 (1986): 3–22.

Junior, Nyasha and Jeremy Schipper. "Disability Studies and the Bible." Pages 21–37 in *New Meaning for Ancient Texts: Recent Approaches to Biblical Criticisms and their Applications*. Edited by Steven L. McKenzie and Jonathan Kaltner. Louisville: Westminster John Knox, 2013.

Kartzow, Marianne B. and Halvor Moxnes. "Complex Identities: Ethnicity, Gender and Religion in the Story of the Ethiopian Eunuch (Acts 8:26–40)." *Religion and Theology* 17 (2010): 184–204.

Keck, Leander. "The Spirit and the Dove." *New Testament Studies* 17 (1970): 41–67.

Keil, C. F. and F. Delitzsch. *Commentary on the Old Testament.* Vol. 1. Peabody, MA: Hendrickson, 1996.

Kiel, Micah. "Tobit's Theological Blindness." *Catholic Biblical Quarterly* 72 (2011): 281–98.

King, Helen. "Green Sickness: Hippocrates, Galen and the Origins of the 'Disease of Virgins.'" *International Journal of the Classical Tradition* 2 (1996): 372–87.

Klein, Jacob. "Enki and Ninmah." Pages 516–18 in *The Context of Scripture,* vol. 1. Edited by William W. Hallo. Leiden: Brill, 1997.

Kletter, Raz. *The Judean Pillar-Figurines and the Archaeology of Asherah.* BAR International Series 636. Oxford: Tempus Reparatum, 1996.

Knust, Jennifer Wright. *Abandoned to Lust: Sexual Slander and Ancient Christianity.* Gender, Theory, and Religion. New York: Columbia University Press, 2005.

Köhler, Ludwig. *Hebrew Man.* London: SCM, 1956.

Kraemer, Ross S. "Monastic Jewish Women in Greco-Roman Egypt: Philo Judaeus on the Therapeutrides." *Signs* 14 (1989): 342–70.

Kuefler, Mathew. *The Manly Eunuch. Masculinity, Gender Ambiguity, and Christian Ideology in Late Antiquity.* Chicago: University of Chicago Press, 2011.

Kunst, Christiane. *Römische Adoption: Zur Strategie einer Familienorganisation.* Hennef: Marthe Clauss, 2005.

Laes, Christian. "Male Virgins in Latin Inscriptions from Rome." Pages 105–19 in *Religion and Socialization in Antiquity and the Middle Ages.* Edited by K. Mustakallio, S. Katajala-Peltomaa, and V. Vuolanto. Rome: Acta Instituti Finlandiae, 2013.

Lambert, W. G. and A. R. Millard. *Atra-Hasis: The Babylonian Story of the Flood.* Oxford: Oxford University Press, 1969.

Lasker, Judith N. and Harriet L. Parmet. "Rabbinic and Feminist Responses to Reproductive Technology." *Journal of Feminist Studies in Religion* 6 (1990): 117–30.

Launderville, Dale. *Celibacy in the Ancient World: Its Ideal and Practice in Pre-Hellenistic Israel, Mesopotamia, and Greece.* Collegeville, MN: Liturgical Press, 2010.

Lefkowitz, Mary R. and Maureen B. Fant. *Women's Life in Greece and Rome: A Source Book in Translation.* 3rd ed. Baltimore: Johns Hopkins University Press, 2005.

Leutzsch, Martin. "Eunuch und Intersektionalität: ein multiperspektivischer Versuch zu Apg 8, 26–40." Pages 405–30 in *Doing Gender—Doing Religion: Fallstudien zur Intersektionalität im frühen Judentum, Christentum und Islam*. Edited by Ute E. Eisen, Christine Gerber, and Angela Standhartinger. Wissenschaftliche Untersuchungen zum Neuen Testament 302. Tübingen: Mohr Siebeck, 2013.

Levenson, Jon D. *The Death and Resurrection of the Beloved Son*. New Haven: Yale University Press, 1995.

Levin, Yigal. "Jesus, 'Son of God' and 'Son of David': The 'Adoption' of Jesus into the Davidic Line." *Journal for the Study of the New Testament* 28 (2006): 415–42.

Levine, Baruch A. *Numbers 1–20*. Anchor Bible 4. New York: Doubleday, 1994.

———. *Numbers 21–36*. Anchor Bible 4A. New York: Doubleday, 2000.

Levinson, Bernard M. "Esarhaddon's Succession Treaty as the Source for the Canon Formula in Deuteronomy 13:1." *Journal of the American Oriental Society* 130 (2010): 337–47.

Lichtheim, Miriam. *Ancient Egyptian Literature: Volume I: The Old and Middle Kingdoms*. Berkeley: University of California Press, 1973.

———. *Ancient Egyptian Literature: Volume III: The Late Period*. Berkeley: University of California Press, 2006.

Lietzmann, Hans. *An die Korinther I, II*. Handbuch zum Neuen Testament 9. Tübingen: Mohr, 1969.

Lipschits, Oded. *The Fall and Rise of Jerusalem: Judah under Babylonian Rule*. Winona Lake, IN: Eisenbrauns, 2005.

Lohfink, Norbert. "'Subdue the Earth?' Genesis 1:28." Pages 1–17 in *Theology of the Pentateuch*. Minneapolis: Fortress, 1994.

Löwisch, Ingeborg. "Gender and Ambiguity in the Genesis Genealogies: Tracing Absence and Subversion through the Lens of Derrida's *Archive Fever*." Pages 60–73 in *Embroidered Garments: Priests and Gender in Biblical Israel*. Edited by Deborah W. Rooke. Hebrew Bible Monographs 25. Sheffield: Sheffield Phoenix, 2009.

Luther, Martin. "Vom ehelichen Leben." *WA* 10/2.

Lutz, Cora E. "Musonius Rufus: 'The Roman Socrates.'" *Yale Classical Studies* 10 (1947): 85–87.

Maier, Christl. *Daughter Zion, Mother Zion: Gender, Space, and the Sacred in Ancient Israel*. Minneapolis: Fortress, 2008.

———. "Zion's Body as a Site of God's Motherhood in Isaiah 66:7–14." Pages 225–43 in *Daughter Zion: Her Portrait, Her Response*. Edited by Mark J.

Boda, Carol J. Dempsey, and LeAnn Snow Flesher. Society of Biblical Literature Ancient Israel and Its Literature 13. Atlanta: Society of Biblical Literature, 2012.

Malina, Bruce J. *The New Testament World: Insights from Cultural Anthropology.* Atlanta: John Knox, 1981.

Marcus, Joel S. *Mark 1–8.* Anchor Bible 27. New York: Doubleday 2000.

——. *Mark 8–16.* Yale Anchor Commentary 27. New Haven: Yale University Press, 2002.

Marsmann, Hennie J. *Women in Ugarit and Israel: Their Social and Religious Position in the Context of the Ancient Near East.* Oudtestamentische Studiën 49. Leiden: Brill, 2003.

Martin, Dale B. *The Corinthian Body.* New Haven: Yale University Press, 1995.

——. "Paul without Passion: On Paul's Rejection of Desire in Sex and Marriage." Pages 201–15 in *Constructing Early Christian Families: Family as Social Reality and Metaphor.* Edited by Halvor Moxnes. London: Routledge, 1997.

——. *Sex and the Single Savior.* Philadelphia: Westminster John Knox, 2006.

Matthews, R. and A. M. Matthews. "Infertility and Involuntary Childlessness: The Transition to Nonparenthood." *Journal of Marriage and the Family* 48 (1986): 641–49.

Matthews, Victor H. "Honor and Shame in Gender-Related Legal Situations in the Hebrew Bible." Pages 97–112 in *Gender and Law in the Hebrew Bible and the Ancient Near East.* Edited by Victor H. Matthews, Bernard M. Levinson, and Tikva Frymer-Kensky. Journal for the Study of the Old Testament Supplement Series 262. Sheffield: Sheffield Academic, 1998.

May, Simon. *Love: A History.* New Haven: Yale University Press, 2011.

Mazar, Amihai. *Archaeology of the Land of the Bible.* Vol. 1. Anchor Bible Reference Library. New York: Doubleday, 1992.

McCarter, P. Kyle. *II Samuel.* Anchor Bible 9. New York: Doubleday, 1984.

McKenzie, John L. *Second Isaiah.* Anchor Bible 20. Garden City, NY: Doubleday, 1968.

Meier, John P. *The Vision of Matthew: Christ, Church, and Morality in the First Gospel.* New York: Paulist, 1991.

Merklein, Helmut. *Der erste Brief an die Korinther.* Vol. 2. Ökumenischer Taschenbuchkommentar zum Neuen Testament 7. Gütersloh: Gütersloher Verlagshaus Gerd Mohn, 2000.

Meyer, Marvin and Richard Smith, eds. *Ancient Christian Magic: Coptic Texts of Ritual Power.* Princeton: Princeton University Press, 1999.

Meyers, Carol. *Discovering Eve: Ancient Israelite Women in Context.* New York: Oxford University Press, 1988.

———. "The Family in Early Israel." Pages 1–47 in *Families in Ancient Israel.* The Family, Religion, and Culture. Louisville: Westminster John Knox, 1997.

———. *Rediscovering Eve: Ancient Israelite Women in Context.* New York: Oxford University Press, 2013.

Milgrom, Jacob. *The JPS Torah Commentary: Numbers.* Philadelphia: Jewish Publication Society, 1990.

Miller, Patrick D. *Deuteronomy.* Interpretation. Louisville: Westminster John Knox, 1990.

Milton, H. "The Structure of the Prologue to St Matthew's Gospel." *Journal of Biblical Literature* 81 (1962): 175–81.

Mitchell, Christopher Wright. *The Meaning of BRK "To Bless" in the Old Testament.* Society of Biblical Literature Dissertation Series 95. Atlanta: Scholars, 1987.

Mitchell, Margaret M. *Paul and the Rhetoric of Reconciliation: An Exegetical Investigation of the Language and Composition of 1 Corinthians.* Hermeneutische Untersuchungen zur Theologie 28. Tübingen: Mohr Siebeck, 1991.

Montague, George T. *First and Second Timothy, Titus.* Catholic Commentary on Sacred Scripture. Grand Rapids, MI: Baker, 2008.

Morgenstern, Julian. "Isaiah 49–55." *Hebrew Union College Annual* 36 (1965): 1–35.

Moss, Candida R. "Heavenly Healing: Eschatological Cleansing and the Resurrection of the Dead in the Early Church." *Journal of the American Academy of Religion* 79, no. 3 (2011): 1–27.

———. "The Man with the Flow of Power: Porous Bodies in Mark 5:25–34." *Journal of Biblical Literature* 129, no. 3 (2010): 507–519.

———. *The Myth of Persecution: How Early Christians Invented a Story of Martyrdom.* New York: HarperOne, 2013.

———. "Nailing Down and Tying Up: Lessons in Intertextual Impossibility from the Martyrdom of Polycarp." *Vigiliae Christianae* 67 (2013): 117–36.

Moss, Candida R. and Joel S. Baden. "1 Thess 4.13–18 in Rabbinic Perspective." *New Testament Studies* 58 (2012): 199–212.

Moss, Candida R. and Jeremy Schipper. "Introduction." Pages 1–13 in *Disability Studies and Biblical Literature.* New York: Palgrave Macmillan, 2011.

Moxnes, Halvor. *Putting Jesus in His Place. A Radical Vision of Household and Kingdom.* Louisville: Westminster John Knox, 2003.

———. "What Is Family? Problems in Constructing Early Christian Families." Pages 13–41 in *Constructing Early Christian Families: Family as Social Reality and Metaphor.* Edited by Halvor Moxnes. London: Routledge, 1997.

Nelson, Richard D. *Deuteronomy.* Old Testament Library. Louisville: Westminster John Knox, 2002.

Nesselhauf, Herbert. "Die Adoption des römischen Kaisers." *Hermes* 83 (1955): 477–95.

Nielsen, Kirsten. *Ruth.* Old Testament Library. Louisville: Westminster John Knox, 1997.

Nutton, Vivian. *Ancient Medicine.* 2nd ed. Abingdon: Routledge, 2013.

O'Hagan, Angelo P. *Material Re-creation in the Apostolic Fathers.* Texte und Untersuchungen zur Geschichte der Altchristlichen Literatur 100. Berlin: Akademie-Verlag, 1968.

Olyan, Saul M. *Disability in the Hebrew Bible: Interpreting Mental and Physical Differences.* New York: Cambridge University Press, 2008.

Osiek, Carolyn A. and David L. Balch. *Families in the New Testament World: Households and House Churches in Context.* Louisville: Westminster John Knox, 1997.

Parker, Holt N. "Love's Body Anatomized: The Ancient Erotic Handbooks and the Rhetoric of Sexuality." Pages 90–110 in *Pornography and Representation in Greece and Rome.* Edited by Amy Richlin. Princeton: Princeton University Press, 1992.

Parry, D. C. "Work, Leisure, and Support Groups: An Examination of the Ways Women with Infertility Respond to Pronatalist Ideology." *Sex Roles* 53 (2005): 337–46.

Parsons, Mikeal C. *Body and Character in Luke and Acts. The Subversion of Physiognomy in Early Christianity.* Grand Rapids, MI: Baker, 2006.

Peppard, Michael. *The Son of God in the Roman World: Divine Sonship in Its Social and Political Context.* New York: Oxford University Press, 2012.

Perdue, Leo G. "Household, Theology, and Contemporary Hermeneutics." Pages 223–57 in *Families in Ancient Israel.* The Family, Religion, and Culture. Louisville: Westminster John Knox, 1997.

———. "The Israelite and Early Jewish Family." Pages 163–222 in *Families in Ancient Israel.* The Family, Religion, and Culture. Louisville: Westminster John Knox, 1997.

Petronius. *Petronius.* Translated by Michael Heseline. Loeb Classical Library. Cambridge, MA: Harvard University Press, 1975.

Pliny. *Natural History.* Translated by H. Rackham. Loeb Classical Library. Cambridge, MA: Harvard University Press, 1961.

Porteous, Norman W. "Jerusalem-Zion: The Growth of a Symbol." Pages 235–52 in *Verbannung und Heimkehr: Beiträge zur Geschichte und Theologie Israels im 6. und 5. Jahrhundert v. Chr.* Edited by Arnulf Kuschke. Tübingen: J. C. B. Mohr, 1961.

Porter, Stanley E. "What Does It Mean to Be 'Saved by Childbirth' (1 Timothy 2.15)?" *Journal for the Study of the New Testament* 49 (1993): 87–102.

Portier-Young, Anathea. " 'Eyes to the Blind': A Dialogue between Tobit and Job." Pages 14–27 in *Intertextual Studies in Ben Sira and Tobit.* Edited by J. Corley and V. Skemp. Washington, DC: Catholic Biblical Association, 2005.

Raphael, Rebecca. *Biblical Corpora: Representations of Disability in Hebrew Biblical Literature.* Library of Hebrew Bible/Old Testament Studies 445. London: T&T Clark, 2008.

Reiner, Erica. "Babylonian Birth Prognoses." *Zeitschrift für Assyriologie (und Vorderasiatische Archäologie)* 72 (1982): 124–38.

Rengstorf, K. H. "Doulos." *Theological Dictionary of the New Testament* 2 (1962): 266–69, 273–79.

Ringrose, K. M. *Eunuchs and the Social Construction of Gender in Byzantium.* Chicago: University of Chicago Press, 2003.

Ritner, Robert K. "A Uterine Amulet in the Oriental Institute Collection." *Journal of Near Eastern Studies* 43 (1984): 209–21.

Robertson, Archibald, and Alfred Plummer. *A Critical and Exegetical Commentary on the First Epistle of St. Paul to the Corinthians.* 2nd ed. International Critical Commentary. Edinburgh: T&T Clark, 1971.

Robins, Gay. *Women in Ancient Egypt.* London: British Museum, 1993.

Roller, L. E. "The Ideology of the Eunuch Priest." Pages 118–35 in *Gender and the Body in the Ancient Mediterranean.* Edited by M. Wyke. Oxford: Blackwell, 1998.

Rose, Charles Brian. *Dynastic Commemoration and Imperial Portraiture in the Julio-Claudian Period.* Cambridge: Cambridge University Press, 1997.

Roth, Martha. "Marriage and Matrimonial Property in the First Millennium B.C." Pages 245–60 in *Women's Earliest Records from Ancient Egypt and Western Asia.* Edited by B. S. Lesko. Brown Judaic Studies 166. Atlanta: Scholars, 1989.

Rowlandson, Jane. *Women and Society in Greek and Roman Egypt.* Cambridge: Cambridge University Press, 1998.

Sanders, James A. "The Ethic of Election in Luke's Great Banquet Parable." Pages 245–71 in *Essays in Old Testament Ethics.* Edited by James L. Crenshaw and John T. Willis. New York: Ktav, 1974.

Sarna, Nahum. *The JPS Torah Commentary: Genesis.* Philadelphia: Jewish Publication Society, 1989.

Satlow, Michael. *Tasting the Dish: The Rabbinic Rhetorics of Sexuality.* Brown Judaic Studies 303. Atlanta: Scholars, 1995.

Sawyer, John F. A. "Daughter of Zion and Servant of the Lord in Isaiah: A Comparison." *Journal for the Study of the Old Testament* 44 (1989): 89–107.

Schipper, Jeremy. *Disability and Isaiah's Suffering Servant.* Oxford: Oxford University Press, 2011.

———. *Disability Studies and the Hebrew Bible: Figuring Mephibosheth in the David Story.* Library of Hebrew Bible/Old Testament Studies 441. New York: T&T Clark, 2006.

———. "Disabling Israelite Leadership: 2 Samuel 6:23 and Other Images of Disability in the Deuteronomistic History." Pages 103–13 in *This Abled Body: Rethinking Disabilities in Biblical Studies.* Edited by Hector Avalos, Sarah M. Melcher, and Jeremy Schipper. Atlanta: Society of Biblical Literature, 2007.

Schneemelcher, Wilhelm. "The Acts of Peter." Pages 285–317 in *New Testament Apocrypha.* Edited by Wilhelm Schneemelcher and R. McL. Wilson. Cambridge: James Clark, 1991.

———. "The Acts of Peter: Introduction." Pages 271–85 in *New Testament Apocrypha.* Edited by Wilhelm Schneemelcher and R. McL. Wilson. Cambridge: James Clark, 1991.

Scurlock, JoAnn and Burton R. Andersen. *Diagnoses in Assyrian and Babylonian Medicine: Ancient Sources, Translations, and Modern Medical Analyses.* Urbana-Champaign: University of Illinois Press, 2005.

Senior, Donald. "With Swords and Clubs: The Setting of Mark's Community and His Critique of Abusive Power." *Biblical Theology Bulletin* 17 (1987): 10–20.

Setzer, Claudia. *Resurrection of the Body in Early Judaism and Early Christianity.* Leiden: Brill, 2004.

Shauf, Scott. "Locating the Eunuch. Characterization and Narrative Context in Acts 8:26–40." *Catholic Biblical Quarterly* 71 (2009): 762–75.

Shaw, Teresa. *The Burden of the Flesh: Fasting and Sexuality in Early Christianity.* Minneapolis: Fortress, 1998.

Solevag, Anna Rebecca. "Disability and Sexuality in the *Acts of Peter.*" Paper presented at the annual meeting of the Society of Biblical Literature, Chicago, November 18, 2012.

Sommer, Benjamin D. *A Prophet Reads Scripture: Allusion in Isaiah 40–66.* Stanford: Stanford University Press, 1998.

Spencer, F. S. *The Portrait of Philip in Acts: A Study of Roles and Relations.* Journal for the Study of the New Testament Supplement Series 67. Sheffield: Sheffield Academic Press, 1992.

Stager, Lawrence E. "Jerusalem as Eden." *Biblical Archaeology Review* 26 (2000): 36–47.

———. "Jerusalem and the Garden of Eden." *Eretz-Israel* 26 (1999): 183*–94*.

Steinberg, Naomi. *Kinship and Marriage in Genesis: A Household Economics Perspective.* Minneapolis: Fortress, 1993.

Stol, Marten. *Birth in Babylonia and the Bible: Its Mediterranean Setting.* Groningen: Styx, 2000.

Stoppard, Tom. *The Invention of Love.* Boston: Faber and Faber, 1997.

Strack, H. L. and Paul Billerbeck. *Kommentar zum Neuen Testament aus Talmud und Midrasch.* 6 vols. Munich: Beck, 1924–56.

Strathmann, Hermann. *Geschichte der früchristlichen Askese bis zur Entstehung des Mönchtums, vol. 1: Die Askese in der Umgebung des wedenden Christentums.* Leipzig: Deichert, 1914.

Strauss, M. L. *The Davidic Messiah in Luke-Acts: The Promise and Its Fulfillment in Lukan Christology.* Journal for the Study of the New Testament Supplement Series 110. Sheffield: Sheffield Academic Press, 1995.

Su, T.-J. and Y.-C. Chen. "Transforming Hope: The Lived Experience of the Infertile Woman Who Terminated Treatment after In Vitro Fertilization Failure." *Journal of Nursing Research* 14 (2006): 46–53.

Sunderland, Ruth. "Childless Is Not a Synonym for Weird." *Guardian,* May 23, 2009. http://www.guardian.co.uk/commentisfree/2009/may/24/women-feminism-childless-ruth-sunderland.

Thomas, Christine M. *The Acts of Peter, Gospel Literature, and the Ancient Novel: Rewriting the Past.* Oxford: Oxford University Press, 2003.

Thompson, Charis M. "Fertile Ground: Feminists Theorize Infertility." Pages 53–57 in *Infertility Around the Globe: New Thinking on Childlessness, Gender and Reproductive Technologies.* Edited by Marcia C. Inhorn and Frank van Balen. Berkeley: University of California Press, 2002.

Tiemeyer, Lena-Sofia. "Isaiah 40–55: A Judahite Reading Drama." Pages 55–75 in *Daughter Zion: Her Portrait, Her Response*. Edited by Mark J. Boda, Carol J. Dempsey, and LeAnn Snow Flesher. Society of Biblical Literature Ancient Israel and Its Literature 13. Atlanta: Society of Biblical Literature, 2012.

Tigay, Jeffrey. *The JPS Torah Commentary: Deuteronomy*. Philadelphia: Jewish Publication Society, 1996.

Tomson, P. J. *Paul and the Jewish Law: Halakha in the Letters of the Apostle to the Gentiles*. Compendia Rerum Iudaicarum ad Novum Testamentum. Section III: Jewish Traditions in Early Christian Literature 1. Assen: Van Corcum, 1990.

Treggiari, Susan. *Roman Marriage: Iusti Coniuges from the Time of Cicero to the Time of Ulpian*. Oxford: Clarendon, 1991.

Ulrich, M. and A. Weatherall. "Motherhood and Infertility: Viewing Motherhood through the Lens of Infertility." *Feminism & Psychology* 10 (2000): 323–26.

Urbach, Efraim. *The Sages: Their Concepts and Beliefs*. 2 vols. Jerusalem: Magnes, 1975.

van der Toorn, Karel. *Family Religion in Babylonia, Syria, and Israel*. Studies in the History and Culture of the Ancient Near East 7. Leiden: Brill, 1996.

——. *From Her Cradle to Her Grave: The Role of Religion in the Life of the Israelite and the Babylonian Woman*. Biblical Seminar 23. Sheffield: JSOT, 1994.

——. *Sin and Sanction in Israel and Mesopotamia: A Comparative Study*. Assen: Van Gorcum, 1985.

van dijk-Hemmes, Fokkelien. "The Great Woman of Shunem and the Man of God: A Dual Interpretation of 2 Kings 4.8–37." Pages 218–30 in *The Feminist Companion to Samuel and Kings*. Edited by Athalya Brenner. Sheffield: Sheffield Academic Press, 1994.

Van Seters, John. "The Problem of Childlessness in Near Eastern Law and the Patriarchs of Israel." *Journal of Biblical Literature* 87 (1968): 401–8.

Vermes, Geza. *Jesus the Jew: A Historian's Reading of the Gospels*. Philadelphia: Fortress, 1973.

von Rad, Gerhard. *Genesis*. Old Testament Library. Philadelphia: Westminster, 1972.

von Tischendorf, Constantin, Max Bonnet, and Richard Adelbert Lipsius. *Acta Apostolorum Apocrypha*. Vol. 1. Darmstadt: Wissenschaftliche Buchgesellschaft, 1959.

Wahl, Harald M. "Ester, das adoptierte Waisenkind. Zur Adoption im Alten Testament." *Biblica* 80 (1999): 78–99.

Walls, Neal H. "The Origins of the Disabled Body: Disability in Ancient Mesopotamia." Pages 13–30 in *This Abled Body: Rethinking Disabilities in Biblical Studies*. Edited by Hector Avalos, Sarah M. Melcher, and Jeremy Schipper. Atlanta: Society of Biblical Literature, 2007.

Weaver, Dorothy Jean. "Barrenness & Fertility." Pages 156–58 in *The IVP Women's Bible Commentary*. Edited by Catherine Clark Kroeger and Mary J. Evans. Downers Grove, IL: InterVarsity Press, 2002.

Weinfeld, Moshe. *Deuteronomy and the Deuteronomic School*. Winona Lake, IN: Eisenbrauns, 1992.

Weisberg, Dvora. *Levirate Marriage and the Family in Ancient Judaism*. Waltham, MA: Brandeis University Press, 2009.

Westbrook, Raymond. "The Female Slave." Pages 214–38 in *Gender and Law in the Hebrew Bible and the Ancient Near East*. Edited by Victor H. Matthews, Bernard M. Levinson, and Tikva Frymer-Kensky. Journal for the Study of the Old Testament Supplement Series 262. Sheffield: Sheffield Academic, 1998.

Westermann, Claus. *Isaiah 40–66*. Old Testament Library. Philadelphia: Westminster, 1969.

White, Benjamin L. "Reclaiming Paul? Reconfiguration as Reclamation in 3 Corinthians." *Journal of Early Christian Studies* 17 (2009): 497–523.

White, L., J. McQuillan, and A. L. Greil. "Explaining Disparities in Treatment Seeking: The Case of Infertility." *Fertility and Sterility* 85 (2005): 853–57.

Whitekettle, Richard. "Human Reproduction in the Textual Record of Mesopotamia and Syria-Palestine during the First and Second Millennia B.C." Ph.D. dissertation, Yale University, 1995.

Willey, Patricia Tull. *Remember the Former Things: The Recollection of Previous Texts in Second Isaiah*. Society of Biblical Literature Dissertation Series 161. Atlanta: Scholars, 1997.

Williams, D. K. "Acts." Pages 225–28 in *True to Our Native Land: An African-American Commentary on the New Testament*. Edited by B. K. Blount. Minneapolis: Fortress Press, 2007.

Wilson, Robert R. *Genealogy and History in the Biblical World*. New Haven: Yale University Press, 1977.

Wire, A. C. *The Corinthian Women Prophets: A Reconstruction through Paul's Rhetoric*. Minneapolis: Fortress, 1990.

Yong, Amos. *The Bible, Disability, and the Church: A New Vision of the People of God.* Grand Rapids, MI: Eerdmans, 2011.

———. *Theology and Down Syndrome: Reimagining Disability in Late Modernity.* Waco, TX: Baylor University Press, 2007.

Zwelling, Elaine. "The History of Lamaze Continues: An Interview with Elisabeth Bing." *Journal of Perinatal Education* 9 (2000): 15–21.

PRIMARY SOURCE INDEX

BIBLE

Genesis
1............... 82, 85, 87, 88, 90, 91, 101,
           232, 267n13
1:22............... 74
1:28............... 30, 70, 71, 72, 76, 85, 87,
           261n10, 261n14, 263n29,
           263n30
2–3............... 85, 263n34, 267n13
2:4b–5........... 111
2:7............... 55
2:10–14........ 111
3............... 56, 88, 89, 91, 101
3:15............... 89
3:16............... 85, 86, 88, 162, 232,
           263n29, 267n13,
           270n32
3:16b 263n34
3:17............... 86, 89
3:20............... 87
4:1............... 55
4:25............... 55
5............... 87
5:2............... 82
5:3............... 82, 261n14
5:4............... 76
6:11............... 78

7:7............... 83
9............... 87
9:1............... 70, 71, 73, 76, 261n10
9:7............... 70
9:11............... 65
9:13............... 65
9:16............... 66
9:25............... 84
10............... 78, 82
10:32............. 79
11............... 23, 90
11:8............... 79
12............... 75
12:2............... 29, 59, 74
12:3............... 84
12:10............. 45
15............... 127
15:2............... 34
16:1............... 104
16:2............... 31, 57, 61, 121
16:4............... 40
17............... 65, 83, 159
17:6............... 65, 70
17:11............. 65
17:17............. 64, 158
17:20............. 70, 71

18:11............ 158
18:12............ 46, 119
18:14............ 51
20................. 45
20:17–18...... 45
20:18............ 56, 99
21:1.............. 67
21:6.............. 65
21:7.............. 112, 123
22................. 142
22:17............ 71, 77, 118
24................. 23
24:60............ 43, 118
25:2.............. 73
25:21............ 23, 34, 51, 104
26:1.............. 45
26:4.............. 77
27:45............ 109
28:3.............. 71
28:14............ 118
29:31............ 23, 58, 104
29:35............ 61
30:1–2.......... 37, 56
30:1.............. 24, 25, 34, 104
30:2.............. 42, 57
30:3.............. 31, 61
30:9.............. 61
30:14............ 24
30:18............ 65
30:20............ 65
30:22............ 51, 56, 67
30:23............ 39
31:38............ 109
34:14............ 39
35:9.............. 71
35:11............ 70, 73, 76
35:22............ 261n8
35:23............ 260n8
35:25............ 261n8
35:26............ 260n8, 261n8
37:2.............. 28, 261n8
38................. 244n5
41:54............ 45
42:49–50...... 43
43:14............ 109
46................. 81

46:15............ 260n8, 262n24
46:17............ 262n24
46:18............ 260n8, 261n8
46:25............ 261n8
47................. 79
47:27............ 79
48:3–4.......... 71
49:7.............. 84
49:31............ 260n8

Exodus
1.................. 91, 98
1:1................ 91
1:7................ 80, 91
1:12.............. 91
12:37............ 91
15:26............ 51
22:27............ 84
23:25–26...... 94
23:25............ 93
23:26............ 96, 109, 270n35

Leviticus
10:1–3.......... 44
13–14........... 44
20................. 252n89
20:17............ 41, 253n89
20:20–21...... 253n89
26................. 108, 109
26:6.............. 93
26:8.............. 93
26:9.............. 95
26:16............ 94
26:22............ 93, 109
26:26............ 93
26:29............ 93

Numbers
5.................. 252n89
5:28.............. 254n94
11:25............ 272n3
12:10............ 44
13–14........... 46
14:29–35...... 44
16................. 44

22:28............. 56
22:6............... 84
27:1–11........ 81, 249n57
36................... 249n57
36:1–12........ 81

Deuteronomy
7:13............... 264n37
7:14............... 38, 96
22:21............. 41
22:23–24...... 115
23:2............... 13
24:1............... 32
24:17............. 115
25:5–6.......... 276n28
25:5–10........ 37
28................... 108
28:4............... 95
28:10............. 93
28:11............. 95
28:12............. 93, 94, 256n116
28:23–24...... 94
28:24............. 93
28:27–28...... 94
28:27............. 93
28:32............. 108
28:39–40...... 93
28:41............. 108
28:53–57...... 93
28:59............. 94
29:13–14...... 92
30:19............. 92

Judges
3:10............... 272n3
13................... 159
13:2............... 23, 60, 266n3
13:23............. 48
13:5............... 59
14:6............... 272n3
14:19............. 272n3

1 Samuel
1:2................. 26
1:5–6............ 13, 56

1:5................. 42, 57, 243n1
1:6................. 40
1:8................. 22
1:10–16........ 22
1:11............... 34, 48, 67
1:18............... 159
10:6............... 272n3
10:10............. 272n3
11:2............... 39
16:13............. 272n3
17:26............. 39
17:43............. 84
28:17–19...... 44

2 Samuel
6................... 252n89
12:15–18...... 44
13:13............. 39
14:7............... 29
18:18............. 29
20:3............... 269n27
21:1–2.......... 44

1 Kings
14:1............... 44
17:17............. 45

2 Kings
2:24............... 84
4................... 129
4:8................. 259n144
4:14–17........ 259n144
4:20............... 45
5:27............... 44
13:14............. 45
18:5............... 52
20:1............... 45
20:3............... 52
23:29............. 45

Isaiah
7:14............... 152
23:4............... 41, 113
23:9............... 41

26:18............. 267n10
33:24............. 44
40–55........... 265n1
40–66........... 103, 265n1
42:1............... 142
42:17............. 41
44:24............. 55
47:3............... 41
47:9............... 113
49:5............... 55
49:7............... 120
49:14–19...... 268n18
49:14............. 269n28
49:16............. 126
49:21............. 104, 109, 110, 113, 119,
                  123
50:4–5.......... 56
51:2............... 110, 118, 268n17
51:3............... 110, 111, 118
53................... 204
54................... 115
54:1............... 104, 120, 123, 126, 129,
                  133, 136, 267n16
54:2............... 118
54:3............... 118
54:4............... 115, 121, 268n24
54:6............... 116
54:7–8.......... 116
54:11............. 270n41
54:14............. 120
55:10............. 247n49
56–66........... 265n1
56:3............... 204
56:4–5.......... 135
61:1–2.......... 143, 273n5
65:17............. 126
65:20............. 270n35
65:23............. 108
65:25............. 120
66................... 112
66:7............... 131
66:8............... 118
66:9............... 121
66:11............. 112
66:12............. 118

Jeremiah
1:5................. 55
13:26............. 41
15:7............... 109
18:21............. 109
24:9............... 41
48:20............. 41

Ezekiel
3:12............... 272n3
3:27............... 56
4:14............... 256n115
8:3................. 272n3
11:1............... 272n3
24:27............. 256n115
33:22............. 256n115
37................... 216, 289n47

Hosea
2:12............... 41
9................... 204
9:12............... 109
9:14............... 13
9:16............... 203

Joel
2:16............... 280n6

Zephaniah
3:18–19........ 250n63
12:12–24...... 280n6

Malachi
3:10............... 256n116

Psalms
2:7................. 142
22:1............... 269n28
105:41........... 56
109:29........... 41
113:7............. 30
113:9............. 123, 266n5
127:3............. 56
128:3............. 13

132:14........... 133
139:13........... 55

Job
3:7................ 110
15:34............. 110
21:10............. 109
24:21............. 31
30:3............... 110
31:15............. 55

Proverbs
30:15–16...... 27

Ruth
1:3................ 45
1:4–5............ 37
1:11–12........ 250n57
4:11.............. 261n8, 261n19
4:13.............. 58

Song of Songs
7:14.............. 243n3

Ecclesiastes
3:5................ 280n6
11:5.............. 54

Lamentations
1:1................ 268n24
1:8................ 268n24
1:9................ 268n24

Daniel
8:27.............. 45
12................. 217

Nehemiah
2:17.............. 39

1 Chronicles
7:13.............. 261n8

2 Chronicles
26:19–20...... 44

Matthew
1:1................ 275n26
1:3................ 155
1:5a.............. 155
1:6................ 155
1:16.............. 153, 156
1:20.............. 153, 275n26
1:22–23........ 151
1:24–25........ 153
9:27.............. 275n26
12:3.............. 275n26
12:23............ 275n26
13:55............ 153
15:22............ 275n26
19:12............ 210
20:30–31...... 275n26
21:9.............. 275n26
21:15............ 275n26

Mark
1:1................ 273n4
1:7................ 140
1:10–11........ 141, 142
2:17.............. 220
3:1................ 203
3:4................ 286n15
3:31–35........ 191
4:6................ 203
5:28.............. 286n15
5:34.............. 286n15
6:56.............. 286n15
8:35.............. 286n15
9:18.............. 203
9:43–48........ 272n58
10:26............ 286n15
10:52............ 286n15
11:20–21...... 203
12:13–17...... 217
12:19–23...... 215
12:24–25...... 216
13................. 212
13:13............ 286n15

13:17............. 212
13:20............. 286n15
15:30............. 286n15
15:31............. 286n15
19:29–30...... 191

Luke
1.................... 159
1:5–6............ 158
1:5–25.......... 158
1:26–28....... 158
1:27............. 151
1:34............. 151
1:35............. 161
1:36............. 13
1:37............. 161
1:38............. 159
1:46–55........ 159
1:57–80........ 158
2:1–21.......... 158
2:21–24........ 153

John
1:1................. 165
2:1–11.......... 165
2:1–12.......... 165
1:14............. 165
19:25–27...... 165, 166

Acts
8.................... 209, 212
8:27............. 208
8:34............. 209
8:36............. 209
8:37............. 209
8:38............. 209
8:39............. 209

1 Corinthians
7.................... 190, 278n1
7:1................. 171
7:1–5............ 172
7:2–3............ 279n3
7:5................. 172
7:6................. 172
7:7................. 172
7:8................. 171
7:9a.............. 171
7:21............. 160
7:25–35........ 242n22
7:28............. 173
7:28–31........ 174
7:32–34........ 190
15................. 214, 219, 226,
15:42–44...... 215
15:42............ 214

Galatians
4:25–26........ 126
5:23.............. 280n8

Philemon
2:6–11.......... 278n50

1 Thessalonians
4:16–17........ 214, 289n43

1 Timothy
2:15............. 13

Hebrews
11:11............ 13

James
2:20.............. 13

SECOND TEMPLE AND EARLY CHRISTIAN SOURCES

1 Enoch
22–27............. 216
98:5............... 251n71

2 Enoch
31:7............... 263n33

2 Baruch
4:3................. 126
4:3–5............. 127
29................. 216

4 Ezra
7:28–44........ 216
16:44–46...... 280n11

Acts of Paul (Coptic MS version)
Para. 14 .... 288n40
Para. 39 .... 288n40

Acts of Peter
192, 193, 194, 283n50, 284n51

Augustine
Against Faustus
22.30............. 290n62

City of God
22.17.1145, 290n60
22.19.1149, 290n58
22.19.1149–1150, 290n57
22.20.1152, 290n59, 290n60

Civ.
16.28............. 259n140

Manichean Ways of Life
15.37............. 290n62
16.49............. 290n62

18.65–66...... 290n62
19.73............. 290n62

Ben Sira
16:3............... 272n58
42:9–10........ 268n20

Clement of Alexandria, *Paedagogus*
2.10.83.......... 260n2

Clement, *Stromateis*
3.48.1............ 290n61

Eusebius, *Church History*
7.18............... 285n2

Irenaeus, *Adversus Haereses*
4.33.11.......... 289n51
5.12.6............ 220
5.13.1............ 289n52

John Chrysostom, *On Virginity*
125.126......... 290n63

Josephus, *Jewish Antiquities*
II.218............ 277n43

Justin Martyr
2 Apology
1–2............... 283n46

Dialogue with Trypho
80.................. 289n48

Origen
Contra Celsum
1.28............... 276n34
1.69............... 278n48

On First Principles
2.10.3............ 289n48

Philo
   De Congressu Eruditionis gratia
   3.................... 272n60

   De Praemiis et Poenis
   158–59......... 272n62

   De Vita Contemplativa
   68.................. 272n61

Joseph
43.................. 283n41

Spec. Laws
3:36.............. 283n42

Pseudo-Justin, On the Resurrection
   3.................... 290n55, 290n56
   4.................... 289n54

Wisd. of Sol.
   3:13.............. 135
   3:13–14........ 207
   3:14.............. 135
   4:1................ 49, 136

RABBINIC SOURCES

Ag. Ber.
   106–7............ 272n56

b. Avod. Zar.
   5a.................. 247n44

b. B. Bat.
   116a.............. 245n17
   12a................ 271n49

b. Ber.
   10a................ 254n98
   17a................ 272n55
   31b................ 254n94
   51b................ 262n22

b. Eruv.
   100b............. 263n32

b. Kallah Rabbati
   52a................ 272n53

b. Ket.
   62b................ 257n125

b. Meg.
   27a................ 260n1

b. Nid.
   69b................ 289n44
   70b................ 289n44

b. Pes.
   54a................ 271n47

b. Roš. Haš.
   16b................ 251n73

b. Sanh.
   21a................ 253n89
   100a............. 259n139, 272n52

b. Shek.
   17a................ 272n52, 272n53

b. Sot.
12a................ 277n44

b. Ta'an
2a.................... 256n118
6b.................... 247n49
8a–b............. 264n40
11a................ 260n1

b. Yeb.
62a–b........... 271n46
64a................ 250n58
64b................ 257n125
65a................ 257n125
65b................ 263n27
80b................ 258n126

Deut Rab.
7.6................. 256n118

Exod. Rab.
1.20............... 277n44

Gen. Am.
675................ 283n40

Gen. Rab.
1.4................. 271n47
8.12............... 262n26
12.7............... 272n54
20.6............... 263n32
45.2............... 247n44, 259n139
45.4............... 251n77, 251n64, 251n72
45.5............... 247n39
47.2............... 255n101
47.3............... 259n142
53.5............... 255n101
60.13............. 251n74
63.5............... 255n101
71.1............... 247n46
71.5............... 247n38
71.6............... 251n75, 247n44
71.7............... 251n75

73.4............... 256n118
77.1............... 271n48, 271n49

m. B. Bat
8.6................. 276n28

m. Eduy.
1.13............... 245n21

m. Gitt.
4.8................. 258n126

m. Ned
5.6................. 280n6

m. Nid.
2.1................. 272n58

m. Soṭ
4.3................. 253n89

m. Yeb
6:5................. 188
6.6................. 246n27, 250n58, 260n1,
                    262n26,
8:5................. 258n126

MHG
Gen 30:23.... 251n64

Num. Rab.
10.5............... 249n55

PDM
xiv. 956–60 ....286n11

Pes. Rab.
42.3............... 257n121
42.4............... 255n101, 271n51
42.7............... 256n118
43.3............... 254n94

43.4............... 251n76, 257n124, 272n57
43.5............... 252n78
43.6............... 245n24
43.8............... 251n64

PRK
18.3............... 270n41
20.1............... 270n39
20.3............... 270n42
20:1............... 257n120
22.1............... 271n51
22.2............... 262n26, 271n49

Song Rab.
II.14,8........... 251n72, 251n74, 251n77

T. Chullin
2.22–24........ 278n49

T. Naph
8.8..................... 280n6

t. Ned
5.6..................... 280n6

t. Yeb.
8.4..................... 246n30

Tanḥ. B.
Bereishit 39.... 260n1
Noah 18........... 262n26
Wayyera' 32... 251n73
Wayyera' 34... 253n91, 254n97
Wayyera' 35... 256n118

GRECO-ROMAN SOURCES

Achilles Tatius, *Leucippe and Clitophon*
5.20.5............ 282n37

Aristotle, *Historia Animalium*
3.19............... 285n4

Athenagoras, *On the Resurrection*
1..................... 289n48

Athenaeus, *Deipnosophists*
10.444d........ 281n22

Cassius Dio, *Roman History*
54.16.1.......... 282n29
69.20............. 274n13

Catullus, *carmina*
63................. 287n27

Dio. Or.
3.34.................... 282n35

Dionysius, *Ach. Tat.*
2.3.3.................. 281n21

Gaius
1.103................. 288n38

Galen
On the Affected Parts
6.5..................... 281n21

On the Preservation of Health
1.1..................... 281n20
1.11................... 281n21
1.5..................... 281n19
2.2..................... 281n20
5.5..................... 281n21

On the Usefulness of the Parts
of the Body
4.190.16........ 283n44

Herodotus, *Histories*
8.105............. 288n34

Hippocrates, *Airs, Waters, Places*
4..................... 285n10

Historia Augusta, *Severus Alexander*
23.7............... 288n39

Juvenal, *Satiries*
3.66–78........ 283n44

Lucian
De Syria dea
51.................. 287n27

Eunuch
6–11............. 211

Martial, *Epigrams*
3:81............... 211

Musonius Rufus, *On Sex*
frag. 12........ 283n39

Ovid, *Fasti*
4.183–86...... 287n27
4.351–366.... 287n27

Petronius, *Satyricon*
131................ 284n53

Plato, *Cornutus*
34.................. 284n56

Laws
5.740b–d...... 286n17

Theaetetus
149B............. 284n56

Pliny the Elder, *Natural History*
7.64............... 286n13

Plutarch, *Moralia, The Face
of the Moon*
938 F............. 284n55

Morals
701F............. 281n21

On Affection for Offspring
493 E–F........ 282n32
493 F............. 282n33

Polybius, *Histories*
10.19.6.......... 282n36

Propertius, *Elegy*
2.7................. 282n30

Ps-Aristotle, *Problems*
30.1............... 281n22

Sophocles, *Oedipus Tyrannus*
1502.............. 284n58

Soranus, *Gynecology*
I.42................ 282n24, 282n25

Suetonius, *Life of Augustus*
34.................. 282n27

Tacitus, Ann.
12.25.2.......... 274n14

Hist.
1.38............... 274n14

Ulpian, *Digest*
  50.16.126...... 210

Virgil, *Aeneid*
  2.693–97....... 211

Xenophon, *Cyropaedia*
  7..................... 288n34

SUBJECT INDEX

1 Enoch, 42, 274n23

2 Baruch, 126–27

2 Maccabees, 216

3 Corinthians, 213, 288n41

abandonment: divine, 17, 116, 132, 269n28; of infants, 145; spousal, 32, 116, 192, 269n26

Abimelech, 45, 49, 56, 60, 98–99, 113–14, 252n88

able-bodiedness, 195, 220

abortion, 43, 181

Abraham, 14, 23, 26, 29, 33–34, 45–47, 51, 59, 60, 61, 64–66, 70, 73, 75, 77–78, 80, 83–84, 91, 95, 101, 106, 110, 112, 114, 118, 127, 142, 151–53, 158, 232, 245n24, 247n39, 251n73, 252n88, 267n10, 268n17, 278n50

Acts of Paul, 213

Acts of Paul and Thecla, 192

Adam, 70, 72, 75–79, 82, 85–87, 89–90, 101, 127, 133, 172, 232, 263n33

adoption, 17, 20, 144–49, 153–54, 169–70, 181, 208, 234, 257n122, 273nn9 and 12, 274nn14, 15 and 17, 276n28, 286n17, 288n37

amulet, 54–55, 57

Ando, Clifford, 145, 147, 273n11, 274n15

annunciation, scenes of, 51, 158–69

Atrahasis, 99–101

Avalos, Hector, 250n62, 252n88, 254n100

Baskin, Judith, 252n78, 263n28

"Beloved Disciple," 166–67

Bergmann, Claudia D., 256n114

Bilhah, 47, 61, 73, 81, 261n8

Bing, Elisabeth, 163

"Birth of Man, The". *See* Enki and Ninmah

Bloch-Smith, Elizabeth, 244n15

Block, Daniel I., 249n57, 261n13, 264n41

Boaz, 38, 156

Boda, Mark, 270n29

Borocin-Knol, S., 269n27

Bovon, Francois, 157

Brenner, Athalya, 243n4, 247n37

Brown, Raymond E., 275n24

Brueggemann, Walter, 269n29

Burrus, Virginia, 209

Bynum, Caroline Walker, 220

Callaway, Mary, 252n93, 270n40

Candace, queen of the Ethiopians, 208

Cassuto, Umberto, 261n17

castration, 3, 210, 212, 283n44, 287n28

celibacy, 17, 33, 173, 175, 184, 186, 189–92, 195–96, 198–99, 207, 217, 222–24, 235–36, 246n34, 262n20, 280n5

Chadwick, Henry, 279n5

childlessness, stigma of 2–7, 9, 11, 40, 69, 231, 242n21

Christianity, 12, 135, 156, 176, 190, 217,
224, 226
Clark, Helen, 239n2
Cohen, Jeremy, 261n16
coins, 148, 154, 178
Collins, Adela, 215, 289n47
concubine, 31–32, 61, 192
contraception, 3, 7, 181, 225

Darr, Katheryn Pfisterer, 268n23
Deutero-Isaiah, 103, 113, 119, 122
Dinah, 47, 61, 80–81, 90–91, 262n24
disability: 2–7, 15, 88, 194, 209–10,
218, 220–22, 226, 243n25, 250n63,
290nn58 and 64; cultural model
of, 239n5; religious model of, 15,
88; theory, 4, 15
divorce, 32–33, 183, 197, 246n32, 250n58,
257n124, 264n27, 271n49, 283nn46
and 54
Dixon, Edward, 143
DNA, 155, 168, 234
Douglas, Mary, 286n14
dreams, 153–55

Eden, Garden of, 12, 72, 85–87, 110–11,
126–27, 131,133, 172–73, 263nn30
and 34, 267nn13 and 15
Eilberg-Schwartz, Howard, 66
Elijah, 84, 129
Elisha, 45, 129, 259n144
Elizabeth, 13, 157, 159–61
Elkanah, 21–23, 35–36, 40, 245n24
Enki and Ninmaḥ, 100
ethics, sexual, 157, 160, 189, 190,
283nn38 and 45
Ethiopian Eunuch, 208–9, 212
eunuchs, 100, 135, 185, 188, 204–5,
207–12, 288, 248n50, 283n44,
286n19, 288nn34 and 36
Evans, James G., 9
Eve, 12, 55, 72, 75–77, 79, 84–90, 101, 133,
162–63, 172, 232, 263n32, 270n32
Exodus, the, 91, 106
Exum, J. Cheryl, 257n123

family, nonbiological, 17, 144, 153,
167–69
femininity, 8, 185, 198, 239n2
feminism, 11, 18–19, 175, 181
Fiore, Benjamin, 242n22
Fitzmyer, Joseph A., 279n3
flood, the, 65–67, 70, 73, 78–79, 82,
93–94, 99–101
Frankfurter, David, 255n111
Frymer-Kensky, Tikva, 265n2
Fuchs, Esther, 244n5, 253n92, 262n25

Gatrell, Caroline, 8
genealogy, 32, 81–82, 87, 147, 151–53,
155–56, 260n8, 262n25, 277n35
Glancy, Jennifer, 162, 163, 277nn42
and 45
Greil, Arthur L., 240n6
guilt, 22, 41, 49, 52, 63, 84, 90, 115, 117,
177, 230, 234, 269n28
Gundry-Volf, Judith M., 280n6

Hagar, 23, 31, 40, 53, 61, 126, 161, 231,
245n24
Hammond, Mason, 273n12
Hannah, 12–13, 21–26, 28, 30–36,
38–43, 48, 51, 53, 56, 58, 67, 69, 123,
124, 134, 159–60, 250n62, 253n93,
254n94, 256n120
Havrelock, Rachel, 257n124, 259n138
Holy Family, 141, 150, 152–62

impotency, male, 36, 38, 196–97,
248nn50 and 52, 288n38
incantation, 36, 54, 138
infertility, biological, 2–4, 10–11, 15,
38–39, 197–99, test of, 26, 204,
258n132
inheritance, 16, 34, 37, 81, 87, 145, 184,
249n57, 262n22, 278n50
Inhorn, Marcia C., 256n112
Isaac, 13, 23, 26, 40, 47, 51, 59, 65, 71,
73, 75–78, 80, 91, 106, 136, 142,
159, 250n58, 267n17
Ishmael, 47, 70, 73, 75, 77, 83, 107

Islam, 71, 258n137; muslim culture, 43, 246n27, 271n49

Jacob, 23–24, 26, 28, 33–34, 37, 42, 47, 56–57, 59, 61, 70, 71, 73–84, 91, 106–7, 109, 118–19, 232, 257n120, 261n9, 262n24
Jesus, 140–44, 148–59, 161–63, 165–71, 191, 200, 205–6, 208, 212, 214–17, 219–24, 226, 234, 275nn25 and 26, 277n42, 278n50
Jesus Movement, 13, 191, 206. *See* christianity
John the Baptizer, 140, 142, 157, 159
Jones, Beth Felker, 290n58
Judaism, 135, 258n137; ancient, 280n5; Hellenistic, 214

Kiel, Micah, 284n51
Kingdom of Heaven, 212, 225, 227, 228
Koran, 43

Law: 225; ancient, 31, 251n66, 252n89; Greco-Roman, 145, 148, 187; of levirate marriage, 37–38, 62, 81, 215, 249n57; rabbinic, 31–32, 70, 124, 216, 258n126, 260n1, 271n49, 276n28
Laws, Julian. See *lex Iulia*
Leah, 24, 33, 34, 47, 53, 58, 60, 61–62, 65, 73, 81, 106, 112–13, 120, 123, 251n75, 256n120, 260n8, 261n19
Levin, Yigal, 276n28
lex Iulia, 181–82
Lohfink, Norbert, 262n21
Luther, Martin, 1

Maier, Christl, 267n13, 267n16, 270n32
mandrake, 24, 63
Mary, 12, 150–66, 232, 275n24, 277n45
medicine, 4, 24
Meier, John P., 275n24
Merkel, Angela, 1, 7, 51, 201–2, 204
Meyers, Carol, 86, 270n32
Milton, H., 275n25
Miriam, 25–26, 44, 90, 257n124

Mitchell, Margaret, 279n5
Montague, George, 242n22
Morgenstern, Julian, 270n29
Moses, 93, 107, 127, 151, 163, 257n124

Naomi, 45, 250n57
Noah, 70, 72–79, 82, 84, 87, 232, 260n1, 261n10

Paul, 17, 126, 149, 160, 166, 170–76, 178, 189, 190–92, 194, 196–97, 213–19, 226, 235, 242n22, 275n24, 278nn50, 1 and 2, 279nn3 and 5, 280nn6, 7 and 8, 281nn13 and 15, 289n43
Peninnah, 13, 21–23, 33, 40, 42, 53, 58, 88, 124, 231, 245n24
Peppard, Michael, 147, 273n9, 274n15
Perdue, Leo, 264n41
Philip, 208–9, 212
Pope Francis, 6
population, 9, 27, 28, 85, 95, 99, 286n17
prophecy, 129, 143, 152, 207–8, 229, 272n3
prophets, 122, 124, 140, 152, 252n88, 271n49
prostitutes, 155–56, 177, 188–89, 277n35
prostitution, 178, 188

Rachel, 22–24, 26, 31, 33–35, 37, 39–40, 42–43, 47–48, 51, 53, 56–58, 61, 63–64, 67, 69, 73, 81, 104, 106–7, 115, 118–9, 121, 123, 129, 131, 160, 251nn64 and 75, 256n120, 259n138, 261n19
Rebekah, 13, 22–23, 25–26, 43, 47, 51, 69, 104, 107, 109, 118–21, 123, 129, 255n101, 256n120
remarriage, 32, 249n57
Reno, Janet, 239n2
Reuben, 34
Rice, Condoleezza, 239n2
Ruth, 239n2

Samson, 28, 59, 159
Samson, mother of, 22–23, 25–26, 48, 51, 60–61, 69, 249n55, 253n92

Sanders, James A., 254n96

Sarah, 22–23, 25–26, 31, 33, 39, 40, 42, 45–47, 51, 53, 57, 61, 64–65, 67, 69, 75, 83, 104–5, 107, 110–12, 119–21, 123–24, 126, 129–30, 133, 136, 153, 158, 160–61, 245n24, 247n39, 250n64, 251n73, 253n91, 255n101, 256n120, 257n122, 259n139, 267nn11 and 17, 270n36

Satan, 172

Sawyer, John F. A., 269n29, 270n32

Schipper, Jeremy, 29

self-restraint, sexual, 172, 176, 179, 186, 193

Septuagint, 152, 158–60, 203–4

serpent. *See* snake, the

sexuality, 175–77, 184, 189, 263n30, 283n44

shame, 33, 39–42, 115–16, 121–22, 138–39, 177, 185, 198, 233, 247n46, 251n68, 268nn22, 23 and 24

Shiomura, Ayaka, 7

sin, 12, 14–15, 43–49, 63, 67–69, 71–72, 113–17, 121, 134–35, 137, 162–64, 173, 202, 230, 232–33, 251n54, 252nn87 and 89, 263n30, 272n58

slavery, 160, 210, 277n40

slaves, 31, 33, 45, 147–48, 160–61, 177, 182, 210, 263n33, 277n41, 288n34

snake, the, 56, 72, 85, 89, 263n33

Solevag, Anna Rebecca, 283n50

surrogate, 31, 32, 112, 148, 160–62, 164, 170, 257n122

Tamar, 155, 276n33

Tomson, P. J., 279n5

Treggiari, Susan, 282n23

van der Toorn, Karel, 246n33, 252n87

virgin birth, 141, 150–52, 155, 157, 159, 224, 275nn24 and 25

virginity, 136, 174, 195–99, 226, 242n22, 262n20, 263n32, 282n37, 284n57

Westermann, Claus, 268n22, 270n33

widowhood, 30, 115–16, 268nn23 and 24, 270n29

widows, 37, 45, 115–16, 155, 166, 182, 215, 249n57, 269nn26 and 27

Wilson, Robert R., 262n25

Wire, A. C., 279n5

womb, divine opening of, 56–58, 63, 66

Yong, Amos, 209–10, 212

Zechariah, 157–59

Zilpah, 34, 47, 61, 73, 81, 261n8

2016.02.12   35. M